Development and
Disorders of Written Language

——————Volume One——————

Picture Story Language Test

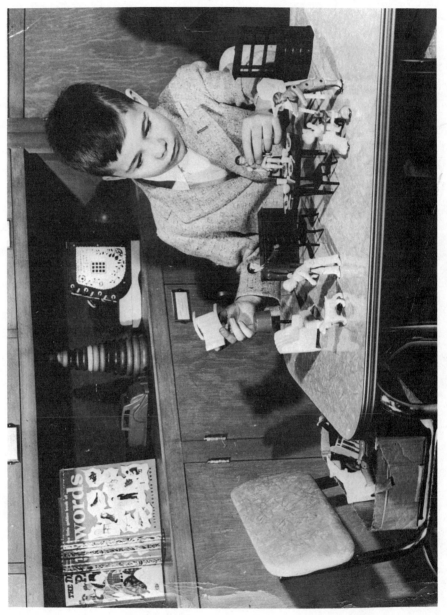

PICTURE STORY LANGUAGE TEST

Development and Disorders of Written Language

Volume One

Picture Story Language Test

HELMER R. MYKLEBUST

Professor of Language Pathology and Psychology
Director, Institute for Language Disorders
Northwestern University

GRUNE & STRATTON • NEW YORK AND LONDON

Grune & Stratton, Inc.
111 Fifth Avenue
New York, New York 10003

Library of Congress Catalog Card Number 65-23996
International Standard Book Number 0-8089-0335-7

Printed in the United States of America

Contents

PART ONE: Background and Purposes

Preface . . . xi

I. Written Language . . . 1
Theoretical Constructs . . . 1
Psychoneurological Aspects . . . 5
Psychological Processes . . . 8
References . . . 10

II. Disorders of Written Language—Differential Diagnosis . . . 12
Developmental Deviations . . . 13
Psychomotor Aspects . . . 14
Paralytic Disorders . . . 15
Ataxia . . . 15
Agraphia . . . 17
Visual Processes . . . 21
Auditory Processes . . . 23
Dysnomia . . . 25
Formulation Aphasia . . . 26
Receptive Aphasia . . . 27
Reauditorization of Letters . . . 28
Sequentializing Auditorially . . . 30
Syllabication and Auditory Blending . . . 31
Spoken versus Written Language Ability . . . 33
Auditory Superior . . . 33
Written Superior . . . 34
Spoken and Written Equal . . . 35
Disorders of Written Language in Handicapped
Children . . . 36
Reading Disability . . . 37
Illustrative Stories . . . 38
Speech Defective . . . 42
Illustrative Stories . . . 43
Mentally Retarded . . . 47
Illustrative Stories . . . 48
Socially-Emotionally Disturbed . . . 52
Illustrative Stories . . . 53
Deaf . . . 57
Illustrative Stories . . . 58

Culturally Deprived . . . 64
Inadequate Teaching . . . 64
Diagnostic Studies of Adults . . . 65
Cross-Cultural Studies . . . 65
Summary . . . 66
References . . . 67

III. Picture Story Language Test, Purpose-Standardization-
        Results . . . 69
        Purpose of the Test . . . 70
        Selection of the Picture . . . 71
        Aspects of Language Measured . . . 72
        The Sample . . . 74
        Results for Normal Children . . . 75
            Productivity . . . 75
            Syntax . . . 78
            Abstract-Concrete . . . 80
            Sex Differences . . . 81
            Illustrative Stories by Normal Children . . . 81
        How to Administer the Test . . . 92
        References . . . 93

PART TWO: Directions for Scoring

IV. Productivity Scale . . . 95
        Total Words . . . 95
            Principles for Scoring . . . 95
        Total Sentences . . . 99
        Words per Sentence . . . 105
        Summary . . . 106
        References . . . 107
V. Syntax Scale . . . 108
        Syntax . . . 109
        Morphology . . . 109
        Word Choice . . . 110
        Punctuation . . . 110
            Summary . . . 110
        Principles for Scoring . . . 111
            Stringency Level . . . 112
            Intended Meaning . . . 113
            Score Accuracy Only . . . 113
        Scoring Error Types . . . 114
            Word Usage . . . 115

Word Endings . . . 118
Punctuation . . . 120
Special Situations . . . 123
Penalty Score Values . . . 123
Designation of Syntax Errors . . . 124
Error Type Symbols . . . 124
Word Usage . . . 125
Word Ending . . . 125
Summary . . . 127
Rationale for the Syntax Score . . . 128
Syntax Quotient . . . 129
References . . . 131

VI.   Abstract-Concrete Scale . . . 133
Directions for Scoring . . . 135
Level I: Meaningless Language . . . 135
Level II: Concrete-Descriptive . . . 136
Level III: Concrete-Imaginative . . . 138
Level IV: Abstract-Descriptive . . . 140
Level V: Abstract-Imaginative . . . 142
References . . . 146

PART THREE: Norms for Written Language

VII.   Validity and Reliability . . . 147
Validity . . . 147
Reliability . . . 149
Interscorer Reliability . . . 151
Productivity Scale . . . 152
Syntax Scale . . . 153
Number of Sentences Required for Reliability . . . 154
Abstract-Concrete Scale . . . 158
Summary . . . 160
References . . . 161

VIII.   Interpretation of Scores . . . 162
Conversion of Raw Scores . . . 165
Total Words . . . 166
Total Sentences . . . 171
Words per Sentences . . . 175
Syntax . . . 179
Abstract-Concrete . . . 183
Summary . . . 187
References . . . 187

PART FOUR: Scoring Guide

Productivity and Syntax . . . 188
    Illustrative Scored Stories . . . 189
Abstract-Concrete . . . 233
    Illustrative Scored Stories . . . 233
Use of Record Form . . . 256
Tables for Converting Raw Scores into Age Equivalents . . . 263
Tables for Converting Raw Scores into Percentiles . . . 264
Tables for Converting Raw Scores into Stanine Ranks. . . 269
Name Index . . . 273
Subject Index . . . 275

Figures, Illustrations, Tables

Figure

1. The hierarchical relationships among Man's verbal systems.   3
2. The psychoneurosensory processes involved in facility with the written word.................................... 4
3. Growth in Total Words as age increases................ 77
4. Growth in Total Sentences as age increases............ 77
5. Growth in Words per Sentence as age increases......... 78
6. Growth in Syntax as age increases.................... 79
7. Growth in Abstract-Concrete as age increases.......... 80

Illustration

1. Story written by a nine-year-old boy with Cerebellar Ataxia... 17
2. Words written from dictation by a nine-year-old boy..... 18
3. Story written by a 13-year-old dysgraphic boy........... 20
4. Phonetic writing of an eight-year-old boy with a deficiency in ability to visualize............................. 24
5. Sentence written by a dysnomic adult as he viewed a picture of people entering a church................... 26
6. Story written by a nine-year-old boy with Formulation Aphasia.. 27
7. The written story by a receptive aphasic boy ten years of age... 28
8. Words written by a 16-year-old dyslexic boy............ 29
9. Words written by a 16-year-old boy with an auditory spelling disorder.................................... 31
10. The writing of a 17-year-old boy with a severe auditorizing defect... 32
11. Stories by an 11-year-old dyslexic boy showing comparative superiority with spoken language............. 34
12. Stories by a 15-year-old boy with moderate receptive aphasia, showing comparative superiority with written language.. 35
13. Stories by a ten-year-old boy with receptive aphasia showing equivalency with spoken and written language..... 36
14. Illustrative Stories: Reading Disability................. 38-41
15. Illustrative Stories: Speech Defective.................. 43-46
16. Illustrative Stories: Educable Mentally Retarded........ 48-51

Illustration

17. Illustrative Stories: Socially-Emotionally Disturbed...... 53-56
18. Illustrative Stories: Deaf............................... 58-63
19. Illustrative Stories: Normal........................... 82-91
20. Scored Illustrative Stories written by normal children.... 189-207
21. Scored Illustrative Stories written by speech defective children... 208-211
22. Scored Illustrative Stories written by reading disability children... 212-215
23. Scored Illustrative Stories written by socially-emotionally disturbed children................................. 216-220
24. Scored Illustrative Sories written by educable mentally retarded children.................................. 221-224
25. Scored Illustrative Stories written by deaf children....... 225-232

Table

1. Sample used in standardizing the Picture Story Language 74
2. Results for Productivity by age and sex................. 76
3. Results for Syntax by age and sex...................... 79
4. Results for Abstract-Concrete by age and sex........... 80
5. Comparison of Picture Story Test results for Words per Sentence with findings of others..................... 148
6. Odd-even reliability coefficients for Words per Sentence... 150
7. Odd-even reliability coefficients for the Syntax scores..... 150
8. Results from repeated administration of the Picture Story Language Test to children with language disorders..... 151
9. Distribution of Stories used in determining inter-scorer reliability.. 152
10. Inter-scorer reliability for Productivity scores as determined for three trained examiners.................... 152
11. Inter-scorer reliability for Productivity scores as determined for seven untrained examiners................. 152
12. Inter-scorer reliability for Syntax for three trained examiners... 153
13. Inter-scorer reliability for Syntax for three untrained examiners... 153
14. Comparison between the Syntax Quotient for the first three sentences (Quo. 3) and the quotient for the total story (Quo. k) as determined by the correlated *t test* technique... 155
15. The approximate error in the Syntax Quotient when one up to 20 sentences are scored...................... 156

Table

16. The Pearson Product-Moment correlations between scores for the first three sentences and for the total story 158
17. Inter-scorer reliability for Abstract-Concrete for three trained examiners 159
18. Inter-scorer reliability for Abstract-Concrete for seven untrained and nine trained examiners 159
19. The mean Abstract-Concrete scores as derived by trained examiners 160
20. Total Words—mean and midpoint scores by age and sex . . 167
21. Total Words—percentile equivalents for males 167
22. Total Words—percentile equivalents for females 168
23. Total Words—percentile equivalents for total group, males and females combined 169
24. Total Words—stanine equivalents for males 170
25. Total Words—stanine equivalents for females 170
26. Total Words—stanine equivalents for total group, males and females combined 170
27. Total Sentences—Mean and midpoint scores by age and sex 171
28. Total sentences—percentile equivalents for males 172
29. Total Sentences—percentile equivalents for females 172
30. Total Sentences—percentile equivalents for total group, males and females combined 173
31. Total Sentences—stanine equivalents for males 174
32. Total Sentences—stanine equivalents for females 174
33. Total Sentences—stanine equivalents for total group, males and females combined 175
34. Words per Sentence—Mean and midpoint scores by age and sex 175
35. Words per Sentence—percentile equivalents for males 176
36. Words per Sentence—percentile equivalents for females ... 176
37. Words per Sentence—percentile equivalents for total group, males and females combined 177
38. Words per Sentence—stanine equivalents for males 178
39. Words per Sentence—stanine equivalents for females 178
40. Words per Sentence—stanine equivalents for total group, males and females combined 179
41. Syntax—Mean and midpoint scores by age and sex 179
42. Syntax—percentile equivalents for males 180
43. Syntax—percentile equivalents for females 180

Table

44. Syntax—percentile equivalents for total group, males and females combined 181
45. Syntax—stanine equivalents for males 182
46. Syntax—stanine equivalents for females 182
47. Syntax—stanine equivalents for total group, males and females combined 183
48. Abstract-Concrete—Mean and midpoint scores by age and sex 183
49. Abstract-Concrete—percentile equivalents for males 184
50. Abstract-Concrete—percentile equivalents for females 184
51. Abstract-Concrete—percentile equivalents for total group, males and females combined 185
52. Abstract-Concrete—stanine equivalents for males 186
53. Abstract-Concrete—stanine equivalents for females 186
54. Abstract-Concrete—stanine equivalents for total group, males and females combined 187

To HELEN
for her patience
and
understanding

Preface

IN THIS MANUAL, the first of a two-volume work on the Development and Disorders of Written Language, the purpose is to provide a standardized procedure for appraising normal facility with the written word as well as a means whereby disorders of this type of verbal behavior can be studied, diagnosed and categorized. Included are the normative data and illustrations representing typical disorders encountered in children with language disabilities.

Because Volume I is to be used in conjunction with the Picture Story Language Test, it also comprises instructions for use of this test and material on its validity and reliability. Volume II is a compilation of data comparing the growth of language in the written from in the normal, in those with learning disabilities, mental retardation, speech defects, social-emotional disturbance and in those with reading disabilities.

It is assumed that Volume I, though not written as a textbook, will be useful in courses in Education, Psychology, Psycholinguistics, Language Pathology, Learning Disabilities, Neurology, Pediatrics, Psychiatry and in others concerned with the treatment and management of children with language disorders. It is intended to be most useful in courses that emphasize differential diagnosis. The material has been presented with this purpose in mind.

Progress in the study of language, nationally and internationally, is being achieved rapidly. Nevertheless, standardized procedures for appraising its development, normal and abnormal, have been slow in materializing. It is my hope that the Picture Story Language Test might provide an impetus and be a contribution toward the development of more efficacious diagnostic instruments.

This study of written language, extending over more than a decade, has been greatly facilitated by my graduate students. Their untiring efforts, criticisms and encouragement is acknowledged with deep feelings of indebtedness. Immeasurable assistance also came from my associates at The Institute for Language Disorders, despite their many other painstaking duties and responsibilities. I gratefully acknowledge suggestions and criticisms from Miss Doris Johnson, Drs. Arthur Neyhus, Harold McGrady, Naomi Kershman, and Mrs. Katherine McGlynn. It is a pleasure to reiterate that James H. McBurney, Dean, School of Speech, Northwestern University, has furnished the guidance, counsel and opportunity that has made this work possible.

HELMER R. MYKLEBUST

Northwestern University
Evanston, Illinois
August 2, 1965

PART ONE

BACKGROUND AND PURPOSES

Chapter I

Written Language

DESPITE THE SIGNIFICANCE of language in Man's history and its importance in relation to his learning and adjustment, science has given only limited attention to this aspect of human behavior. Scales for its measurement have been essentially lacking. Except for tests of reading achievement, the principal measures available have been the verbal subtests found in tests of intelligence. Not only has there been a lack of standardized scales upon which many scientific insights depend, but available knowledge is limited largely to the spoken word.[21] Remarkably few studies on the development and disorders of written language have been reported, nor is it mentioned in recent publications on communicative disorders.[3,20] Because of the dearth of information, as well as for clinical, scientific and theoretical reasons, we thought it was of importance to develop a scale for measuring facility with the written word.

When studied propitiously, language behavior offers an unusual avenue through which to gain insight into human development and its aberrations. Yet it is mentioned only rarely in discussions of growth. With the exception of the spoken word,[11,21] most studies of verbal behavior as it pertains to maturation, learning disabilities and reading were accomplished two or three decades ago.[2,5,6,13]

There is an urgent need for emphasis on the importance of language behavior in relation to learning and adjustment. Perhaps a new emphasis is approaching because there is an increased awareness of the effects of cultural deprivation and of learning disabilities resulting from dysfunctions of the brain.

THEORETICAL CONSTRUCTS

The Picture Story Language Test evolved on the basis of a number of theoretical constructs. One of the first of these entailed the meaning of the term *language*. This term is used variously, depending upon the discipline involved, the purpose and point of view of the investigator. In all of our efforts, clinical and scientific, we have found it rewarding to view language as "symbol-making" behavior. This is to say that to use words is to

1

represent experience symbolically. Words are not simply signals; hence, communication and language are not synonymous. Lower forms of animal life, as Langer[9] emphasizes, can communicate and "signify" states such as fear and hunger, but they cannot use language to symbolize experience, as does Man. The principal difference is that Man through words is capable of representing experience when the experience in question has no immediate relevancy.

Mowrer's[14] discussion is revealing when he states: ". . . it is suggested that animals cannot 'abstract' in the sense of making or reacting to a sign when they have no interest in the significate. In other words, they cannot separate or detach the sign and employ it for reasons which are motivationally unrelated to the object or event which the sign represents. Thus, we may say, a *symbol* is an *abstracted* sign. And here, perhaps, lies one of the reasons why its precise identification and definition has been so difficult: a symbol is not distinguishable from an ordinary sign in terms of its *form*; it is only when the *motivation* behind its usage is taken into account that the difference clearly emerges." Language, then, encompasses the ability to abstract, to attach meaning to words and to employ words as symbols for thought, for the expression of ideas.

Another theoretical construct which has influenced this investigation is that verbal language is of two types, spoken and written (auditory and visual). Moreover, though there are various definitions of writing, there is agreement that Man acquired the auditory language long before he began to read and write.[4,7] Similarly, the child first acquires spoken language, not reading and writing. In other words, Man's language systems, the auditory and the written, develop sequentially according to a pattern determined phylogenetically and ontogenetically, neurologically and psychologically. He first acquires the spoken word and he comprehends before he speaks; reception precedes expression, output follows input.

After auditory language has been achieved and after the required additional maturity has been attained neurologically and psychologically, the normal child acquires the visual language forms; he learns to read and write. But as with auditory language, he first establishes the receptive aspects. He does not learn to write and then learn to read. The written form assumes that the *read* form has been achieved. Written language is the expressive component of read language. Normally, that is developmentally, the child does not speak until he comprehends the spoken word. Likewise, he does not use the written form until he reads. Again, output follows input. Moreover, this relationship between the auditory and visual language forms is hierarchical in nature, meaning that to develop normally, the read form is dependent on the auditory or spoken form and the written is dependent on the integrity of both the auditory and the read.

The congenitally deaf reflect this hierarchical dependency of verbal behavior. Because they are deaf and do not acquire auditory language, learning to read and write is exceedingly arduous, and in most deaf children is accomplished only after great effort and to an extent considerably below the average hearing child. When the form acquired first phylogenetically and ontogenetically is not established, then acquisition of those which follow, the read and written, is impeded developmentally.[17]

From this point of view, as shown in Figure 1, Man has a total complex of language consisting of three forms, spoken, read, and written, each having a reciprocal affiliation with the other. This reciprocal, hierarchical relationship is manifested in the sequentialness of the developmental pattern. By implication, when a deviation in facility with the written word occurs, it may be the result of a disturbance in either of the other two (auditory and read) which normally precede its acquisition or by a combination involving components of each. In Chapter II we stress these possibilities and the need for the diagnostician to be alert to the reciprocalities of verbal behavior.

Another facet of our theoretical construct concerns the psychoneuro-

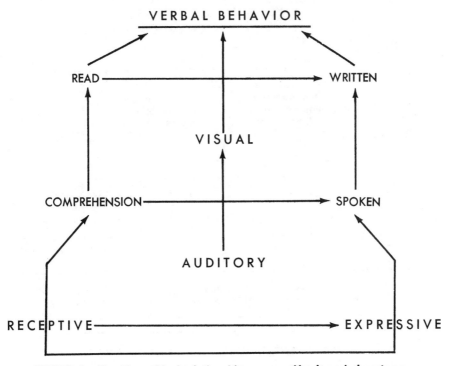

FIGURE 1. The hierarchical relationships among Man's verbal systems.

sensory processes through which Man acquires verbal facility; see Figure 2. The spoken form appears to be dependent only on the integrity of auditory learning and experience. Visual or tactile learning, if involved, seems to be incidental. Vision may be absent, as in the congenitally blind, but spoken language is acquired. Similarly, a child may be unable to read, yet he acquires auditory language.

Achieving the read and written forms, however, assumes greater complexity and maturity of psychoneurosensory processes. From research and experience with normal as well as with mentally deficient children, it is apparent that additional maturation both psychologically and neurologically are required for reading and writing in comparison with the spoken word. Not only is more intelligence required, but a higher degree of intersensory perception and facilitation are essential. Both auditory and visual integrity in learning to read must be assumed psychoneurologically because normally the child initially "translates" what appears on the printed page into the auditory equivalents which he learned previously.

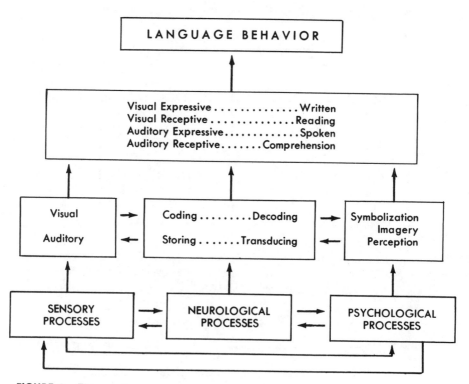

FIGURE 2. The psychoneurosensory processes involved in facility with the written word.

Likewise, initially learning to write entails precisely the ability to combine the visual and auditory word images. Only those sophisticated in verbal behavior, only those who have attained mature use of language can really "bypass" the auditory and truly engage in silent reading and writing. In fact, even the mature regress and auditorize when they encounter an unfamiliar word on the printed page and when they attempt to spell (write) uncommon words.

In the discussion of differential diagnosis in Chapter II we again consider these relationships. Here we are concerned only with the postulation that acquiring the three verbal forms, the spoken, read, and written, assumes integrity for learning through certain modalities, not only in terms of each modality separately but also in being able to convert that which is learned through one of these into equivalents learned through other channels. It is such transmodal learning which often is deficient in children with learning disabilities.

PSYCHONEUROLOGICAL ASPECTS

Learning is dependent upon both psychological and neurological processes: it is psychoneurological in nature. Though the association between the neurological and psychological is not on a one to one basis, there is a body of knowledge which clearly indicates that such a relationship exists.[1] Because of this interdependence of psychological and neurological aspects, specific types of learning cannot be achieved normally unless certain integrities of the brain are present. This association appears most obviously in verbal behavior, as stressed by Penfield and Roberts.[18] They state: ". . . there are definite differences in the types of aphasia produced by lesions in different portions of the speech cortex. In some instances there is more involvement of the sensory side of speech, and in others, more of the motor elements. Thus there is what clinicians have called *motor aphasia*, in which speaking is severely involved while understanding of speech is relatively and comparatively intact. There is also *sensory aphasia* in which the reverse is true. This strongly suggests that the motor units for words and phrases are separated somehow, spatially, from the sensory units. But it is also clear that they are both located in the general region of the cortico-thalamic speech areas of the left side, where they are closely interrelated in function."

These neurologists state further ". . . writing is carried out by one hand, which is called dominant. It is controlled through the motor hand mechanism in the cortex of the opposite hemisphere. Writing must be considered voluntary in regard to each move, at the beginning. But in time it comes to be automatic. The image of the movement required to produce each word, taken together with the execution of the movement, becomes a skill that is eventually automatic but can be controlled voluntarily. It is so automatic that in time, a man can summon a word and discover that his hand has written it."

Another statement made by these authorities is "The ideational part of speech, whether spoken, heard, written or read, depends upon the employment of a certain portion of one hemisphere alone—normally the left hemisphere. This localization of function in one hemisphere is, in itself, something new in mammalian evolution. Other intellectual functions, such as perception, the recording of current experiences, and the storing of generalizations or concepts in memory, are made possible by the utilization of homologous areas of cerebral cortex on the two sides, together with the coordinating and integrating work of the higher brain stem."

Consistent with this neurological point of view is the semiautonomous systems concept, as propounded by Hebb[8] and the concept of transmodal learning as presented by Pimsleur and Bonkowski.[19] The assumption made by these psychologists and by us in our studies of the development and disorders of language, is that the brain is made up of systems that can, and sometimes do, perform semi-independently from others. At times a given system functions in a supplementary way with another, and at times all of the systems function interrelatedly as a unit. This concept has many implications for better understanding of learning as it occurs in normal children as well as in those having neurogenic disorders of learning. It is especially relevant to differential diagnosis as discussed in Chapter II because it follows that it is necessary to appraise each system as it functions semiautonomously in coordination with other systems, and as all of the systems function simultaneously.[15] This concept of psychoneurosensory processes, as it relates to learning and differential diagnosis, is shown schematically in Figure 2.

This schema shows that written language is acquired last. Because it is acquired last, ostensibly it is Man's highest achievement verbally and is achieved only when all of the preceding levels have been established. In view of this inference, we assumed that knowledge regarding the written form should have implications for all of the other systems. In other words, greater awareness of the patterns of development and the disorders of written language should provide insights into Man's total complex of behavior linguistically.

From Figure 2 we note that for written language to develop normally there must be integrity of sensory processes, particularly in regard to auditory, visual and motor functioning because each of these is involved in acquisition and use of the written word. Hearing and vision are the channels through which the two basic receptive verbal systems, spoken and read, are acquired; it is these upon which the written depends. They are the means whereby information critical to verbal behavior reaches the brain. Significantly, because these are receptive processes (input), both may function normally so that comprehension of the spoken word, as well as of the written, may be achieved but the expressive (output) may be deficient; see the discussion of apraxia in Chapter II. Oral and written expression are dependent not only on the adequacy of receptive functions but on the integrity of motor processes. Therefore, seemingly, in comparison with the auditory and the read, written language entails a higher and more complex level of sensory functioning.

Hebb's neuropsychological theory of learning, more than others, was used in developing postulations relative to the function of the brain in language acquisition, especially concerning the written word. In brief, according to Hebb,[8] this theory holds that "The key conception is that of *cell assembly*, a brain process which corresponds to a particular sensory event, or a common aspect of a number of sensory events. This assembly is a closed system in which activity can 'reverberate' and thus continue after the sensory event which started it has ceased. Also, one assembly will form connections with others, and it may therefore be made active by one of them in the total absence of the adequate stimulus. In short, the assembly activity is the simplest case of an *image* or an idea: a representative process. The formation of connections between assemblies is the mechanism of association."

This theory has the advantage of indicating that certain learning (auditory, visual, tactile) can occur independently, even though association with other assembly systems leads to learning which is cross-modal in nature. It is in these terms that we view the neurological processes as indicated in Figure 2. Both intrasensory and intersensory learning must occur for writing to ensue. Initially at least, and perhaps indefinitely when unfamiliar words are encountered, the writer must have the capacity to learn (code) and recall (decode) both the auditory and visual aspects of words, and then convert (transduce) these images into the motor pattern for writing.

According to this postulation, an inability to write may derive from a number of "breaks" in this sequence or chain of events in learning. The individual may not be able to learn auditorially, so he cannot associate the names of letters or the sounds they make with their appearance, though he recognizes them when he sees them. Or the opposite may occur; he cannot learn to associate their appearance with their names and sounds, though he recognizes them when he hears them.

We see, therefore, that psychoneurologically it must be possible to learn each aspect separately, the auditory and the visual, and also to learn the equivalents of each. Associations must be formed among the "assemblies" in order that transducing can occur. It is interesting that clinically it is not uncommon to see persons who have learned intrasensorially but who cannot learn intersensorially. Moreover, there are many children who readily learn the auditory and visual aspects of words but who cannot convert these aspects into motor patterns. When this occurs for the written word it is referred to as *dysgraphia*.

PSYCHOLOGICAL PROCESSES

Considerable progress has been made in recent years in understanding the psychological processes underlying language learning.[10,14,20,22] Most of the studies, however, pertain only to the spoken word. Much less has been learned about the processes involved in learning to read and very little attention has been given to written language. The work of Herrick[8a] et al. suggests a new interest in handwriting. Nevertheless, though related, it is not equivalent to study of the written word as a language system.

Perhaps the most striking aspect of a concept of the psychology of written language is the generalized integrity and maturity which seemingly must be assumed for its development. Although the precise mental age levels necessary for acquisition of the written word and its use at various stages of proficiency are not known, it is apparent that more intelligence is required for its attainment than for the spoken form, and perhaps also than for the read. In comparison with the normal, our studies of educable mentally retarded children reveal a marked inferiority in facility with written language.[16] They were deficient in Total Words, Total Sentences, Words per Sentence and in Syntax; their greater limitation was in Productivity, not Correctness.

If we assume that intellectual capacity is associated with facility in the written word we are inferentially postulating that developmental factors are of importance. Perhaps no other single consideration was more influential in our theoretical formulations. These factors were viewed as being significant in all three of the processes shown schematically in Figure 2: sensorially, neurologically and psychologically. Hence, we theorized that "readiness" was consequential to acquiring written language, rudimentally as well as at the level achieved in adulthood. Because we view language behavior as an organismic, psychoneurological process, we considered readiness not only in psychological terms but also in terms of the maturation of both the peripheral and central nervous systems. Perhaps this point of view should be stressed because verbal functions, spoken, read, and written, often are viewed as separate or isolated elements developmentally. This implies that language acquisition and learning can be fostered by using a given method or procedure. In other words, it is assumed that readiness per se can be environmentally produced.

Despite the importance of environment, including proper methods of teaching, from our point of view readiness for learning includes genetic factors that sequentially follow a time pattern of their own and which are essentially not subject to change by training or other environmental influences. Acquisition of the written word, therefore, should adhere to patterns of the type found for other aspects of learning and maturation. For example, after initial readiness has been established, the child should gradually increase in proficiency as he matures organismically—that is, as he grows intellectually, motorically and in other ways. Moreover, this being true, it should be possible to determine the level of facility with the written word attained from one year to the next. In addition it might be possible to disclose that certain aspects, such as the number of word produced under certain conditions and correctness of usage, mature at different rates. Some aspects of the written word may require greater maturation, hence, greater complexity and more integrity than others. This concept was fundamental to the development of the Picture Story Language Test.

Specific psychological processes also were considered, especially perception, use of imagery and ability to symbolize; see Figure 2. These processes appear to be highly related to all verbal behavior. Clinically we have observed that children with learning disabilities often are incapable of discriminating between words that sound or appear alike. We have noticed that they are deficient in ability to normally identify and interpret everyday experience sensorially. We attributed these deficiencies to a lack of normal perceptual development or as a disturbance of these processes. Therefore, we postulated that acquisition of written language was dependent upon a minimal level of integrity of perceptual functioning.

Though in recent decades psychologists have thought otherwise, we find that Mowrer,[14] Werner and Kaplan,[22] as well as Miller, Galanter and Pribram,[12] rely heavily on the concept of imagery. Imagery, conceived as mediation or in other terms, is unusually relevant to verbal behavior, be it spoken, read, or written. In our formulation it has bearing both psychologically and neurologically. Psychologically it entails learning and memory. The basis of the image must be learned; facility with letters, words and sentences must be acquired. After it has been learned it must be available as needed; it must be recallable. When letters and words are to be used it must be possible to bring them into the foreground of attention. It is this process which distinguishes between reception and expression, input and output. Neurologically this process may be referred to as decoding. Children with neurogenic learning disabilities often have disturbances in this function and are deficient in ability to auditorize and visualize. Normal facility with written language entails these processes;

further discussion of the importance of imagery is reserved for the following chapter.

Theoretically, we are in agreement with those who distinguish between signals (signs) and symbolic (representational) behavior.[9,14,22] Moreover, we postulated that written language is Man's highest attainment in verbal symbolization. Although symbolization as a psychological process has not been adequately defined or described, various correlates of its use are well-known. It assumes certain degrees of intelligence, opportunities for learning, and as shown by study of the aphasias, dyslexias and dysgraphias, certain neurological integrities. Because language behavior is defined and discussed throughout this volume, detailed analysis of symbolic behavior is not given here. Fundamentally, however, this study of written language was viewed as a study of representational behavior symbolically, as a study of verbal behavior in the written form. Therefore, ours was an attempt to devise a test that measured this type of learned behavior developmentally.

REFERENCES

1. Council for International Organization of Medical Sciences. Brain Mechanisms and Learning, Springfield, Ill., Charles C. Thomas, 1961.
2. Dearborn, W., Carmichael L. and Lord, E. E.: Special disabilities in learning to read and write. Harvard Monogr. Educ. 2: 1, 1925.
3. de Reuck, A. V. S. and O'Connor, Maeve (eds): Disorders of Language. London, J. & A. Churchill, 1964.
4. Diringer, D.: Writing. New York, Frederick A. Praeger, 1962.
5. Fernald, Grace M.: Remedial Techniques in Basic School Subjects. New York, McGraw-Hill, 1943.
6. Gates, Arthur I.: The Improvement of Reading. New York, Macmillan Co., 1947.
7. Gelb, I. J.: A Study of Writing. Chicago, University of Chicago Press, 1963.
8. Hebb, D. O.: A neuropsychological theory. In Psychology: A Study of a Science, Vol. I, Sigmund Koch (ed.). New York, McGraw-Hill, 1959.
8a. Herrick, V. and Okada, Nora: Practices in the Teaching of Handwriting. In New Horizons for Research in Handwriting, Virgil E. Herrick (ed). Madison, University of Wisconsin Press, 1963.
9. Langer, Susanne K.: Philosophy in a New Key. Cambridge, Harvard University Press, 1957.
10. Lenneberg, E. H. (ed): New Directions in the Study of Language. Cambridge, The M.I.T. Press, 1964.
11. McCarthy, Dorothea: Language development in children. In Manual of Child Psychology, 2nd Ed. Leonard Carmichael (ed), New York, John Wiley & Sons, 1954.
12. Miller, G. A., Galanter, E. and Pribram, K. H.: Plans and the Structure of Behavior. New York, Henry Holt & Co., 1960.
13. Monroe, Marion: Children Who Cannot Read. Chicago, University of Chicago Press, 1932.
14. Mowrer, O. H.: Learning Theory and the Symbolic Processes. New York, John Wiley & Sons, 1960.

15. Myklebust, H. R.: Learning disorders: Psychoneurological disturbances in childhood. Rehabilitation Literature 25: 12, 1964.
16. ———: Development and Disorders of Written Language, Vol. II. New York and London, Grune & Stratton. In press.
17. ———: The Psychology of Deafness, 2nd Ed. New York and London, Grune & Stratton, 1964.
18. Penfield, W. and Roberts, L. Speech and Brain Mechanisms. Princeton, Princeton University Press, 1959.
19. Pimsleur, P. and Bonkowski, R. J.: Transfer of verbal material across sense modalities, J. Educ. Psychol, 52: 104, 1961.
20. Rioch, D. and Weinstein, E.: Disorders of Communication. Baltimore, Williams & Wilkins, 1964.
21. Templin, Mildred C.: Certain Language Skills in Children. Minneapolis, University of Minnesota Press, 1957.
22. Werner, H. and Kaplan, B.: Symbol Formation. New York, John Wiley & Sons, 1963.

Chapter II

Disorders of Written Language—
Differential Diagnosis

THE DISORDERS of written language have received only minor attention on the part of psychology and special education although diagnostically this verbal deficiency has been both recognized and stressed by neurology for almost a century.[26] School programs have been inaugurated for the deaf, blind, crippled, speech defective, mentally retarded, emotionally disturbed, and for those with reading disabilities, but provisions are lacking for children who have disorders in use of the written word. Programs for these children may not have developed because an objective means whereby such disabilities might be identified has not been available. Because of the importance of written language in daily life, as well as culturally, and because of the high incidence of deficiencies in this type of verbal functioning, there is a great need for establishing diagnostic and remedial educational programs.

In the preceding chapter we suggested that the written word was developmentally dependent upon the spoken and read forms. The implication is that when a deficiency in written language appears the diagnostic evaluation must determine whether it derives reciprocally from a defect in spoken language, in reading ability or from a disorder in the written form per se. To do so often entails a complex diagnostic process. In addition, a lack of proficiency in written language may be caused by at least four types of disturbances: peripheral nervous system impairments, such as hearing loss and partial sightedness; central nervous system involvements, resulting in neurogenic learning disabilities; emotional disturbance, causing an imposition on learning; and cultural deprivation, that is, lack of opportunity for proper training.

Inasmuch as written language deficiencies involve organismic functioning, that is, the child as a whole, and because they might result from developmental anomalies, dysfunctions in the brain, sensory impairment, emotional disturbance as well as cultural and educational factors, a number of disciplines are required for making adequate diagnostic studies. Such deviations usually are recognized in school, so the teacher-educator is the first to observe the problem. Next the child might be seen by the psychologist, the language pathologist, and the pediatrician. If a neurogenic involvement is indicated he then would be examined by a neurologist, an electroencephalographist, and often by a psychiatrist. It is necessry to stress that written language deficiencies almost without exception *must* first be identified by school personnel. Therefore, it is of critical importance that children be *screened* for these deficiencies, much in the same way as screening tests are used for identifying reading disabilities, a loss of hearing, or an impairment of vision; the Picture Story Language Test can be used for this purpose. After the child with a written language problem has been identified he should have a thorough diagnostic evaluation, sometimes including all of the specialties indicated above. Our discussion is limited to the ways in which children who are presumed to have disorders of written language can be appraised *behaviorally* in order to ascertain the nature and extent of their problem. It is not our intention to discuss the use of mental, personality, motor and other standard tests, but rather to suggest areas of learning that might be explored in addition to those typically evaluated by psychologists.

Various factors can interfere with normal facility in use of the written word, one of which is lack of opportunity and training. Though cultural deprivation is important to many children it is not included for detailed discussion because our primary concern is the conditions and disabilities that lead to inadequate use of the written word despite average or better educational advantages; albeit the Picture Story Language Test can be used to study the effects of cultural deprivation. We also wish to emphasize the importance of written language in understanding the needs of children who have deficiencies of learning such as reading disabilities, speech defects or mental retardation. If the specific type of disorder is properly identified and described diagnostically, remedial training can be pursued in the most beneficial manner. Moreover, objective studies of written language, normal and abnormal, promise to furnish new insights into the process of learning, especially as they relate to language behavior.

DEVELOPMENTAL DEVIATIONS

We have noted that to learn normally the child must have minimal integrity of the peripheral nervous system, of the central nervous system, of his emotions, as well as adequate training. Another way in which to view the essentials for learning, including the written word, is that he must have the necessary intelligence, motor ability, sensory capacity and social-emotional maturity. Before the child will write there is much that must transpire developmentally. He must attain a certain level of intellectual competence, psychomotor coordination, emotional maturity and psychosensory integration. Should any of these aspects of development be retarded or impeded, the readiness pattern for writing will be altered.

The work of Doll[9] and Gesell and Ilg[13] is highly relevant. To illustrate, Gesell and Ilg have shown that at six years the average child copies capital letters; at seven his writing is large, awkward, uneven in size and irregular in position (confirmed by our own studies; see examples in the Scoring Guide); at eight spoken language is still far more basic than written but he enjoys reading aloud and *sounds out* the words; at nine he uses the written form more as a tool, and as a motor skill writing is relatively under good control, penmanship becomes smaller and more uniform and the written word is established as a means of communication.

The normative studies in social maturity by Doll show that from five to six years the child prints simple words, from six to seven he uses a pencil for writing, but on the average he does not write for communication, in the form of short letters, until about ten years of age, long after he has begun to read.

These developmental studies are in close agreement and reveal the degree of integrity or maturity required for fluent use of written language. They also furnish evidence indicating that acquisition of the written word, even rudimentally, requires the mental capacity, psychomotor ability and social-emotional maturity of approximately seven years. But not until about ten years is use of the written word firmly established, a result which is consistent with the findings given in this manual. The diagnostician therefore, when studying children with deficiencies in written language, must consider the child's developmental status. As Birch and Lefford[1] have emphasized, children vary in the manner in which they mature; hence, there is a *normal* range of deviation. Intelligence may be adequate in a given child but motor ability immature and below average, or vice versa. Our concern is with those in whom the deviation falls outside the variabilities that can be considered normal. We now consider these developmental prerequisites in more detail.

PSYCHOMOTOR ASPECTS

All expressive language entails motor activity. Cobb,[5] Orton,[28] Gesell and Amatruda,[12] and Penfield and Roberts[29] stress that verbal behavior assumes a type of specialized motor ability uniquely present in Man, and that this ability is related to cerebral dominance. Both spoken and written language develop naturally when cerebral dominance occurs. When laterality is confused, delayed, or disturbed, expressive language functions might be disordered. One reason Man has attained verbal symbolic behavior is that he is capable of a specialized type of motor function. An example, as Halverson[15] has demonstrated, is thumb opposition. At 12 months of age the child has difficulty grasping a crayon even with the whole hand. By 24 months, through use of the thumb, the grasp is already much more intricate. But what Gesell refers to as crayon and writing behavior, or manipulation of writing tools, is not established even by six years of age. He states: ". . . it may be said that the course of development in writing is proximo-distal. The gradual decrease in the size of writing movements with age is paralleled by corresponding reduction in the number and magnitude of superfluous movements." It is apparent that children cannot write until they have attained the necessary maturity motorically. It follows that in differential diagnosis it is necessary to establish whether this degree of motor maturation has been attained. In doing so we have found the Heath[17] and Oseretsky[27] tests beneficial, as well as the Gesell Developmental Schedule.[13] These procedures are useful in differentiating between developmental deviations and disorders of written language that derive from other causations.

Paralytic Disorders

Perhaps the most obvious motor involvements relating to the act of writing are the paralyses. There are various types but one of the most common is hemiplegia, a paralysis of one side of the body, usually including both the arm and the leg. Sometimes the condition is severe and necessitates learning to write with the left hand. This motor problem is mentioned here because it is frequently associated with the language disorders seen in adults. It is not a symbolic disorder, hence not an apraxia, and should be distinguished from other incapacities affecting use of the written word. Paralytic disturbances are influential principally in regard to speed and legibility of writing. All degrees of involvement are found and children may also be affected. Various tests of laterality and strength of grip are useful in exploring the relative integrity of the right and left limbs; the dynamometer is especially applicable.[20]

Ataxia

Another motor disorder, affecting the ability to write and occurring with some frequency in both children and adults having learning disabilities, is *cerebellar ataxia.*[8] This condition which results from disturbances in the cerebellum does not cause paralysis but an inability to coordinate motor movements in a normal manner. Frequently it is observed clinically as awkwardness in walking, the gait being characterized by poor balance and by the appearance of lunging. It is seen also as poor coordination of the hands and fingers, with tremor and choreiform movements being common. Finger dexterity and grasp may be seriously disturbed so that clumsiness is observed in buttoning, in manipulating eating utensils, and in other motor acts.

Children with ataxia of the hand and fingers find writing extremely difficult; again it is legibility and speed that are affected, not meaning and syntax. Sometimes tragic consequences are observed in these children because the nature of the condition often is undiagnosed and neat, legible writing is demanded. Though the ataxia often relieves with growth and maturation, in some instances the involvement is not overcome even with medical treatment and training. When the child is expected to learn to write in a manner impossible for him, he becomes emotionally disturbed, if not mentally ill.

Henry is a case in point. He was referred for being a behavior problem and was unable to write at the age of nine years. Neurological, electroencephalographic and behavioral studies disclosed a brain dysfunction, including cerebellar ataxia. Appraisal of mental ability revealed near average intelligence. The ataxia also caused a marked articulation defect but there was no language disorder. He was seriously emotionally disturbed. When given the Picture Story Language Test he wrote as shown in Illustration 1. Because his writing was illegible he was asked to read the story and the examiner copied what he read.

To further analyze this boy's verbal facility, he was given the Gates[11] spelling test with the results as presented in Illustration 2. Some of the words are legible, but scoring required the child's assistance; he helped the examiner identify what he had written. Seven words were spelled correctly.

These specimens, the story and the words written from dictation, were of considerable value in ascertaining diagnostically that the basic condition was cerebellar ataxia, that there was no receptive aphasia, no dysgraphia (no apraxia), and that the child had learned both the visual and the auditory aspects of the written word. Furthermore, except for legibility, his written language was within normal limits as indicated by Words per Sentence and Syntax. Productivity was reduced because of his severe problem of incoordination.

Conditions such as cerebellar ataxia, as well as other motor disorders, do not affect language per se, but often greatly decrease legibility. It is here that the disorders of written language and handwriting overlap, so the diagnostician must recognize the importance of legibility if for no other reason than that it is necessary to distinguish these problems from others. The studies of Herrick and Okada,[18] Callewaret[4] and Harris and Rarick[16] are refreshing and challenging precisely in this connection. Herrick and Harris have shown that the average child cannot judge or evaluate his handwriting by adult standards until he reaches the fifth or sixth grade. Their results and ours agree in indicating that writing is a complex act requiring substantial maturity. Smith and Murphy[30] also should be mentioned because they have presented evidence on the nature of writing that goes beyond most studies of handwriting ability. They investigated the feedback mechanisms involved and formulated a neurogeometric theory of writing. This work is pertinent to both research and diagnosis in relation to the written word.

ILLUSTRATION 1. Story written by a 9-year-old boy with cerebellar ataxia.

▶ **AS WRITTEN**

▶ **AS READ**

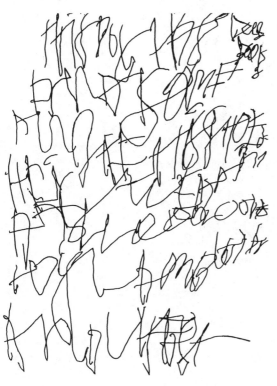

This boy has dolls and some books. He has shoes. He is wearing a warm coat and has a toy lamp shade. . . .

Agraphia

The act of writing entails neurological and psychological complexities; it involves the integration of auditory, visual and motor capacities. In no condition is this more apparent than in *agraphia*. It is this problem that the neurologist Exner[10] described and that perhaps is the "grandfather" of all disorders of written language. Here we suggest the importance of this condition in differential diagnosis; evidently it is more common in children than has been assumed.

Agraphia refers to a total inability, whereas dysgraphia refers to a partial inability to write because of a dysfunction in the brain. It is not a paralysis nor is it an incoordination such as ataxia, but rather a defect that is symbolic in nature. Though the individual has all aspects of the word in mind and though the motor system is normal, he cannot associate

**ILLUSTRATION 2. Words written from dictation by a
9-year-old boy with cerebellar ataxia.**

▶ **AS WRITTEN**   ▶ **AS SCORED**

1. *do
2. *or
3. *hen
4. *net
5. come
6. *year
7. *child
8. *point
9. scratch
10. frighten
11. shephard
12. elegant
13. brilliant

*correct

the two. He cannot relate the mental images of the word and the motor system for writing. Therefore dysgraphia is a type of *apraxia*. Cobb[5] states: ". . . no learned motor skill can be practiced without an ideational plan. This is a psychic elaboration necessary as a precursor to the carrying out of any complex motor act. This ideational plan is called eupraxia; the normal person knows how to do a thing quickly and automatically when requested. A defect in such performance in response to a command is *apraxia*. It is a symptom of injury to the sensorimotor elaboration areas of the cortex, corresponding to agnosia from a lesion in the more strictly sensory area."

In biomedical engineering terms apraxia can be described as an inability to transduce auditory and visual information into motor activity. As Cobb stresses, however, memory, the storing processes in the brain, may be involved. If this is true, it is a deficiency in remembering the motor sequences for writing, not the words to be written. The individual knows the words he wishes to write; he can recall what they sound like as well as what they look like, but he cannot produce the necessary motor movements. Because those having this problem have no difficulty with either the auditory or visual aspects of the word, they are not helped by having someone dictate or sound out the word, nor are they helped by seeing it; hence, *they cannot copy*. In other words, providing them with the auditory and visual aspects of the word does not benefit them; they have these. Their need is for assistance with the motor plan aspects.[22]

The story in Illustration 3 was written by a dysgraphic boy when he was 13 years of age and after he had received remedial training for approximately six years. He was of high average intelligence with comparable ability to read, but he had other apraxias and a marked dyscalculia.[7] Essentially his only problem was of visuomotor coordination, of legibility. The sentences are of adequate length and he is proficient in Syntax though Total Words is below average. In some instances the dysgraphic involvement persists residually into adulthood.

Agraphia and expressive aphasia are parallel conditions, both being types of apraxia and both being disorders of language, one for written and the other for spoken. Because these conditions may be partial, not total, we have need for the terms *dysgraphia* and *dysphasia*. Hinsie and Campbell[19] define agraphia as "Loss of the power, or the inability, to communicate (ideas) in writing, and thus is a subdivision of aphasia. This is the motor (or expressive) aspect of the ailment of which the sensory (or perceptive) counterpart is alexia." In Blakiston's New Gould Medical Dictionary[2] we find dysgraphia defined as "Loss of ability to write; a form of aphasia; absolute-inability to write even unconnected letters; acoustic—inability to write from dictation; amnemonic—inability to write connected sentences, although letters and words can be written; cerebral—incapacity to express a thought in writing; motor—loss of ability to write because of ataxia; musical—loss of ability to write musical notes; optic—inability to copy; verbal—inability to write words although single letters can be written." These definitions are useful in denoting the way in which dysgraphia is viewed here. It comprises a number of problems organic in origin that can be attributed to minimal dysfunctions in the brain.

Like aphasia, dysgraphia was first recognized in adults; Nielsen[26] states that this term was introduced by William Ogle in 1867. The condition was identified because it became apparent that adults who previously were capable of normal written language lost this ability after having a vascular illness. Otherwise the patients were of good intelligence and had no paralysis. In 1881, Exner,[10] on the basis of clinical evidence, stated that

ILLUSTRATION 3. Story written by a 13-year-old dysgraphic boy.

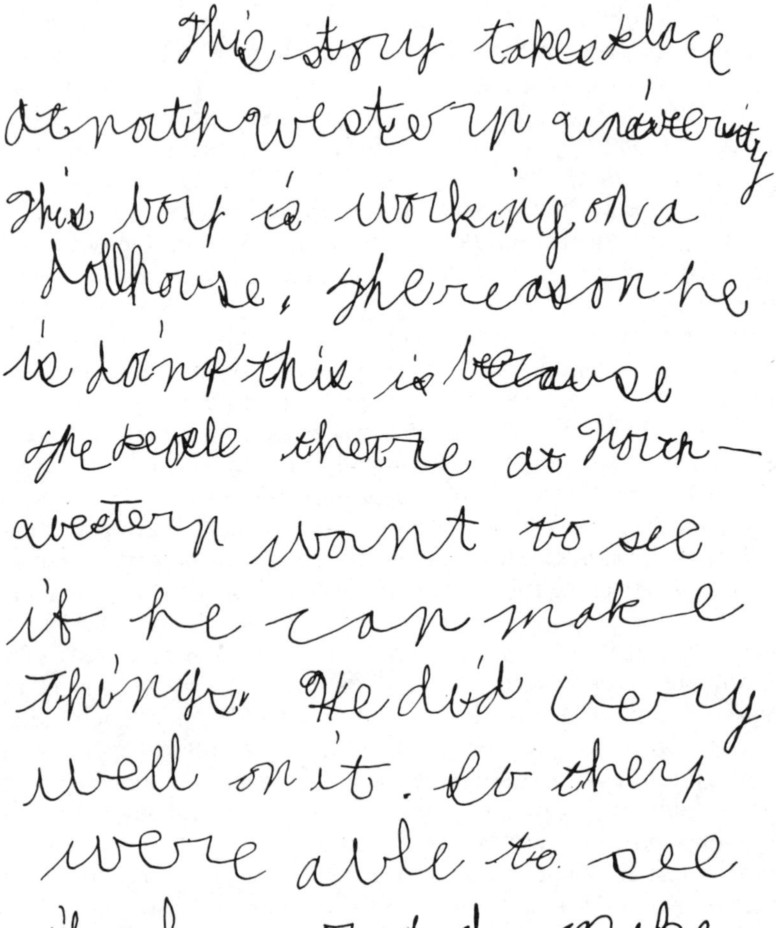

This story takes place at northwestern university. This boy is working on a dollhouse, the reason he is doing this is because the people there at North-western want to see if he can make things. He did very well on it. So they were able to see if he could make things, which he did.

the reason for such patients no longer being capable of writing was that damage had been sustained at "the foot of the second frontal convolution" in the left hemisphere of the brain. This is the traditional basis for the concept of dysgraphia as a type of apraxia. Disturbances of written language were first understood only in these terms. In neurology Nielsen has enlarged this concept as it pertains to adults by showing that brain involvements affecting auditory or visual processes also might interfere with use of the written word.

Orton[28] stressed that dysgraphia was common in children having a reading disability and who were confused in use of the right hand. His position, for which there is an increasing amount of evidence is that some children are developmentally retarded in learning to write because the necessary areas of the brain do not develop in the normal manner, or at the usual rate. He designated this condition as *developmental agraphia*. Conceivably this is the most common type of dysgraphia found in children.

Dysgraphic children frequently present no other obvious symptoms, except their inability in writing, so it is the teachers and other school personnel who carry the major responsibility for their identification. Although a formal test of written language is not always necessary, the Picture Story Language Test makes possible the comparison with normative data. Unless the disability is severe such comparison is beneficial because it furnishes objective evidence and makes finer clinical differentiation practical. In order to further screen the possibility of a dysgraphia being present after the child with a deficiency of written language has been identified, it is advantageous to ascertain whether he can copy and whether he profits from being given assistance auditorially. When given a model to go by visually, which is what is done when he is given a unit to copy, typically the dysgraphic shows little benefit. Likewise, when the words are spelled for him, he shows no advantage. Under these circumstances in an otherwise essentially intact child, dysgraphia should be suspected. The specific diagnosis requires additional information, including neurological and electroencephalographic findings. Usually dysgraphic children respond well to appropriate remedial training.

VISUAL PROCESSES

That visual functions are involved in the act of writing is obvious. However, the obviousness pertains mainly to visual acuity, to vision as it relates to the peripheral nervous system and not to visual perception, to imagery or to other psychoneurological processes. Acuity is a significant factor, as manifested by the difficulties in writing encountered by the blind and the partially sighted, but this aspect is not our primary concern. Rather, we stress those deficiencies commonly associated with learning disabilities because it is these that more often require careful consideration in identification, differential diagnosis and remedial education.

First we give a brief description of the visual processes involved psychoneurologically in producing the written word. Let us assume that a child is to write: *I see a boy*. Initially he scans the situation in general. He sees the paper and the pencil, makes a judgment as to how the pencil should be grasped, where the paper should be placed, where to begin writing on it and the direction in which to write. (At this point if the writer is a child at the stage of learning to write, he may utter letters or words as he writes them; see the discussion below of auditory processes.) Before beginning to write, however, he has engaged in visual-spatial perception, visual-size discrimination, right-left orientation and visuomotor coordination. If one or more of these processes are deficient or disturbed the child may not be capable of the act of writing.

Let us assume, nevertheless, that all of these processes have been completed successfully. The next step is to write the word *I*. Before he can do so, he must have the image of this word in mind. Lacking such an image, he will not be able to write it unless the image is presented to him and he copies it from the model. When we present material to be copied it is the visual aspect which is provided. As suggested above, providing this aspect does not benefit the apraxic because it is not the visual image which he lacks. The child who lacks this aspect usually writes immediately when given a model to go by. An individual may lack the visual image because he has not learned it or because he cannot recall it; these are separate psychoneurological processes. Learning alone does not assure one of being able to call it to mind, to visualize it. Visualizing assumes not only learning, receiving and storing, but ability to bring it back into mind as needed. A brain dysfunction might impede any one of these processes as well as combinations of them.

If we assume that the child can visualize, the next step is to coordinate the visualized word *I* with the motor system for writing. The ideational aspects must be transduced or converted into motor behavior. Should there be deficiencies at any point in this chain of events he might produce a different word, an illegible equivalent, or even no word at all. If the production is not adequate, he may not be aware of its inadequacies. Such awareness assumes that he is capable of visually monitoring what he produces because through monitoring he is continuously aware of the correctness of what he writes. Such monitoring includes legibility, spelling, syntax, spacing between words and sentences, punctuation, paragraphing, appropriateness of vocabulary, clarity of meaning, and other aspects. Disturbances of the feedback process might include any of these, including an inability to read one's own writing. In terms of differential diagnosis, the diagnostician scrutinizes the written production, looking for errors of the type that characterize groups or individuals having certain language disorders. For example, those having a "syntactical aphasia" write in an agrammatical style, whereas the most common error of persons deaf from early life consists of omitting necessary words.[25]

The visual processes entailed in facile use of the written word are intricate and encompassing. One of the most important of these processes as seen in children with learning disabilities is the inability to mentally visualize letters and words. Also common are deficiencies of memory and poor ability to perceptually discriminate between letters that look alike. Although the memory defects are various, there are two distinct types, immediate and delayed, conforming to the disturbances found in lower animals when certain areas of the brain have been experimentally impaired.[6] Some children learn to recognize letters but only momentarily and only when they remain in view. Hence, they continue to encounter letters as though they are being seen for the first time. Presumably this is the result of a dysfunction in the recording or storing process in the brain.

In contrast, some children are deficient in recall of what is learned, though initially they learn adequately. In this instance, storage takes place but recall is disturbed. When presented to them, these children immediately identify the letter and word as the correct one, the one they have tried to recall, but they cannot bring it into mind themselves.

The example in Illustration 4 is characteristic of a disturbance in immediate learning and memory, inasmuch as these children tend more to be the "phonetizers"; they write phonetically. This story was written by an eight-year-old boy, above average in intelligence, and able to read both silently and orally about one grade above his age level. He was referred for diagnostic study because he seemed incapable of learning to spell. His written language reveals that he has learned what the letters sound like but not what they look like. Therefore, he writes phonetically, writing words the way they sound; note *kereen* for *Korean, avree one* for *everyone, kernal* for *colonel, chines* for *Chinese*, etc. Otherwise vocabulary, syntax, sentence length, punctuation, and meaning fall at the average for his age. He read beautifully what he wrote but was unable to identify his spelling errors. When informed that a word was spelled incorrectly, his only recourse was to again write it the only way it appeared in his mind, which was auditorially.

AUDITORY PROCESSES

Many of our inferences relative to diagnosis are based on the semi-autonomous systems concept as discussed in Chapter I. This assumes that each of the major senses has attained a degree of automony and specialization in the central nervous system, and a major goal diagnostically is to determine the integrity of function in each of these separately and in unison. Other hypotheses that serve as a background to our approach derive from the hierarchy of the verbal systems as portrayed in Figure 1. A disorder might occur at any of these levels, at one or at more than one level. It is necessary diagnostically to determine the degree of intactness

ILLUSTRATION 4. Phonetic writing of an 8-year-old boy with a deficiency in ability to visualize

▶ **ORIGINAL**

John Jerrects was a peravet
in the kerceen war.
it camp avree one wold muke
fun of him, becous he wus
Lowe runke. one day they
went out to war, wen
they came to pork chop
hill the chines suroded
them. Without thinging the
kennal gjave the order to
shot, the chines fell buck,
hopeing they wold wen,
then. the chines sueroded
them agen, and pouted in
for a masev atecke bouth
saedes,

▶ **CORRECTED**

John Jerrects was a private in the Korean War. At camp everyone would make fun of him, because he was low rank. One day they went out to war. When they came to pork chop hill the Chinese surrounded them. Without thinking the colonel gave the order to shoot. The Chinese fell back, hoping they would win. Then the Chinese surrounded them again and poured in for a massive attack on both sides.

at all levels and not to infer deviations simply on the basis of the presenting symptomatology. Diagnostically, the need is to appraise each level of function to the extent possible because disorders of written language may derive from a number of conditions—receptive and expressive.

That it is necessary to hear in order to normally acquire spoken language has been recognized for decades, perhaps for centuries. That auditory integrities are necessary also for learning to read and for acquisition and use of the written word has not been acknowledged in the same manner. From study of language learning by deaf children,[25] and from the results of investigations of children with learning disabilities,[24] it is apparent that auditory processes play a significant role in all verbal functioning, perhaps a leading role. To distinguish these processes from acuity, the ability to hear, we use the term *auditorization*. The ability to auditorize experience is a part of total auditory behavior. Because we have discussed this type of behavior elsewhere we will not analyze it in detail. It involves the manner in which audition serves as a basic alerting system throughout the life span, including while we are asleep. This sensory modality is psychologically nondirectional, permissive, and a manditory channel through which to acquire the most basic verbal system—the spoken word. Vision comparatively is a much less adequate channel for language learning.

Auditorization is less inclusive, referring principally to the use of auditory experience after it has been learned. Hence, perhaps without exception, it entails auditory memory. It is involved in speaking, initially in learning to read and whenever unfamiliar words are encountered on the printed page, and in use of the written word as illustrated repeatedly by spelling disorders. Nonverbally it plays a role in music and in rhythm. We now consider this process more specifically as it relates to the acquisition and use of written language and, accordingly, its importance in differential diagnosis. Sometimes when we read or write we must "sound out" the word before it can be fully understood or meaningfully integrated. In the written form a word, phrase or paragraph must both look and sound right before it is identified as satisfactory.

Dysnomia

To achieve normal auditory function psychoneurologically the individual must hear and learn the spoken language of his culture. He must be able to discriminate between sounds that are similar and to organize them into the sequences that form words. The speech sounds must be "stored" and be available when needed. When they are stored but not recallable instantly because of a dysfunction in the brain, the condition is referred to as *dysnomia* (anomia). The individual knows the word he is trying to remember and recognizes it immediately when it is said for him, but he cannot recall it at will. Usually the person is also unable to produce the word in written form. Unless he can recall it auditorially, unless he can auditorize the word, he can neither speak it nor write it. However, his expressive language is not agrammatical. When he finally recalls the word, he uses it appropriately in relation to other words and he speaks and writes in sentences.

The example in Illustration 5 includes these features. When shown a picture of people (all ages) entering a church, a middle-aged, highly competent professional person who had sustained a vascular illness and which resulted in a dysnomia, wrote as shown below. To be correct he should have written, *The people went to church.* The sentence he wrote is syntactically correct, without misspellings and correctly punctuated except for not dotting the *i*. Experience with this man reveals clearly that he knows that what he has written is incorrect. He writes in this manner because he has no alternative inasmuch as he cannot recall the proper words. The Picture Story Language Test is helpful in identifying language disorders of this type.

ILLUSTRATION 5. Sentence written by a dysnomic adult as he viewed a picture of people entering a church.

The children went to school.

Formulation Aphasia

Another type of language disorder which manifests itself equally in the spoken and written forms is *formulation aphasia,* also referred to as syntactical aphasia.[14,26] It is not characterized by an inability to remember words but by an inability to properly formulate sentences. Words are used in the wrong relationship to each other, tenses are confused and the unit is generally agrammatical. Typically the person with formulation aphasia is aware that he has made errors, that his expressive language is not like that of others. This condition too is caused by a dysfunction in the brain.

A sample of the written language of a nine year old boy with formulation aphasia but who is above average in intelligence is given in Illustration 6. His spoken language was equally lacking in Syntax, so again we note the circumstances of being unable to normally produce both spoken and written language.

ILLUSTRATION 6.   Story written by a 9-year-old boy with formulation aphasia.

Father give I bike.
I Broke rope
I like my boy because.
I ready my vork.
I cry. I don't no.
I not have grandfather
sometimes in
prospect Heights rain.
I have chickens lay
eggs.

Receptive Aphasia

We have indicated that some persons cannot write because they are dysgraphic. An analogous condition, expressive aphasia, occurs for spoken language. There is a deficit in ability to relate the auditory image of the word to the motor system for speech. As would be expected the expressive aphasic, without other involvements, writes normally.

In contrast, when the disorder is in comprehension of the spoken word, when a *receptive aphasia* is present, there is a marked effect on written language if the aphasia is present from early life. If the receptive aphasia is incurred *after* spoken, read and written language has been acquired, the effect on the written form varies, whereas the child having an aphasia of this type preverbally is usually deficient in both read and written language. Though there are many variations, irrespective of the age of onset, children and adults having this condition are incapable of monitoring what they write. Presumably if they cannot monitor what they say, they cannot monitor what they write. What is written cannot be monitored only by the way it looks because it also must sound right. Perhaps the final, the most fundamental check on what is written is the way it sounds. This may be the reason that professional writers often advise their students to read aloud what they have written. Supposedly they can criticize their own productions more effectively when they do.

The story in Illustration 7 was written by a receptive aphasic boy when he was ten years of age. Because his condition was congenital, he had virtually no spoken language until he was four years old. Gradually after acquiring considerable function at the level of spoken language, he attained some ability to read and later to use written language to a degree. He continues to make progress in all of the verbal functions. The illustration given portrays his difficulty with verb tense (syntax).

ILLUSTRATION 7. The written story by a receptive aphasic boy 10 years of age.

The little girl is make
dog food. the dog want
seme food.

Reauditorization of Letters

An intriguing instance of a psychoneurological learning disability involving the auditory process is found in the child who lacks the auditory aspect of letters of the alphabet. Though he has learned and can recall what the letters look like, he has not learned their auditory equivalents. There are at least two forms of this problem, one being the inability to learn the names of the letters and the other a deficiency in learning the sounds associated with them. These do not necessarily appear concomitantly.

An example of this learning problem is given in Illustration 8. It was written by a 16-year-old boy of average intelligence who was referred for study because of a marked inability to read and to use the written word. Spoken language was excellent. When asked to write words from dictation he immediately and with vehemence stated, "I can't write." The examiner gave encouragement, then asked whether he could write if the words were spelled aloud for him. His reply was, "Of course." The illustration shows his ability to write with and without this assistance. As can be seen, when the words were spelled aloud he had no difficulty in writing them. Moreover, he could copy normally, hence, cannot be considered a dysgraphic of the apraxic type. Without assistance, however, he was severely limited in ability to produce written language.

ILLUSTRATION 8. Words written by a 16-year-old dyslexic boy with a deficiency in ability to auditorize.

▶ **DICTATED NORMALLY** ▶ **SPELLED ALOUD**

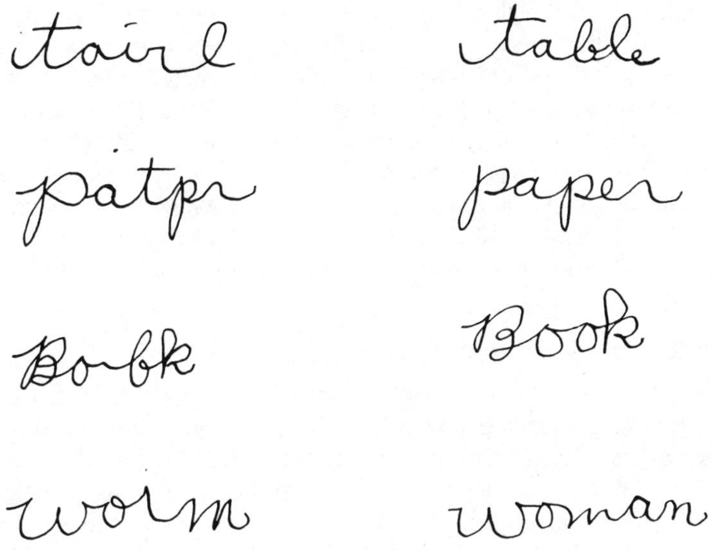

As in other instances the exact nature of this learning disability is unknown but several observations seem apropos. This behavior is not characteristic of emotionally disturbed children who sometimes resist or reject certain facets of academic learning. Supplementary observation and evaluation confirmed this opinion. This boy, typical of those presenting this deficiency, had excellent motor ability. He was characteristic also in that he had a marked dyslexia, scoring at approximately the second grade on tests of reading. We noted, therefore, that his deficit in written language was reciprocal to his limited capacity to internalize the read word; he could not have output without input.

It must be stressed that he had acquired a certain facet of the reading process. He was not without facility with the visual-verbal system because when given assistance with the *auditory* aspect only, he readily produced the written form. More specifically, it was a facet of the auditory aspect, the names of the letters which was supplied, not the visual. He was not shown a model of the letters or of the words. Rather, first the word was dictated and he wrote it as best he could. Second, he was asked to write it again but this time the examiner spelled the word aloud and he wrote each letter as it was spoken by the examiner.

We may infer that it was the auditory aspect that was lacking and which he had been unable to learn. When this aspect was provided, he could write because the visual properties had been learned and were available to him without assistance. We see here the importance of evaluating the deficit as manifested in the written form in order to gain insight into the reading disability. We classified his learning disability as a type of *auditory* dyslexia. The dysfunction in the brain was shown by neurological and electroencephalographic studies. A broader generalization seems warranted to the effect that if the child cannot learn both the auditory and the visual aspects of letters, he will not learn to read normally. This boy could not acquire the auditory equivalents of the appearance of the letters, he could not "translate" the visual into the auditory and so he did not learn to read. Inasmuch as the written form also initially assumes that both are available, neither could he produce the written word. There are many implications for remedial education.

Sequentializing Auditorially

A disturbance in the auditory process, similar but not identical to the problem of reauditorizing letters, is the inability to *auditorially sequentialize* syllables. Though syllabication tests, such as are found on diagnostic tests of reading, are beneficial in diagnostic study of this condition, the written form as produced by the child often is more revealing.

In Illustration 9 we see how a 16-year-old boy wrote when the words were dictated in the usual manner and how he wrote them when *not* the words but the syllables were dictated. In other words, when the whole word, *transportation*, was dictated he could not accurately produce the written equivalent. However, when this word was dictated syllable by syllable, *trans-por-ta-tion*, he had no difficulty in writing it correctly.

This problem cannot be viewed as being of the same type as the one discussed above, Reauditorization of Letters. First, the boy whose writing appears in Illustration 9 was not dyslexic. His ability to read was above average, as was his intelligence (I.Q. 125). Moreover, his Productivity (Total Words, Total Sentences and Words per Sentence), Syntax and Abstract-Concrete scores were not substantially below average. His deficiency, therefore, was in an exceedingly specific aspect of the written form. Why could he not spell more correctly when he used written language? Again the learning disability was found to be related to a dysfunction in the brain; neurological and electroencephalographic findings were

ILLUSTRATION 9. Words written by a 16-year-old boy with an auditory spelling disorder.

▶ **DICTATED NORMALLY**   ▶ **DICTATED ONE SYLLABLE AT A TIME**

positive. This dysfunction precluded ability to sequentialize words auditorially, syllable by syllable, even though he had learned both the auditory and visual equivalents of the letters and had no difficulty with reading.

We note that when words of more than one syllable are presented as a whole and at one time through dictation, he cannot hold them in mind so that he can "transduce" and produce them in the written form. He "forgets" essential parts of the words, apparently because of a disturbance in the ability to hold all of them in mind in the proper order. When the syllables are sequentialized for him he has no difficulty in producing them in writing, manifesting that it is not the letters themselves in which he is deficient. This too is a disturbance of the ability to auditorize.

Syllabication and Auditory Blending

Among others, Monroe[23] and Gates[11] have stressed the importance of auditory processes in learning to read. These processes have received less attention as they pertain to the written word. Their significance in children with learning disabilities is gradually being documented. In a neurological and behavioral study of these children, Boshes and Myklebust[3] found that ability to syllabicate and blend word sounds correlated with neurological status. *Syllabication* consists of the ability to divide words into syllables whereas *auditory blending* entails the facility to combine isolated syllables into words. These functions are mentioned here because it is not uncommon to see children with disturbances of written language that are related to inabilities of this type.

ILLUSTRATION 10. The writing of a 17-year-old boy with a severe auditorizing defect.

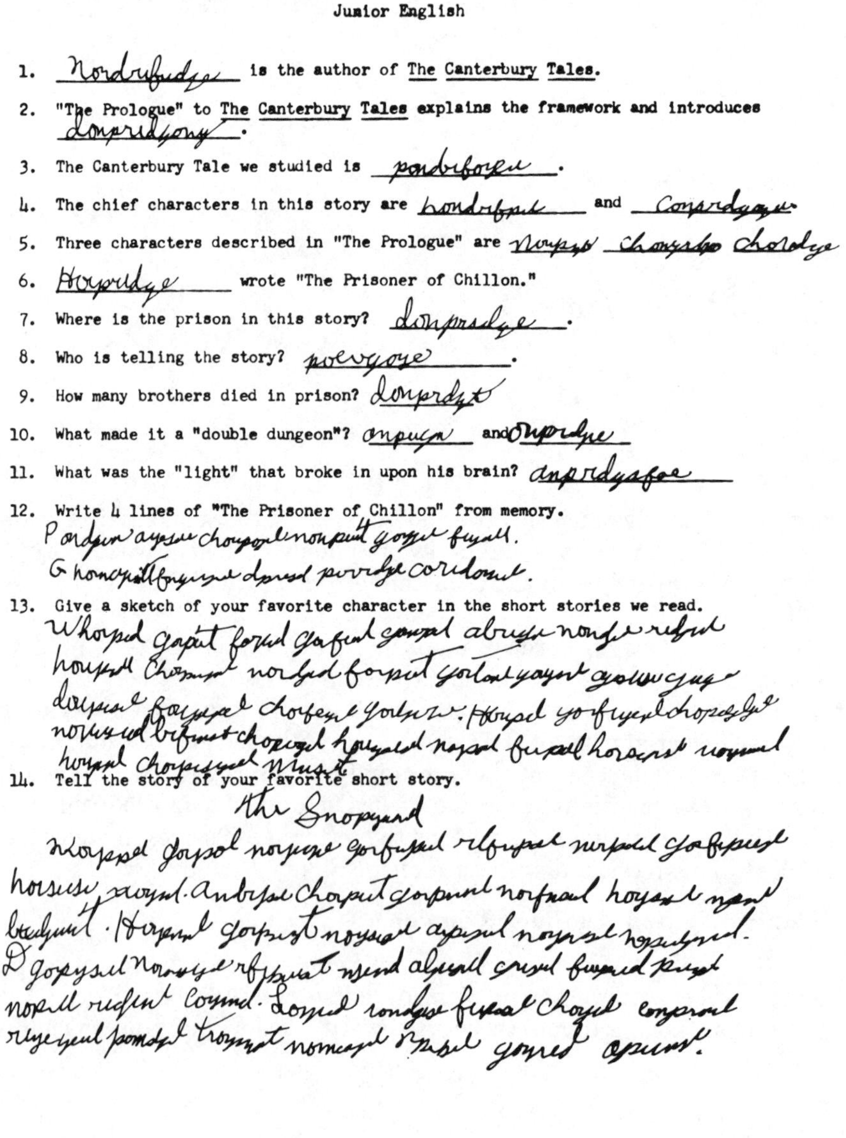

Junior English

1. _____ is the author of The Canterbury Tales.
2. "The Prologue" to The Canterbury Tales explains the framework and introduces _____.
3. The Canterbury Tale we studied is _____.
4. The chief characters in this story are _____ and _____
5. Three characters described in "The Prologue" are _____
6. _____ wrote "The Prisoner of Chillon."
7. Where is the prison in this story? _____.
8. Who is telling the story? _____.
9. How many brothers died in prison? _____
10. What made it a "double dungeon"? _____ and _____
11. What was the "light" that broke in upon his brain? _____
12. Write 4 lines of "The Prisoner of Chillon" from memory.
13. Give a sketch of your favorite character in the short stories we read.
14. Tell the story of your favorite short story.

The 17-year-old boy who wrote as he did on a Junior English Test is an intriguing case in point. We provided remedial instruction for this young man for more than seven years, beginning at 17 years of age when his written language was as shown in Illustration 10. He had a marked auditory dyslexia. He could not auditorize any aspect of words, hence was at a loss to syllabicate and blend them. He made good but arduous progress with reading and writing and attained the seventh to eighth grade level after seven years of training.

As can be noted, his written language is the opposite from those who write phonetically. When he lacks ability to auditorize, when he cannot "sound out" words, he can produce letters only as they appear and not as they sound and thus cannot form syllables. The result is a "hodge podge" of letters run together that do not form words so even he, the writer, is unable to read them.

Spoken Versus Written Language Ability

Though the Picture Story Language Test has not been standardized for spoken language, often it is beneficial diagnostically to compare an individual's facility with the spoken and the written word. The lack of norms for spoken language is not critical because facility with the spoken should be at least equal to facility with the written. Variations in ability to use these verbal systems are not uncommon. Nevertheless, if the involvement of auditory language is receptive and has persisted from early life, the acquisition of the read and written word also is impeded. On the other hand, if the auditory receptive language disorder is sustained after the spoken, read, and written systems have been acquired, the impairment may vary from one system to the other.

Auditory Superior

In working with children who have learning disabilities, it is common to find those in whom auditory language is superior to the written. Illustration 11 characterizes this type of child. These samples are from an 11-year-old boy who was found to have a moderately severe dyslexia with a concomitant spelling problem and a deficiency in revisualization. He was otherwise a mentally bright and alert boy with an I.Q. of 121.

In comparing his spoken and written language, the greater fluency in the spoken is obvious; his level of Productivity in this form is much higher. As is common for dyslexics, the written form is tedious and laborious. Though sentence length is adequate, he wrote only two sentences. Syntax also is adequate but spelling is inferior and this too characterizes children who have this type of language disorder.

Written Superior

When diagnostic comparison is made, written language in some instances is found to be superior to the spoken. This occurs most often in adults in whom language functions had been normal until the onset of brain disease. However, it is also seen in children as shown by Illustration 12. These stories represent the spoken and written language levels of a 15-year-old boy with a moderate involvement of receptive aphasia. Because of high intelligence (I.Q. at least 130), excellent home management, special training and a good school program, he was able to compensate for his disability. Hence he became a good reader and achieved a level of facility with the written word that exceeded his spoken language.

ILLUSTRATION 11. Stories by an 11-year-old dyslexic boy showing comparative superiority with spoken language.

▶ SPOKEN

Early Monday morning I woke up—me and my friend, Pete. We were going to go to a field and build our fort. We went—we left with our lunches and were going to eat in the fort after we got finished and we had three stories in the fort and we were finishing up on the third, and then we—then my mom said we had to go some place after we got home. So she took—she took me to Northwestern University, and we pulled through the parking lot and saw that they were working on a new addition. They were filling in sand—they were filling in the lake with sand. So we—we went in and then I met the teacher at the door and then I was listening to my transistor radio and the Dodgers just hit a four-run homer. Then the teacher took me into a room, and there were—I sat down at a table and there was a box of toys and then I sat up a dinner room with the plates and a baby and a scooter and a high chair and lamps and a dresser, and it was a little table just my size. And there was a shoe, just like I learned on, how to tie my shoes with, and a tower and a car and some books just like I have at home. The room was just about the same size as my bedroom at home only there wasn't a bed in the middle of it. There were lots of cabinets and they all had labels on them. And then I had to go home and we ate dinner and then I watched a movie on TV and then I had to go to bed.

▶ WRITTEN

Monday

Early Monday morning I got up and turned on the TV and I watched Bugs Bunny and Elmer thud and they had the turtle races and some cartoons. later then Mom told me to get in the car. then we whent to the store then we whent to Northwestern University.

It should be noted that "superior" in this case is relative. The number of words in each of these stories is considerably below average. The superiority of the written form is largely in the higher level of ideation expressed. The spoken language story is "concrete," somewhat redundant and lacking in narrative; it is a description of that which is portrayed. The written language story is more in harmony with this boy's ability, showing narration and abstract ideation. Such differences frequently are of unusual importance diagnostically and provide a basis for planning remedial instruction. It is pertinent to stress that he shows evidence of residual auditory dysfunctioning in his written language, both in word usage and in spelling.

ILLUSTRATION 12. Stories by a 15-year-old boy with moderate receptive aphasia, showing comparative superiority with written language.

▶ **WRITTEN**

"why do they keep takeing pictures?" Billy thought "dont they have enough by now? Then he lost himself in his work. The time befor he was given something to p/ay with here were almost imbearable but now he was allowwed to be to himself. At least thats what he thought at the time when they gave him the worn box of dolls now they were takeing Pictures like mad.

▶ **SPOKEN**

Well, there's a worn box of dolls and doll furniture on a chair next to the table and there's a boy in a suit playing with some dolls and doll furniture on the table. Behind him are some marked cabinets—wooden cabinets with shelves with toys on it. The boy is about five years old and he's putting a girl—a toy girl next to a toy table and there's a boy doll going after a dog and—uh—a cabinet on the table—toy cabinet with no back to it.

Spoken and Written Equal

Children with receptive aphasia commonly reflect the interdependence of spoken and written language. The illustrations below are by a boy ten years of age who initially had a moderately severe receptive aphasia. These samples represent his verbal facility after three years of training with considerable improvement in language behavior. His Syntax and Abstract-Concrete scores for the auditory and written forms are equivalent but he has 111 words in the spoken as compared with 69 in the written story.

ILLUSTRATION 13.   Stories by a 10-year-old boy with receptive aphasia showing equivalency with spoken and written language.

▶ **SPOKEN**

Well, the boy is playing house with his toys. He has a mother—a mother, a father, a baby, dog, sister and a brother. Mother is setting the table for dinner so she calls the family in and everybody—body goes in the house—goes in the house in the bathroom wash their hands and their faces. Then they sit down at the table—then they sit down at the table on the chairs. They they—then they are ready to eat but first they have to say their prayer. This is how it goes: "Come Lord Jesus, be our guest. Let this food to us be blessed. Amen." That's all.

▶ **WRITTEN**

The little boy is playing house with his toys. He has a father, a mother, baby, dog, brother, and a sister and a dog. It's is about time for dinner call mother Everyboby gose into the house to wash their hands and faces. Dinner is set on the table. Everybody is sitting down on a chair. Then they say their pray, "Come Lord Jease be our gusse let this food to us be bless Amen.

DISORDERS OF WRITTEN LANGUAGE IN HANDICAPPED CHILDREN

In addition to clinical information of the types discussed above, the Picture Story Language Test provides five scores that are useful when making diagnostic studies of individuals or of groups. Three of these scores are derived from the Productivity Scale (Total Words, Total Sentences and Words per Sentence) and furnish quantified evidence relative to the amount of language written when the Test is administered in the standardized manner. Scores also are obtained for Syntax, the correctness of the language written and for Abstract-Concrete, the nature of the content or meaning expressed.

This Test has been used extensively in the study of groups of handicapped children and a number of differences have been revealed in comparison with normal children.[24,25] Only a brief discussion of these differences will be given here in an attempt to suggest the usefulness of the scores in making diagnostic studies of children who have specific handicaps. Illustrative Stories are presented for each of the groups and these should be reviewed in detail by the examiner; see also stories in the Scoring Guide.

Reading Disability

Throughout this volume we emphasize the relationship between read and written language. To explore the interdependency of these verbal systems research was conducted on two groups of children who had marked limitations in ability to learn to read. The first group comprised a public school population classified generally as "reading disability," whereas the second consisted of children who had been through an extensive diagnostic evaluation and had been classified as having dyslexia.

While there were differences between these groups as compared with the normal, their scores, in general, showed them to be inferior especially in ability to produce the same quantity of language; they were deficient in Total Words, Total Sentences and Words per Sentence. Moreover, at the lower age levels dyslexia significantly restricted the use of correct syntax. Interestingly, the dyslexic population did not manifest inferiority in expression of abstract ideas, albeit they had been diagnosed as having a dysfunction in the brain. Although it is premature to view these findings as a pattern of performance characterizing dyslexic children, the diagnostician can be confident that their written language typically deviates from the normal.

Illustrative Stories By Reading Disability Children

These stories were selected by age, sex and score as being representative of facility with the written word as manifested by children classified by public school personnel as having a reading disability. As disclosed by these examples, the written language of this population differs widely from the normal; compare their scores with the normative data in Tables 2, 3, and 4.

Little growth occurs for Total Words and Total Sentences from nine through 15 years. The Words per Sentence scores, on the other hand, are erratic. The female at 11 years and the male at 13 years wrote abnormally long sentences, whereas the sentence length for both sexes at the other age levels show a limited increase. The Syntax Quotients also reveal a deficiency in four of the subjects, with the remaining four attaining normal proficiency in correctness of usage. More generally, these stories reflect the overall findings to the effect that Productivity, not Syntax, is the greater limitation.

ILLUSTRATION 14.   Illustrative Stories: reading disability.

▶ **9 YEARS**

MALE

One Time I was playing with my toys. Ther wase a little dog and a tatro little dwir And fore littlle pekle and gre dodey. And ary todell And two dresro dresser?

Total Words	21 (10)
Total Sentences	2
Words per Sentence	10.5
Syntax Quotient	85
Abstract-Concrete	7

FEMALE

One day a little boy nano allan saw playing whit sone etoys. boll house things there ore girls, boy, and mother, and father and furnitaure. He had some Bood, cars, and a Big Ball, and some blocks.

Total Words	29 (8)
Total Sentences	4
Words per Sentence	7.3
Syntax Quotient	80
Abstract-Concrete	9

ILLUSTRATION 14—Continued.

▶ 11 YEARS

MALE

The boy is playing with little people. A baby & boys and girl and father and dog. He is playing house with them. Father is a soldger. The table is set when he comes in. The boy is after, the dog. The girl is standing in a cheer.

Total Words	42	(6)
Total Sentences	6	
Words per Sentence	7.0	
Syntax Quotient	95	
Abstract-Concrete	11	

FEMALE

The boy is playing what toys and he is puting a frnia on the tabl he is makeing a farwing room and he is suting people in the farwing room and a dog and a baby and a mother and a father and a little girl seting on a char.

Total Words	41	(9)
Total Sentences	2	
Words per Sentence	20.5	
Syntax Quotient	88	
Abstract-Concrete	7	

ILLUSTRATION 14—Continued.

▶ **13 YEARS**

MALE

This story ics a bout a boy /
playing with some dolls and
some doll functicer. the dog
is washing T.V. and the
mother ~~~~ lunch
how barther is going to the
table and mother is going
to seat donw by the table

Total Words	52
Total Sentences	3
Words per Sentence	17.3
Syntax Quotient	95
Abstract-Concrete	14

FEMALE

Ther was a little boy how had dolls
and girls. He like to play with them.
He sate down and play with them one
day? He had a toy dog, and a play
car he like vear much. So thats what
he did all day.

Total Words	45
Total Sentences	5
Words per Sentence	9.0
Syntax Quotient	96
Abstract-Concrete	8

ILLUSTRATION 14—Continued.

▶ 15 YEARS

MALE

The boy is playing with his sister's doll house. And he's puting it together / Looks to me like he likes to play with things that you have to build up.

Total Words	29
Total Sentences	3
Words per Sentence	9.7
Syntax Quotient	94
Abstract-Concrete	8

FEMALE

Once apon a time there was a boy. and he was all by his self planing house. He was all dress up he look like he was going out and he could not go.

Total Words	34
Total Sentences	3
Words per Sentence	11.3
Syntax Quotient	86
Abstract-Concrete	8

The Abstract-Concrete scores indicate a considerable inferiority in comparison with the normal, a trend found for the total population. Further study must be made to clarify the implications for diagnosis of dyslexia versus other types of reading disability.

Speech Defective

Children having articulatory defects, as classified in a public school system, also were found to have deficiencies in written language.[24] Their greatest deviation occurred in Total Words and Total Sentences. Though inferior in Words per Sentence, their more pronounced limitation was in sheer quantity or length of the total production.

In this study we also applied measures of facility in spoken language and in reading. From the theoretical position stated in Chapter I, it was intriguing to find that they were most adequate in the spoken, with reading next and performance in written language the most deviate. These children were most successful in Syntax and Words per Sentence, the more technical aspects of usage, and they were most inferior in fluency as measured by their total output.

Illustrative Stories By Speech Defective Children

The stories presented here typify those written by children with articulatory defects. The scores for Total Words, Total Sentences and Words per Sentence conform to the mean scores by age for the total population. The greatest deficiency is in Total Words and Total Sentences with Words per Sentence more equal to the levels attained by the normative population; see Tables 2, 3 and 4. These examples, according to our more inclusive findings, accurately reflect that Syntax presents a problem in early life but correct usage is attained, albeit substantially later than found for the normal population.

Use of abstraction is inferior, the highest score (15) being attained by a 13-year-old female. Even her score is below average for normal 11-year-old girls. This limitation in abstract ideation concomitant with poor productivity was common to many of our findings. However, this trend holds only for groups, not individuals.

Although the implications diagnostically are not fully understood, the total pattern of the scores must be carefully scrutinized. Our purpose is to illustrate that children with defects of articulation tend to have difficulties in acquiring facility with written language. There are important implications for comprehensive diagnostic evaluations, as well as for remedial training and education.

ILLUSTRATION 15. Illustrative Stories: speech defective.

▶ **7 YEARS**

MALE

I like to qlay
with a toy.
toys are go
to you.
IS your Mother
go to you ?

Total Words	18
Total Sentences	3
Words per Sentence	6.0
Syntax Quotient	87
Abstract-Concrete	5

FEMALE

The boy has a good time .
can you go ovve ny home
to play .

Total Words	14
Total Sentences	2
Words per Sentence	7.0
Syntax Quotient	81
Abstract-Concrete	8

ILLUSTRATION 15—Continued.

▶ 9 YEARS

MALE

Once that was a boy he had many toy he had a mans made of wood and woman and child he had a lot of books in the toy rome he had many mayy toy

the toy Rome

Total Words	36
Total Sentences	5
Words per Sentence	7.2
Syntax Quotient	82
Abstract-Concrete	9

FEMALE

The boy is playing with the toy in his house. He have book and game to play with it to. He have so much fun with it he like to play with it. He love to play with it.

Total Words	39
Total Sentences	5
Words per Sentence	7.8
Syntax Quotient	81
Abstract-Concrete	8

ILLUSTRATION 15—Continued.

▶ 11 YEARS

MALE

There was a boy who was playing with some toy dolls and dollhouse and he was seting up a table and put a doll in a chaire and he set the some food on the table and there to was a baby in a highchaire and there was a cabent nee by the table. And there was a dog and there was a le boy who was going to pet the dog.

Total Words	68
Total Sentences	6
Words per Sentence	11.3
Syntax Quotient	87
Abstract-Concrete	11

FEMALE

There is a boy playing with a dall. there is some story Books. and a (chore) box with toys. there is a showe an a shilf. the bay has brown eyer blue suit. and brown (heaiyr hary. and he is playing (with) on a table.

Total Words	45
Total Sentences	5
Words per Sentence	9.0
Syntax Quotient	92
Abstract-Concrete	7

ILLUSTRATION 15—Continued.

▶ 13 YEARS

MALE

A boy is sitting down at a table it looks as though if he making up a home with tiny dolls. In the picture he has five statues of people I guess he supposts to be the Father the Mother children and a table a couch some chairs and other furniture.

The boy is wearing a suit and is putting the tiny people in the way he wants to and he even as a dog in the picture

Total Words	77
Total Sentences	7
Words per Sentence	11.0
Syntax Quotient	96
Abstract-Concrete	9

FEMALE

The little boy must enjoy hobbies because in his Room as is the Room in which he is now in are a lot of interesting as things which can lead to hobbies for instance the books there are a small library of Books for Childrens one of his Greatest hobbies must be dollhouse dolls & furniture. On his little Table he has assembled the furniture to make it look like the living Room or Dining room he also has assembled the dolls so each individual one is doing something different.

Total Words	88
Total Sentences	6
Words per Sentence	14.7
Syntax Quotient	96
Abstract-Concrete	15

Mentally Retarded

The influence of mental capacity on language behavior is clearly disclosed by studies of the mentally retarded. However, most research has pertained to the spoken and read language forms.

To evaluate the suitability of the Picture Story Language Test as a diagnostic instrument, as well as to gain further insight into the written word as a verbal system, we investigated the written language behavior of a population of educable mentally handicapped school children. They were markedly inferior on all of the measures—Productivity, Syntax and Abstract-Concrete. The pattern was for the greatest deficiency to appear in the amount of language written, with less deficiency in correctness of usage.[24]

It is apparent that a standardized measure of written language can be used with this group of handicapped children in at least two ways: first, as further evidence regarding the presence of mental retardation, and second, as a means to further explore their verbal limitations as well as their specific educational needs.

Illustrative Stories By Mentally Retarded Children

There are several features that characterize the stories written by the educable mentally handicapped as a group. As mentioned above, and as shown by these Illustrative Stories, Productivity is limited. Scores might vary conspicuously for individuals within the group, however. The story of the 15-year-old male presented below is a case in point. Though he was markedly inferior in total output, he scored at the average level in Words per Sentence. In other words, the mentally retarded can attain normal facility with the written word *in certain respects*. This fact is of importance diagnostically and in terms of remedial education.

All of our data suggest that Syntax is the most readily achieved aspect of facility with written language. The stories presented here conform to this generalization. It was in correctness of usage that the mentally retarded attained their most normal proficiency.

It is not intended to imply that the four stories shown typify all aspects of the problem encountered by the mentally retarded so far as their written verbal behavior is concerned, but diagnostically it is noteworthy that none of these children scored significantly above the seven-year level on use of abstract ideas. Again we note the independence of the scores because though they show an increment by age in the number of words written, they do not show comparable growth in the use of abstraction.

Conceivably, a profile of the relationships among the five scores that characterize this group of handicapped children might be evolved. These possibilities are promising in terms of their applicability in differential diagnosis and from the point of view of gaining further insight into their special needs educationally.

ILLUSTRATION 16.   Illustrative Stories: educable mentally retarded.

▶ 9 YEARS

MALE

I saw a picture the store it had a boy playing the teacher gave hem it to play. the and of the play

Total Words	16
Total Sentences	5
Words per Sentence	5.3
Syntax Quotient	78
Abstract-Concrete	7

FEMALE

an boy was playe wits his toy

Total Words	7
Total Sentences	1
Words per Sentence	7.0
Syntax Quotient	82
Abstract-Concrete	7

ILLUSTRATION 16—Continued.

▶ 11 YEARS

MALE

I see a Boy

I see a Dog

I see a quilt

I see a Book

I see a a

Total Words	20
Total Sentences	5
Words per Sentence	4.0
Syntax Quotient	92
Abstract-Concrete	3

FEMALE

The boy is playing whate Toys

The boy is playing house

The boy has Toys here

The boy is home here

The boy is at home

Total Words	26
Total Sentences	5
Words per Sentence	5.2
Syntax Quotient	94
Abstract-Concrete	7

ILLUSTRATION 16—Continued.

▶ 13 YEARS

MALE

This story is about a boy a he is playing with some of his sisters chairs tables lamp dogs and dolls. The boy is playing on his mother's table in his play room.

Total Words	31	(2)
Total Sentences	3	
Words per Sentence	15.5	
Syntax Quotient	93	
Abstract-Concrete	7	

FEMALE

This boy is playing houses with dolls on the table he has a big table to play with. He has a car and some book and a play toys shoes a dog and boyboc have baby lamb a blocks he has a ball and a father and mother to he has a box of toy.

Total Words	43 (12)
Total Sentences	5
Words per Sentence	8.6
Syntax Quotient	91
Abstract-Concrete	7

ILLUSTRATION 16—Continued.

▶ 15 YEARS

MALE

The boy in the rome for look in the shelf have a car in the shelf in the ball I all a dog I see two men I see two girl I see one boy he have is a big boy in the

Total Words	39
Total Sentences	7
Words per Sentence	5.7
Syntax Quotient	80
Abstract-Concrete	9

FEMALE

There is a little boy and he's playing With his doll's he's playing with them in the kitchen on the table and there are some books too. and there is a car as the cabinet and book on the cabinet. There's furniture to for the dolls to sit on There's a dog to in the picture.

Total Words	56
Total Sentences	5
Words per Sentence	11.2
Syntax Quotient	92
Abstract-Concrete	7

Socially-Emotionally Disturbed

Another type of imposition on acquisition and use of the written word is emotional disturbance. It is remarkable that psychogenicity in association with the spoken and read forms of language has been stressed widely, yet mention of this condition in relation to written language is essentially nonexistent. It seemed necessary therefore to raise the question of the nature and possible incidence of psychogenic involvements of the written word.

To explore this question we studied a population of public school children classified as being socially-emotionally disturbed. It was comprised principally of the "acting-out" type of child and included many who were seriously delinquent. The results indicated significant inferiority in all verbal behavior, spoken, read and written. Typical stories written by these children are presented below. Their written language was characterized by a generalized deficiency, being inferior in amount and correctness, as well as in content. The diagnostician must be alert to what appears as a basic relationship between social-emotional disturbance and facility with written language, particularly in children who present serious behavior and adjustment problems in school.

Illustrative Stories By Socially-Emotionally Disturbed Children

Although as a group, the stories written by the socially-emotionally disturbed showed generalized inadequacy, as indicated by the Illustrative Stories there were wide variations. Of the seven presented here, only one scored within normal limits in Productivity; the 13-year-old female fell at approximately the mean for normal children on Total Words, Total Sentences and Words per Sentence (see Tables 2, 3, and 4). Otherwise, in sheer output, in the amount of language produced, the other six fell far below the norms.

It is worthy of note, nevertheless, that five out of these seven scored within normal limits on at least one of the aspects of written language measured. The seven-year-old male earned average scores on Words per Sentence, Syntax and Abstract-Concrete. The nine-year-old male attained an average score on Words per Sentence as did the 15-year-old female. Both of the 15-year-olds scored at the average level on Syntax.

From the data and on the basis of our clinical experience, we have the impression that many children in this group present problems not only of emotional disturbance but also poor educational achievement as a result of deprivation of opportunity and the presence of learning disabilities. Statistical analysis revealed further that the factor of developmental delay might be involved.

In more diagnostic terms, these children appear to be deficient in verbal behavior generally though many attain normal function in specific respects. The story written by the 13-year-old female is the most adequate of those presented here but despite normal productivity, Syntax and Abstract-Concrete are low. Furthermore, the spelling errors, of which there are several, cause the diagnostician to be suspicious of a disturbance in the visual aspects of learning; these errors suggest a need to unduly depend on the auditory aspects.

More investigation is necessary to clarify the relationships between emotional disturbances and impositions on learning as they affect facility with written language. That such relationships exist, perhaps in many instances in association with other factors, is suggested by our studies. The Picture Story Language Test has been useful in differentiating children with such disturbances from those whose lack of proficiency is caused by other conditions.

ILLUSTRATION 17. Illustrative Stories: socially-emotionally disturbed.

▶ **7 YEARS**

MALE

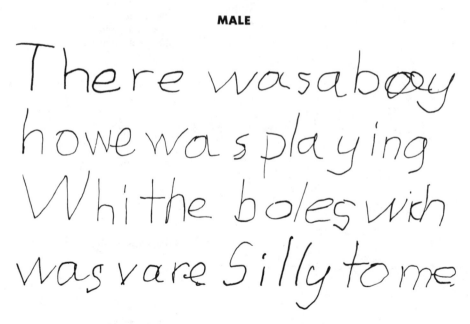

Total Words	15
Total Sentences	2
Words per Sentence	7.5
Syntax Quotient	89
Abstract-Concrete	7

ILLUSTRATION 17—Continued.

▶ **9 YEARS**

MALE

This little boy is playing with girls things he is sitting on a chair there are a lot of books and a ball and a car and some blocks on a shelf

Total Words	29
Total Sentences	3
Words per Sentence	9.7
Syntax Quotient	88
Abstract-Concrete	7

▶ **11 YEARS**

MALE

The boy to play home and he put every Body the table and he have a good time

Total Words	18
Total Sentences	2
Words per Sentence	9.0
Syntax Quotient	82
Abstract-Concrete	8

ILLUSTRATION 17—Continued.

▶ 13 YEARS

MALE

He is playing with those toys. He is pretending that, that is his family

Total Words	14
Total Sentences	2
Words per Sentence	7.0
Syntax Quotient	88
Abstract-Concrete	8

FEMALE

I things, this picture is a bout a boy working with puppets. He has some which is siting down and some is standing up and one is reding in something like a stroller. I things he is trying to make some pupets. He has a lot of figures there of all source of kinds. He has some figures in a box and has a lamp, some chairs and tables he also has a little girl siting on the table in a chair. He has a women standing up talking to a baby in a stroller. He has a chair in one hand and is holding a girl in a chair in the other hand. behind him is a cupboard with books and cars and many other things on it.

Total Words	137
Total Sentences	10
Words per Sentence	13.7
Syntax Quotient	87
Abstract-Concrete	11

ILLUSTRATION 17—Continued.

▶ 15 YEARS

MALE

A boy is playing with some doll house toys he is setting them up on the table the mother is playing the boy is playing with the dog the girl is sitting at the table the father is going to the table this picture shows a boy having fun with his toys

Total Words	52
Total Sentences	7
Words per Sentence	7.5
Syntax Quotient	91
Abstract-Concrete	12

FEMALE

This is a story about a boy about the age of 7 he is a normal boy and seems like a very happy one. At the moment his whole mind is attracted to the house he is arranging. I'm sure he is pretending that he is one of the characters that he is arranging. He is arranging the figures as if they were ready to have dinner, like he would have at his house.

Total Words	73
Total Sentences	5
Words per Sentence	14.6
Syntax Quotient	97
Abstract-Concrete	15

Deaf

We have made extensive studies of the written language of the deaf.[25] When a hearing loss is severe and when it exists from the preverbal age, it has a marked effect on language development, including the read and written word. Furthermore, it results in features and characteristics unique to this handicapped group, referred to as *deafisms*. Some of these are apparent in the Illustrative Stories presented below; see also Scoring Guide.

The Picture Story Language Test has been useful in identifying these characteristics, as well as in revealing the growth in written language that occurs as a result of educational training. It assists in making specific differentiations between the written language of deaf children and those with other handicaps or learning disabilities, as shown by the Total Sentence score. Deaf children by 15 years of age are equivalent to hearing children on this measure, but they are very inferior on Total Words. Though they write fewer words, they write many short simple sentences so they are not inferior in the number of sentences. This conclusion is corroborated by their Words per Sentence score which shows them to be markedly limited in normal sentence length.

Another pattern that typifies the written language of deaf children is their peculiarity in relation to Syntax. One of these, revealed readily by the scoring procedure used in the Picture Story Language Test, is Omissions; essential words are omitted from the sentence. This is the most common error in the sentence structure of the deaf, comprising approximately 50 per cent of all of their Syntax errors. They also have characteristic errors involving Substitutions, Additions and Word Order.

These findings for the deaf demonstrate the need for the diagnostician to consider both the Error Category and the Error Type when analyzing the deviations of a given group. Only when these scores are interpreted in relation to each other and in relation to the pattern for the normal child can the most beneficial distinctions and classifications be made.

Illustrative Stories By Deaf Children

These stories written by profoundly deaf children illustrate a marked problem in the acquisition of written language. The first sentence of the story written by the seven-year-old female is especially characteristic. It manifests many of the errors that can be identified by the Syntax Scale in the Picture Story Language Test, including Additions, Omissions, Word Endings, Word Order, etc.

It is unusual that an authority on language behavior should indicate that deaf children acquire read and written language normally.[21] It is obvious to educators of the deaf that they do not. These stories representing their written language are presented here, not only for their significance diagnostically, but also because they reveal the severe limitation imposed on acquisition of the read and written word when the *auditory* (spoken) verbal system is not available. Presumably, when the read and the written cannot be related to the auditory, it is remarkably difficult to acquire them. It might be inferred that a basic deprivation, such as lack of auditory language, grossly disturbs all language acquisition. We interpret this circumstance as conforming to the hierarchical relationships among Man's verbal systems as schematized in Figure 1.

ILLUSTRATION 18.   Illustrative Stories: deaf.

▶ 7 YEARS

MALE

boy has blca Keyes and black hair.
boy h as o na white, and, white, and
white and blcak pant
yellow sock
brown shons,

Total Words	19 (4)
Total Sentences	2
Words per Sentence	9.5
Syntax Quotient	75
Abstract-Concrete	3

FEMALE

Baby has play some a the books.
boys and girls she some boots.
Sally snow is the some was birt and Father.
girls bress the coat cold.
boy is caot was cold.

Total Words	42
Total Sentences	5
Words per Sentence	8.4
Syntax Quotient	56
Abstract-Concrete	9

ILLUSTRATION 18—Continued.

▶ 9 YEARS

MALE

A boy is playing with something a picture. We watched them.
He put a table, five chairs, a lamp, four books, a dog, a car,
a ball, a toy baby, a toy man, a toy woman, a toy boy, a toy-
girl, four spoons, four forks, four plates, two cups, two
classes and something.

Total Words	21 (34)
Total Sentences	3
Words per Sentence	7
Syntax Quotient	68
Abstract-Concrete	7
(Lists)	

FEMALE

boy has a chair and table.
girl has a chair, eat and table.
Shelf on a ball.
Chair on a box.
Woman and baby saw a chair.
Father said saw a chair.
boy said saw a dog.
On a shelf shoe.
Shelf on a car.
On a tree.

Total Words	48
Total Sentences	10
Words per Sentence	4.8
Syntax Quotient	49
Abstract-Concrete	12

ILLUSTRATION 18—Continued.

▶ 11 YEARS

MALE

A boy played with the little doll this day. The chair is the one doll box. the table is to doll and little and dog little chair, light. the wall was the on books, Car and toy thow hoxy toys shoes.

Total Words	34	(8)
Total Sentences	4	
Words per Sentence	8.5	
Syntax Quotient	64	
Abstract-Concrete	7	

(Lists)

FEMALE

(A boy is fixing) a house room. I don't know a boy years old. He played with toys on the table. A car is toy. A boys family ate some vegetable and fruits. The other boy catch a dog. The other girl looked at a baby play with dog.

Total Words	49
Total Sentences	7
Words per Sentence	7
Syntax Quotient	67
Abstract-Concrete	12

ILLUSTRATION 18—Continued.

▶ 13 YEARS

MALE

a boy play a room,
a boy ploy a dog
a girl ate a lunchroom.
a boy ploy a cart.
a baby doll sit on the table.
a man carry a chair.
a dish is on the table.
a boy sit a chair
a boy carry a little chair.

Total Words	49
Total Sentences	9
Words per Sentence	5.4
Syntax Quotient	68
Abstract-Concrete	11

FEMALE

A boy sat down a chair on the table. He played with a toy. Mother pulled up a baby. She carried him? He sat a chair. She ask to family Come ate in supper. A dog followed him in supper. He told a dog to go out. Father cut a meat. The family were finished, Father read a new paper. A girl help her mother the dishes. She washed the dishes and wipes it,

Total Words	74
Total Sentences	13
Words per Sentence	5.7
Syntax Quotient	72
Abstract-Concrete	14

ILLUSTRATION 18—Continued.

▶ **15 YEARS**

MALE

I saw a little boy play with his toy in the picture. he play with his toy on the table. he hole a chair on his right hand. he hale a little girl on his left hand. he dued 5 family. Father stand behond the table and a little boy follow his dog. other little boy watch the baby. he had book, toy car, ball, and a shoe with a house. he had a box with a toy on the other chair. a little boy like to play with his toy.

Total Words	92
Total Sentences	10
Words per Sentence	9.2
Syntax Quotient	83
Abstract-Concrete	12

FEMALE

About little boy.
One day a little boy have lots of toys. So he get the box of toys to put on the table. So he play with it. And I think he was so lonesome. That why he play with it and he have a book or toy car on shelf. And I think this room for himself. So he had a many of dolls on the table. he wear a clean suit. I think he was 7 or 8 year olde. And maybe he is favor of many of toys and dolls.

Total Words	91
Total Sentences	10
Words per Sentence	9.1
Syntax Quotient	84
Abstract-Concrete	8

ILLUSTRATION 18—Continued.

▶ 17 YEARS

MALE

This picture is about a little boy about ten years old is playing with his toys in kitcher of modern home. He put the toy furnitures, people and dog on the kitchen table. He has more toys in the box on the chair and he takes toys and put them on the table. Under the cupboards there are ball, automobile, books, the other toys. The boy wear his new suits and sport shirt. I think the boy play with his toys on Sunday afternoon and enjoy playing with his toys.

Total Words	90	(1)
Total Sentences	6	
Words per Sentence	15	
Syntax Quotient	94	
Abstract-Concrete	16	

(Lists)

FEMALE

The Playful Boy

One day in March on school days, a little boy named Jack ran home from school for lunch. His mother did not fix lunch yet so she went to the grocery store to buy something for Jack to eat. While she gone for awhile, Jack putted his playhouse's furnitures on the table. He putted the furniture it places and then playd with the dolls and playd with them until mother came back.

Finally, mother call him to take those furnitures off and putted plates and fork on the table. Then mother putted the food on the table and then they ate together. Then Jack kissed mother good-bye and went on to school for his class.

Total Words	116
Total Sentences	7
Words per Sentence	16.6
Syntax Quotient	84
Abstract-Concrete	19

Culturally Deprived

Use of the written word, perhaps all learning, can be impeded in four basic ways: involvement of the peripheral nervous system, of the central nervous system, by psychogenic disturbances and through psychosocial deprivation. The Picture Story Language Test has been useful in differentiating among the types of learning disabilities that result from these various conditions. The two most common impositions on learning that are psychosocial in nature are cultural deprivation and inadequate teaching.

Cultural deprivation refers to lack of opportunity and though other influences are involved, socioeconomic factors play an important role. Despite the high literacy rate in the United States, cultural deprivation is a problem in that both urban and rural children, in many instances, are without adequate opportunities for schooling, and therefore do not learn to use written language except perhaps in a rudimentary manner. It is our experience that they can copy and can acquire facility with written language when adequate teaching is provided, unless they have superimposed handicaps, such as sensory impairment and mental retardation.

Inadequate Teaching

Inadequate teaching is difficult to define because knowledge is, at this time, incomplete in regard to the psychoneurological processes whereby children acquire language. Nevertheless, from our point of view, a major factor in being able to write well is being able to read well, so the question of adequacy of teaching must include both reading and writing. Before a conclusion can be reached diagnostically to the effect that the teaching method is a major factor in a given child's limitation with the written word, it is necessary to secure information as specifically as possible concerning the method or methods to which he has been exposed.

It is not intended to imply that there is only one way in which to teach a child to read and write, or that all children learn equally well by the same method. Rather, we call attention to the possible oversimplification of concepts, such as "look and see" and "hear and say." Both approaches are oriented in terms of sensory modalities, one toward vision and the other toward audition. Neither concept is oriented specifically to child development nor to the relationships among the spoken, read and written forms of language.

In Chapter I we have suggested that phylogenetically and ontogenetically the sequence of language acquisition is first the auditory, then the read and thirdly the written. Study of those with language disorders provides further evidence of this hierarchical, sequential interdependence of these verbal systems. It seems, therefore, that the most effective means whereby children can be assisted in learning to read and write is to employ methods that are not contrary to these sequences followed developmentally by nature. In other words, in the early stages of learning to read and write it is necessary to foster the relating of the visual form to the auditory because the sequence of spoken-read-written seems basic to natural and efficient learning.

The purpose of this discussion is to indicate that the diagnostician must constantly be aware of the importance of the teaching methods to which a child has been exposed and must attempt to distinguish between those showing poor success in written language because of inadequate teaching and those who are deficient for other reasons.

DIAGNOSTIC STUDIES OF ADULTS

Though the Picture Story Language Test has been standardized on children, it has been used in making diagnostic studies of adults, including aphasics, dyslexics, dysgraphics, emotionally disturbed and the aged. Its use has made possible more accurate determination of the disturbance of written language in relation to the spoken and the read. Often this has been done by administering the test in two ways: first, by having the person tell a story and then having him write one. Sometimes these are accomplished on different days to avoid the attempt to provide an identical story. We have shown above that verbal facility in the spoken and written forms may vary considerably and that this finding is of significance, not only in terms of remediation but in relation to the nature of the brain dysfunction that has been sustained.

In addition to being useful in diagnostic studies, the Test offers opportunity for research on language in adults. Because of our theoretical interest in the interdependence of the verbal systems used by Man, we have begun to explore the language deterioration process in the aged. Though many variations must be considered, it appears that as senility progresses, the first verbal function to be affected is the written, then the read and lastly, the spoken. Much more study must be made, however, before conclusions can be drawn.

CROSS-CULTURAL STUDIES

Our research on written language has encompassed cross-cultural studies. We have administered the Picture Story Language Test to children in other countries in an attempt to gain knowledge regarding possible variations in the patterns of language acquisition. The relationships between the spoken, read, and written forms in the Orient presumably vary from those found in the western portion of the world. This assumption is based on the premise that oriental languages are less phonetic;

hence, the spoken form would not be closely associated with the read and the written. Objective data concerning this hypothesis would be revealing relative to the fundamental processes involved in language development.

Cross-cultural studies offer various possibilities. Through comparative data on children having handicaps, much can be learned regarding language behavior, as well as the nature of the impact of culture versus the impact of a handicap. To explore questions such as these we have administered the Picture Story Language Test to deaf children in other countries, Western and Oriental.

Investigation of the diverse written languages used from country to country provides significant data for psycholinguistic analysis. Furthermore, these studies furnish a basis for appraising the relative incidence of language disorders from one written form to another.

SUMMARY

In this chapter our purpose was to outline some of the disorders and deviations of written language and to suggest their importance in the differential diagnosis of learning disabilities. The Picture Story Language Test as a clinical tool has been useful in differentiating between disturbances of the auditory and visual processes as they relate to read and written language, and sometimes even as they relate to involvements of the spoken.

Emphasis has been given to the ways in which the Test can be employed to identify the type of learning disorder in a given individual, as well as the deficiencies that characterize certain groups of handicapped children. These determinations are basic to remedial training and can provide the specific details necessary for revealing agreement among various diagnostic approaches.

Our discussion has emphasized diagnostic study of children with learning disabilities. It has been assumed, however, that the Picture Story Language Test is useful as a measure of progress and educational achievement in normal children because it is a standardized test of facility with the written word. It has been found applicable to adults as a test of literacy and as a diagnostic instrument, especially for those who have language disorders. Moreover, it has been found beneficial in cross-cultural research studies on language behavior.

Differential diagnosis of learning disabilities is an extensive process covering various psychological and neurological functions, including a definitive, objective evaluation of written language. It is in this connection that the Picture Story Language Test has been useful because certain of these disabilities can be revealed only through appraisal of facility with the written word.

REFERENCES

1. Birch, H. G. and Lefford, A.: Two strategies for studying perception in "brain-damaged" children. *In* Brain Damage in Children, Herbert G. Birch (ed.). Baltimore, Williams & Wilkins, 1964.
2. Blakiston's New Gould Medical Dictionary. Philadelphia, The Blakiston Co., 1949.
3. Boshes, B. and Myklebust, H. R.: A neurological and behavioral study of children with learning disorders. Neurology 14: 1, 1964.
4. Callewaret, H.: For easy and legible handwriting. *In* New Horizons for Research in Handwriting, Virgil E. Herrick (ed). Madison, University of Wisconsin Press, 1963.
5. Cobb, S.: Borderlands of Psychiatry. Cambridge, Harvard University Press, 1948.
6. Council for International Organization of Medical Sciences. Brain Mechanisms and Learning, Springfield, Ill., Charles C. Thomas, 1961.
7. Critchley, M.: The Parietal Lobes. London, Edward Arnold, 1953.
8. De Jong, R.: The Neurological Examination. New York, Paul B. Hoeber, 1950.
9. Doll, E. A.: The Measurement of Social Competence. Minneapolis, Educational Test Bureau, 1953.
10. Exner, S.: Untersuchunden über die Lokolisation der Funktronen in der Gross-hirnrinde des Menschen. Cited by von Monakow. Wien, Braumüller, 1881.
11. Gates, A.: Gates Reading Diagnostic Test Manual. New York, Bureau of Publications, T. C., Columbia University, 1954.
12. Gesell, A. and Amatruda, Catherine: Developmental Diagnosis. New York, Paul B. Hoeber, 1947.
13. —— and Ilg, Frances: The Child from Five to Ten. New York, Harper & Brothers, 1946.
14. Goldstein, K.: Language and Language Disturbances. New York and London, Grune & Stratton, 1948.
15. Halverson, H.: Motor development. *In* The First Five Years of Life, Gesell et al. (eds). New York, Harper & Brothers, 1940.
16. Harris, T. L. and Rarick, G. L.: Physiological and motor correlates of handwriting legibility. *In* New Horizons for Research in Handwriting, Virgil E. Herrick (ed.). Madison, University of Wisconsin Press, 1963.
17. Heath, S. R.: Railwalking performance as related to mental age and etiological type among the mentally retarded. Amer. J. Psychol. 55: 240, 1942.
18. Herrick, V. and Okada, Nora: Practices in the teaching of handwriting in the United States. *In* New Horizons for Research in Handwriting, Virgil E. Herrick (ed.). Madison, University of Wisconsin Press, 1963.
19. Hinsie, L. and Campbell, R.: Psychiatric Dictionary, 3rd Ed. New York, Oxford University Press, 1960.
20. Jones, H. E.: Motor Performance and Growth—a Developmental Study of Static Dyamometric Strength. Berkeley, University of California Press, 1949.
21. Lenneberg, E. H. (ed): New Directions in the Study of Language. Cambridge, The M.I.T. Press, 1964.
22. Miller, G. A., Galanter, E. and Pribram, Karl H.: Plans and the Structure of Behavior. New York, Henry Holt & Co., 1960.
23. Monroe, Marion: Children Who Cannot Read. Chicago, University of Chicago Press, 1932.
24. Myklebust, H. R.: Development and Disorders of Written Language, Vol. II. New York and London, Grune & Stratton. In press.

25. ———: The Psychology of Deafness, 2nd Ed. New York and London, Grune & Stratton, 1964.
26. Nielsen, J. M.: Agnosia, Apraxia, Aphasia. New York, Paul B. Hoeber, 1946.
27. Oseretsky, N. I.: Psychomotorik: Methoden zur Untersuchung der Motoric. Beih. Zeitschrift Angewandte Psychol. 17: 162, 1931.
28. Orton, S.: Reading, Writing and Speech Problems in Children. New York, W. W. Norton, 1937.
29. Penfield, W. and Roberts, L.: Speech and Brain Mechanisms. Princeton, Princeton University Press, 1959.
30. Smith, K. V. and Murphy, T. J.: Sensory feedback mechanisms of handwriting motions and the neurogeometric bases. *In* New Horizons for Research in Handwriting, Virgil E. Herrick (ed). Madison, University of Wisconsin Press, 1963.

Chapter III

Picture Story Language Test
Purpose – Standardization – Results

A WIDE INTEREST has developed in language so it is now being studied by various disciplines. Educators, psychologists, neurologists, speech pathologists, specialists in linguistics, language pathologists, anthropologists and communication theorists especially are devoting attention to this unique human attribute. Perhaps the most predominant question is, How can this aspect of behavior be measured more definitively?

Because language is broad and inclusive, it must be separated into its primary components if it is to be measured efficaciously. Although some investigators have done this, it is not uncommon even for the sophisticated to consider language as a single, unitary factor. Perhaps to some extent it is a unitary factor developmentally but only when separated into its major components can it be studied and evaluated adequately. Without stating so specifically, those concerned with the spoken word have concentrated on this language form, usually without stressing its relationship to the read and written forms. However, some investigation has been made of the interdependence of the verbal systems and interest in this phase of the communication process is increasing.[2,24,26]

That language is an important aspect of total behavior is disclosed by the significant role it has played in Man's search for knowledge, but scientific study of this capacity is of recent origin and scales for its measurement are essentially lacking. Even though techniques are available for measuring certain components of the spoken and the read word, in these areas too there is a critical need for precision of the type that can be accomplished only through standardized tests.

Psychologists and educators for several decades have recognized the need for a test of written language ability. The National Council of Teachers of English also has demonstrated extensive interest, especially in terms of the need to objectively evaluate growth and improvement in written composition.[4] Though many have attempted to measure progress in use of the written word, tests for this purpose apparently have not been previously developed. Noteworthy studies that served as a background for the Picture Story Language Test include those of Stalnacker,[28] Boder,[3] Diederich,[10] Anderson,[1] Guiler,[15] LaBrant,[19] Goodman,[14] Thompson,[31] and Heider and Heider.[16] Because of their implications for ontogenetic development of the written word, we gained valuable clues and suggestions

69

from the studies on the phylogenesis of written language by Diringer,[11] Gelb,[13] Ceram,[7] and Clodd.[9]

Studies of "creative writing" ability as well as studies of handwriting are also important but these should not be confused with investigations of developmental growth in facility with the written word, nor with a scale designed to be useful in the diagnosis of language disorders.

The Picture Story Language Test consists of a picture about which a story is written. The objective was to develop a scale for quantitifying one's facility with the written word and thereby provide a measure of this type of verbal behavior in a given individual. The intent was to furnish a developmental scale for children and one which would also be useful in the study of adults.

The Test was evolved on the basis of a theoretical construct. Even though data on the normal as well as on the abnormal support the point of view that was postulated, it can be used to study written language from any frame of reference. It was standardized according to commonly accepted criteria for the study of human behavior. If only a beginning so far as objective evaluation of this intriguing symbol system is concerned, its usefulness in establishing developmental levels in normal children and in making diagnostic studies of persons with learning disabilities has been considerable for more than a decade.

PURPOSE OF THE TEST

The Picture Story Language Test was designed with several purposes in mind, but the major objective was that it should serve as an instrument for the study of language developmentally and diagnostically. We anticipated that it would be of value in the appraisal and classification of both normal and handicapped children so that their educational needs could be met more effectively. Clinical and educational situations in which the test can be applied are:

(1) As a diagnostic instrument for the study of children with language disorders and other types of learning disabilities;

(2) As a research tool to investigate the relationships between written language and aspects of behavior such as intelligence;

(3) To determine the achievement level of a given class or of a larger group in order to note the progress made from one year to another;

(4) To compare the advantages of various educational methods;

(5) To study the range and nature of written language abilities geographically;

(6) To ascertain levels of written language ability for purposes of grouping and teaching;

(7) To define the errors of written language which characterize the

performances of the deaf, asphasic, mentally retarded, speech defective, emotionally disturbed, dyslexic and dysgraphic;

(8) To obtain data for comparatively analyzing facility with the spoken, read, and written word;

(9) As a tool for studying grammar and the syntactical development of sentence structure;

(10) As a measure of the geriatric deterioration of verbal behavior;

(11) As a means for comparing the languages used in various countries psycholinguistically;

(12) As an indication of literacy.

SELECTION OF THE PICTURE

Various methods have been followed in securing samples of written language. Stromzand and O'Shea[29] used materials such as compositions, stories, and the published works of authors. This process has the advantage of wide sampling but it is not reproducible and does not meet the requirements of a standardized test. Heider and Heider[16] showed a movie about which a story was written, a technique that can be reproduced and hence could be standardized. However, it has the disadvantage of encompassing recall of what was seen, thus introducing a variable that complicates the development of a test. Hillocks[18] selected compositions written to fulfill class assignments.

Our approach was to use a picture about which a story is written. This has the expedience of being simple, highly flexible and readily standardized without incorporating recall inasmuch as the picture remains before the individual while he is writing the story. Initially the plan was to use more than one picture but experimentation revealed that the additional samples gained through a longer test were of little advantage; the sample of written language need not be long in order to achieve a high degree of reliability. (See Tables 15 and 16.)

The test Picture was developed on the basis of the following criteria:

(1) It must portray action of a type that provided as much interest and motivation as possible;

(2) It must be appealing to children of school age, from the primary grades through high school or between the ages of seven and 17 years;

(3) It must lend itself to imaginative thinking and be conducive to writing about more than what is actually portrayed;

(4) There should be a definite "foreground" and "background";

(5) The size of the picture must be standardized and large enough to permit continuous viewing by eight to ten persons at one time; the actual size is $10\frac{1}{2}$ by $13\frac{1}{2}$ inches.

ASPECTS OF LANGUAGE MEASURED

There is an obvious need for measuring the ability of individuals to communicate effectively. For purposes of diagnosis and educational classification, language scales are most useful if they make it possible to evaluate this ability developmentally. It was in these terms that we delineated the aspects of language which seemed to furnish greatest insight into effective use of the written word, and therefore should be included in the test.

No single aspect of language manifests an individual's total facility with words, even though workers often employ only one indicator, such as complexity or length. Productivity or complexity has been utilized by many workers.[4] Though not in a traditional way, both of these aspects are measured by the Picture Story Language Test. Our intention was to devise a test which was not based on a single indicator of facility but rather one that provided several measures so that the total result would represent a composite or profile of abilities. The assumption was that individuals, children and adults, might show greater facility in certain aspects of written language than in others; hence, a single indicator would be inadequate and inappropriate. Moreover, a test making it possible to study both the weaknesses and strengths, to see a profile of abilities, was presumed to have maximum value diagnostically.

After exploring a number of alternatives, we concluded that effective use of language rested upon essentially three attributes of its usage: *Productivity, Correctness*, and *Meaning*. For this reason the Picture Story Language Test is comprised of three scales, one devised to measure length (Productivity Scale), another to measure correctness (Syntax Scale), and the third to measure content or meaning (Abstract-Concrete Scale). Each is defined under Directions for Scoring.

Productivity is the amount of language expressed under a given circumstance, or, it is that aspect commonly referred to as length. Unless an expression is of minimum length, effective communication is precluded; an adequate number of words is essential as a prerequisite for useful communication. This prerequisite is measured in three ways on the Picture Story Language Test: by ascertaining the number of words (Total Words), the number of sentences (Total Sentences) and the number of words per sentence (Words per Sentence). Norms were established developmentally for each of these measures (see Results for Normal Children). The data reveal that though all of these are indicators of the amount of language produced, each discloses verbal facility in its own way and must be considered separately to gain maximum insight into an individual's competence with the written word.

When studying efficacious usage of language developmentally as well as diagnostically, all investigators in some way must evaluate the extent to which verbal expressions are used correctly. It is evident that a. language unit can be adequate in length but be so incorrect syntactically, grammatically and morphologically that effective communication, if not all communication, is precluded. For this reason *correctness* was included and is measured by the *Syntax Scale*. This Scale, however, is more inclusive than is indicated by the term *syntax*. Actually it furnishes an indication of correctness in three basic ways: the accuracy of *Word Usage*, of *Word Endings* and of *Punctuation*. An inclusive measure was necessary because a single indicator, such as syntax, does not adequately reveal the extent to which verbal expressions are used correctly. Correctness, per se, was viewed only in terms of its influence on meaning; hence, neither spelling nor handwriting were included. The aspects measured are syntax, grammatical construction, certain morphological factors and punctuation, but these are scored as errors of Word Usage, Word Endings and Punctuation, constituting the *Error Categories*. *Error Types* were defined as Additions, Omissions, Substitutions and Word Order. Both the scores for the Error Categories and Error Types are tabulated on the Record Form. Therefore, profiles of errors and correctness can be derived, although the final score is a composite referred to as the *Syntax Quotient*.

The third attribute of effective communication is content, or *meaning*. This prerequisite must be included because a unit of expression can be of adequate length and be correct syntactically but be partially or totally deficient in meaning. Parroting of words or sentences is not communication and when observed in the spoken form is classified as echolalia. Similarly, for various reasons, with a dysfunction in the brain, mental illness or cultural deprivation, an individual may write an expression that scores within normal limits on length and on correctness but that is devoid of meaning. Since the avowed function of language is to communicate meaning, this becomes a critical criterion of successful communication.

Others have devised systems for evaluating meaning but these seemed unsuitable for our purpose because they are essentially linguistic.[25,27] Our concern was with ideation, the nature of the thoughts expressed. Though we assumed there were relationships between language and thought, we supposed that an individual might be verbose and use language correctly but not be able to effectively communicate his ideas. Hence we devised the Abstract-Concrete Scale to study the effectiveness with which ideas are conveyed. As indicated by the discussion of scoring procedures, this Scale consists of five levels, each manifesting greater facility in the use of abstract ideas. Our results reveal that specific aspects of verbal behavior are more closely related to meaning than others and, moreover, that some groups of handicapped children may be more deficient in certain language functions than in others, yet convey ideas more successfully. Such observations can be made because this Scale is standardized. An individual of any age can be compared with the norms indicating the extent to which an average child between seven and 17 years of age succeeds in communicating ideas—the meanings he has in mind.

To summarize, the three aspects of language measured by the Picture Story Language Test are: Productivity, the length of the expression; Syntax, the correctness of what is expressed; and Abstract-Concrete, the nature and meaning of the ideas being expressed.

THE SAMPLE

Inasmuch as the primary objective was to provide a developmental scale for written language, the Picture Story Language Test was standardized only on children. The subjects were selected from three types of public school populations; metropolitan, rural and suburban. The largest number, 307, was from a metropolitan school system that encompassed a wide range of socioeconomic and ethnic groups. In order that this portion of the Sample be as representative as possible, a group of educators within the system selected six schools from which the subjects were chosen. Each of the schools represented a variation of cultural and socioeconomic influences. The second largest number, 262, was from a rural community; the families lived in small towns or on farms. The remaining segment of the Sample, 178, was from a suburban community composed of upper middle class families.

The total distribution of the subjects is given in Table 1. Approximately an equal number of males and females were included with 61 to 64 of each sex studied at each age level. Because little was known concerning the increment in written language occurring from one year to the next, only alternate age levels were used. The assumption was that the growth change from one age level to the next might be more clearly indicated by this sampling procedure; the results support this assumption. Therefore, alternate age groups from seven through 17 years of age made up the sample. The total consisted of six age groups, with 373 males and 374 females, a total of 747 subjects.

TABLE 1. Sample Used in Standardizing the Picture Story Language Test.

Age	7	9	11	13	15	17	Total
Males	62	61	63	63	63	61	373
Females	61	62	64	62	62	63	374
Total	123	123	127	125	125	124	747

In addition to cultural, ethnic, socio-economic, age and sex factors, other criteria were established for selection of the subjects, the objective being that only normal children should be included. No child was selected who was known to be mentally retarded or to have a physical handicap, a learning disorder, an emotional disturbance or a sensory impairment; the handicapped were studied separately.[22] As a result, the norms derived are higher than would be obtained for a sample where these criteria are not imposed.

Although geographically the Sample was chosen from one Midwestern state, the sampling incorporated children of all socioeconomic levels and a wide variety of cultural backgrounds. Studies will be made of children in other geographic areas but at this time the evidence suggests that the norms are applicable to all children who have had an average school opportunity. Whether developmental differences in the acquisition and use of written language occur in the United States on a geographic basis is not known. Any child who is culturally deprived would be expected to be deficient in language, perhaps especially in the written word. Study of these influences must be made and progress is being achieved both nationally and internationally.

RESULTS FOR NORMAL CHILDREN

Virtually all former studies of language developmentally have concerned the spoken word.[20,30] Though normal children have been included as control groups, it seems that patterns of growth for written language have not been previously investigated. Such growth patterns appear in various forms, as shown by the data and the growth curves presented below. Each area of verbal behavior studied, Productivity, Syntax and Abstract-Concrete, as well as each of the five measures, Total Words, Total Sentences, Words per Sentence, Syntax and Abstract-Concrete reveal maturation as age increases.

Productivity

The results for the measures of Productivity are presented in Table 2 and the growth curves in Figures 3, 4, and 5. Of the three measures, Words per Sentence shows the most stable and continuous growth from age to age. Both the mean scores and the growth curves reveal remarkably uniform increments within each two-year interval. Moreover, maturation continues through the age of 17 years, indicating that the average adult level has not been reached. As such, these results are in agreement with those presented by Stormaznd and O'Shea[29] who studied the length of sentences in compositions written by average adults and obtained a score of 20.9 words. From our results on the basis of the increments per two-year interval, it appears that this level may not be attained until an age of at least 21 or 22 years. In any event, it is of considerable significance psychologically and educationally that this aspect of productivity continues to mature beyond the age usually assumed to represent adult maturity intellectually.

TABLE 2. Results for Productivity by age and sex.

Age		N	TOTAL WORDS		TOTAL SENTENCES		WORDS PER SENTENCE	
			Mean	SD	Mean	SD	Mean	SD
7	Male	62	22.2	14.4	3.6	2.5	6.3	2.2
	Female	61	33.1	18.0	5.0	2.8	6.7	2.3
	Total	123	27.6	17.1	4.3	2.7	6.5	2.3
9	Male	61	83.1	43.1	8.6	4.3	9.9	2.5
	Female	62	97.6	58.1	10.5	6.1	9.5	2.1
	Total	123	90.4	51.5	9.6	5.4	9.7	2.3
11	Male	63	106.8	51.1	10.1	5.2	11.2	2.8
	Female	64	125.1	59.5	11.5	6.7	11.8	3.3
	Total	127	116.0	56.0	10.8	6.0	11.5	3.0
13	Male	63	143.5	64.3	11.1	5.9	13.8	3.6
	Female	62	156.0	75.5	11.5	6.4	14.2	3.2
	Total	125	149.7	70.1	11.3	6.1	14.0	3.4
15	Male	63	123.2	47.4	8.4	3.8	15.4	4.1
	Female	62	153.2	42.1	10.9	4.5	14.8	3.2
	Total	125	138.1	47.1	9.7	4.4	15.1	3.7
17	Male	61	158.5	61.3	9.9	4.4	16.8	4.1
	Female	63	164.2	62.8	11.5	6.0	15.4	3.8
	Total	124	161.4	61.9	10.7	5.3	16.1	4.0

The stability of Words per Sentence as an indicator of verbal facility is further demonstrated by the results obtained for the nine-, 11-, and 13-year-olds. Stormzand and O'Shea[29] and Heider and Heider[16] also studied these age groups and our results are in close agreement with theirs. Considering that the period of time covered by these studies is 40 years, these findings take on added significance and usefulness.

Various authorities have stated that the written form of language follows that already learned or established for the spoken word. This was our hypothesis, too, especially in regard to the acquisition of read and written language developmentally. Nevertheless, from the studies of young children by Templin,[30] and from other observations, we contended that spoken and written words per sentence were not equivalent. In earlier life, before nine years of age, it is apparent that they are not. However, comparing our results with those reported by Fries[12] for the spoken word,

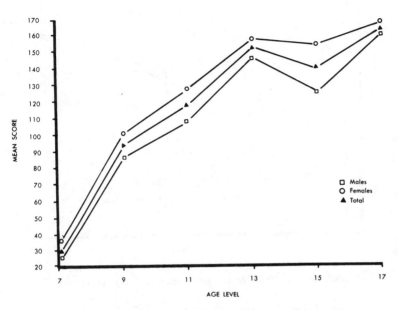

FIGURE 3.   Growth in Total Words as age increases.

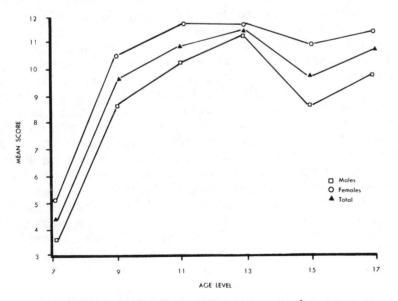

FIGURE 4.   Growth in Total Sentences as age increases.

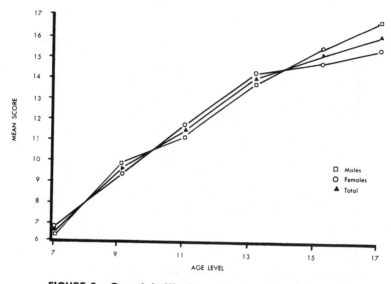

FIGURE 5.   Growth in Words per Sentence as age increases.

at adulthood the differences may be slight. Using the guide of Standard English he reports a score of 21 words per sentence, a finding that is remarkably close to the average for written language reported by Storm-zand and O'Shea, and close to the projected mean for adults were we to extend our norms to older age groups.

Compared with the number of words written per sentence, Total Words and Total Sentences show a "plateau" effect, as manifested both by the mean scores and by the growth curves. However, plateauing is most characteristic of the results for Total Sentences. The number of words written per story grows rapidly up to 13 years of age, then increases more slowly although increments continue through 17 years, with the males showing greatest growth during these later secondary school years. Total Sentences, on the other hand, reveals no further maturation after 11 years of age. After this age, at approximately the fifth grade, even though the stories increase in length, they gradually write longer sentences so the number of sentences shows no further growth. This pattern of relationship, this intercorrelation among the Productivity scores is not characteristic of children having certain types of learning disabilities or sensory handi-caps.[22,23]

Syntax

Correct usage has been the focus of many investigators, including teachers of English,[4] specialists in linguistics[8] and communication theorists.[21] Ours was an inclusive approach, not based on the point of view of a given group, nor was it derived specifically from methods employed by others. Correctness was interpreted in terms of its influence on meaning. The results are presented in Table 3 and in Figure 6.

The principal significance of these data developmentally is that they disclose early maturation of syntax ability. Growth is very rapid between the ages of seven and nine years, with a slight increment between nine and 11 years, and virtually no improvement thereafter. The implication is that the average child attains adult proficiency in correct usage of the written word when he attains approximately the fourth grade level of educational achievement. This is in marked contrast to Total Words and Words per Sentence but in close agreement with Total Sentences. As syntactical ability is achieved, sentences of greater length can be written; hence, both Syntax and Total Sentences show little growth after 11 years of age.

TABLE 3. Results for Syntax by age and sex.

Age	Males			Females			Total		
	N	Mean	SD	N	Mean	SD	N	Mean	SD
7	62	84.6	21.9	61	88.9	18.7	123	86.7	20.4
9	61	94.3	7.8	62	96.4	4.7	123	95.3	6.5
11	63	96.7	4.1	64	98.1	2.9	127	97.4	3.6
13	63	97.4	2.7	62	98.0	3.0	125	97.7	2.9
15	63	97.1	3.5	62	98.7	2.2	125	97.9	3.0
17	61	97.8	3.3	63	99.8	12.8	124	98.8	9.4

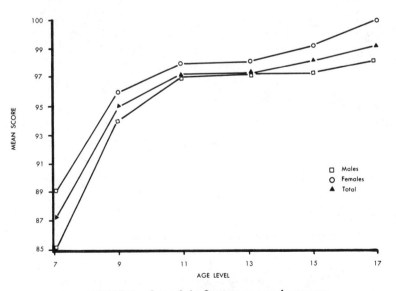

FIGURE 6. Growth in Syntax as age increases.

Abstract-Concrete

For decades, if not for centuries, philosophers, as well as scientists in the fields of psychology and linguistics have been concerned with the definition and measurement of meaning in relation to verbal behavior[5,6,25] To some this has been the "referent," the idea, the mental image to which the word refers. Our measure, the use of abstraction, is based on the nature of the ideas expressed, but, perhaps, more in the sense of Brown's[5] concept when he states that "the meaning of linguistic form appears to be the total disposition to make use of and react to the form." Specifically our objective was to measure the extent to which abstract ideas were expressed through the written word, given a standardized stimulus in the form of a picture, with instructions to write a story about what was portrayed. In this sense, meaning as ideation was established developmentally.

TABLE 4.   Results for Abstract-Concrete by age and sex.

| Age | Males | | | Females | | | Total | | |
	N	Mean	SD	N	Mean	SD	N	Mean	SD
7	62	7.3	3.5	61	8.4	2.9	123	7.8	3.2
9	61	13.0	5.1	62	13.8	4.8	123	13.4	4.9
11	63	14.8	5.2	64	16.2	4.4	127	15.5	4.8
13	63	16.5	4.3	62	16.9	4.5	125	16.7	4.4
15	63	17.4	4.6	62	19.5	3.6	125	18.4	4.3
17	61	19.5	3.7	63	18.2	4.3	124	18.8	4.0

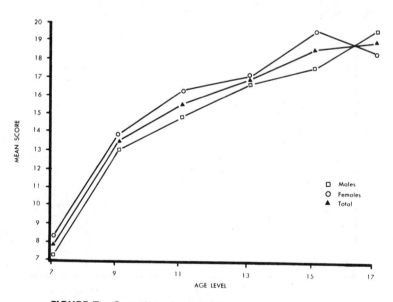

FIGURE 7.   Growth in Abstract-Concrete as age increases.

The results are given in Table 4 and in Figure 7. The data reveal gradual growth in the use of abstract ideas from seven through 15 years for the females and from seven through 17 years for the males. An immediate and intriguing question pertains to the relationships between ability to express abstract meaning and verbal facility. An involved statistical analysis has been made of such relationships and is reported elsewhere.[22] The highest correlations were found with Total Words, the lowest with Words per Sentence and Syntax; generalized fluency, or vocabulary shows significant association with the use of abstract ideas, whereas sentence length and correct usage do not. Other revealing evidence is derived from studies of handicapped children and indicates that language facility and abstract thought, though perhaps mutually interdependent, are not identical. A measure of one does not in and of itself disclose facility in the other. Meaning, the content of that expressed, varies from age to age and this variation apparently cannot be attributed only to facility with the written word.

Sex Differences

As shown by the mean scores and the growth curves, the females achieved proficiency with the written word at a rate that exceeded the maturational progress of the males. The differences were statistically significant as follows: Total Words at 15 years, Total Sentences at seven, nine and 15 years, and Syntax at 11 and 15 years. In contrast, though the sexes were highly similar on Words per Sentence, the males exceeded the females at 17 years of age. In general, the indicated pattern of growth was one in which females attained language proficiency levels earlier than males, with essential equality being reached by 17 years.

Illustrative Stories by Normal Children

The stories presented below are representative in that they fall approximately at the mean for each sex at each of the age levels. They illustrate the growth trends found in the normative data. The measures of Productivity, Total Words, Total Sentences and Words per Sentence all increase by age. There is a tendency for the females to exceed the males in the amount of language written. The early maturation of Syntax can also be observed. Variations occur, however, as illustrated by the nine-year-old female whose Syntax Quotient is 88, being equivalent to the mean for the seven-year-old females.

These Illustrative Stories are beneficial in other ways and should be given attention accordingly; see Illustration 19. For example, they demonstrate a certain independence of the five scores derived from the Picture Story Language Test. There is a significant correlation between Total Words and Abstract-Concrete. Nevertheless, these scores may vary substantially in individuals. At seven years both scores are in the same direction as indicated by the statistical data; the female being superior in abstraction and writing the most words. In contrast, at nine years the male wrote fewer words but scored twice as high as the female in the use of abstract ideas. The same type of independence between these scores is also noted at the age levels of 11 and 17 years. Presumably, these variations reflect the differences among children developmentally both in rate and extent of maturation with respect to the specific factors being measured.

The stories written by the two 17-year-old subjects furnish additional insight into the relationships of the five scores. Though there is a correlation between Total Words and Total Sentences, and between Total

ILLUSTRATION 19.   Illustrative Stories: normal.

▶ **7 YEARS**

MALE

a Boy had some toys.
And he was playing house.
He had a little chair to put a
little girl on it.

Total Words	22
Total Sentences	3
Words per Sentence	7.3
Syntax Quotient	90
Absolute-Concrete	7

Words and Abstract-Concrete, the male at this age level wrote 77 less words and eight less sentences than the female, yet he exceeded her score in the use of abstraction.

These stories exemplify the patterns that characterize acquisition of the written word by normal children. As in all aspects of growth and maturation, these patterns are various and differ from one child to another.

ILLUSTRATION 19—Continued.

FEMALE

There is a boy playing with a doll house. There is a table, chairs and children a dog too. There is a Mother pushing a baby. There is two boys and one girl.

Total Words	31	(2)
Total Sentences	4	
Words per Sentence	7.8	
Syntax Quotient	95	
Abstract-Concrete	11	

ILLUSTRATION 19—Continued.

▶ 9 YEARS

MALE

The Little House Maker

Once there was a little boy who liked to play with toys he had a house with people in it the house had many things in it he was working on the table. The little boy and put a table down a few chairs and put a lamp down. The little boy put father down and two children when the little boy finished he showed his mother and everybody else in the family and they were proud of him.

Total Words	79
Total Sentences	7
Words per Sentence	11.3
Syntax Quotient	94
Abstract-Concrete	17

FEMALE

One day a boy wanted to play with toys. And never played with any thing ele's. And he played with toy's on the kitcienatable. And he played with books, and car's and mostlie with girl's stuff. He has lots of fun with he's toy's. He works in offic and he learn's how to read and do other thing. He just had fun in he's life. And he played with furniture of a doll house. And played with toy shoe's. He always staijed in a suit.

Total Words	85
Total Sentences	10
Words per Sentence	8.5
Syntax Quotient	88
Abstract-Concrete	8

ILLUSTRATION 19—Continued.

▶ 11 YEARS

MALE

A Day at Home

One day little Gary had a cold. So his mother told him to stay at home. But he couldn't of who to do. He don't want to play with his car or read his books. He decides to play with his wooden toys. He took out a man, woman, some children, and a baby and then he took out a chair, desk, table, lamp, plates, cups, and other things. Then he arranged them in order. And had a happy time with his wooden toys.

Total Words	78	(6)
Total Sentences	7	
Words per Sentence	11.1	
Syntax Quotient	91	
Abstract-Concrete	18	

FEMALE

Playing Alone with Imagination

This is a picture showing a boy and his toys. He is setting a room in a home out of his toy furniture. He has a table setting ready for a family of plastic dolls. It shows an infant in a stroller holding his hands to his mother. A man that has pulled out a chair for a lady. Their is boy stooping over and following a dog. He is consentrating where to place a chair. His imagination is on a home. It is a dining room, perhaps like his. Really imagination is important to him now, its his friend

Total Words	99
Total Sentences	10
Words per Sentence	9.9
Syntax Quotient	94
Abstract-Concrete	15

ILLUSTRATION 19—Continued.

▶ **13 YEARS**

MALE

This story takes place in a kindergarden or a his house. This boys name is Tom. He went to school this morning to find that not many of his playmates went because of the snowstorm last night. The teacher didn't want to do much because most of the children weren't at school.

Tom had a table all to himself and looked glad. The teacher gave him some toys to play with. He got out his favorite toys the doll set or house set with all the furniture and moving children with the arms and legs he made them into different shapes. He had a lot of fun. He had five little dolls in the secen he was creating they just got through eating and were starting to play. He worked until it was time to quit and go home.

Total Words	140
Total Sentences	12
Words per Sentence	11.7
Syntax Quotient	92
Abstract-Concrete	18

ILLUSTRATION 19—Continued

FEMALE

Thoughts of a Child.

"What a day," sighed Jim David-
son to himself. Jim is a kindergartener
at the Billings Primary School. "I'll bet
I've played with this stupid dollhouse game a thousand times
before, if only I could do something
more exciting."

Jim is small for his age, and
is left out of many of the rougher
games, due to his delicate health.
The teacher, following Jim's parent's
instructions, is "excluding Jim
from the hartier games". Let's see
what Jim thinks about this!

"If only I was as big as those
other guys. All day long I'm sitting
playing, 'nice quiet games' as
Mother says. Those other games look
like so much fun! I guess I'll just
have to sit here and play 'that
sissy stuff', as the fellas call it.
Some day I'll grow big and strong,
then I'll show them. Right now
I'll have to stay content with just
'sitting around'."

Total Words	150
Total Sentences	12
Words per Sentence	12.5
Syntax Quotient	99
Abstract-Concrete	18

ILLUSTRATION 19—Continued

▶ 15 YEARS

MALE

Tommy liked school he had a lot of fun at play time and got good markets.

In his school room they had may games, books and toys. Tommy liked the games and books but most of all he liked the toys.

School started at 9:00 in the morning with reading and spelling then came recess. After the children returned from recess they would do their English and then go to lunch. In the afternoon came their arithmetic after which came Tommies favoute part of the day, play time. Tommy enjoyed playing with every one of the toys at school. After play time came clean up when the children would clean and tiddy up the room befor going home.

Total Words	117
Total Sentences	9
Words per Sentence	13.0
Syntax Quotient	90
Abstract-Concrete	19

ILLUSTRATION 19—Continued

FEMALE

Johnny had just come home from a rather regular day of school. It was raining and he was unable to think of a way to amuse himself. His older sister Sally was at a friends house and his mother was very tired and upset over her busy day.

While pondering over an idea Johnny's eyes suddenly caught hold of a small box tucked in the corner in the den. He approached it curiously. Upon seeing that it only contained old plastic furniture and people which Sally had cast aside, he turned away. However, in a moments time curiosity got the best of him, and he carried the box over to a table.

At first Johnny kept watching to see if anyone was around to see him. Soon he was so engaged in this new experience that he forgot all else. The dolls walked, sat, and moved in various ways with the slight use of his hands. Here he had found amusement in a simple and different form. Would you have tried it?

Total Words	172
Total Sentences	12
Words per Sentence	14.3
Syntax Quotient	98
Abstract-Concrete	18

ILLUSTRATION 19—Continued

▶ 17 YEARS

MALE

Since the time of his early childhood Raymond Hittendorf had been obsessed by the will to control large masses of people. at the age of five he was buying large amounts of small dolls. which he constantly played with. He did not not greatly enjoy playing with the dolls, but seemed to get a satisfaciton out of it, the more dolls, the more satisfaction he felt at being able to make them do what he wanted. As Raymond became alder he was able to control his friends in the same way. through the use of words, Raymond continued to develope this power until he could sway great masses of people. He soon realized the extreme power that he had, and what it could do for him.

Total Words	126
Total Sentences	6
Words per Sentence	21.0
Syntax Quotient	97
Abstract-Concrete	21

ILLUSTRATION 19—Continued

FEMALE

Johnny was alone in his sister's room. He looked around and spotted some doll house furniture and people on a table. There were more doll house toys in a box on a chair next to the table. He wondered how his sister could sit hours at that table, and play with those toys. He decided to try playing with those toys. He arranged the dinning room table and chair on the corner of the table with the buffet and china cabinet around it. He added a chair and lamp next to the buffet. He put in the doll house people. He put sister at the table, mother bending over and to left baby out of it's stroller. He had father standing next to the chair at the head of the table. Brother was telling the dog to leave the room, because it was dinner time.

Having set up the doll house toys, Johnny played with them a little while and then decided to stop, because he was bored. He put the toys back where he had found them and left his sister's room. He wondered as he left the room, how his sister could spend hours playing with those doll house toys?

Total Words	203
Total Sentences	14
Words per Sentence	14.5
Syntax Quotient	99
Abstract-Concrete	19

HOW TO ADMINISTER THE TEST

Administration of the Picture Story Language Test is simple, requiring only those precautions observed in the proper use of other tests of ability and educational attainment. Cooperation and motivation are essential on the part of the individuals being tested and it is assumed that the examiner will establish a favorable rapport, yet maintain an objective approach.

The standardization studies were conducted by persons trained in the administration of psychological and educational tests, especially as they relate to language development and learning disorders. As shown by the data on Reliability, however, except for Syntax, specific training in the use of this test is not essential, but training in the use of objective tests as well as in the interpretation of test scores is necessary.

Adequate preparations must be made before the test is given. The environmental circumstances should be favorable and conducive to good effort. A room of sufficient size is necessary. Crowded or poorly lighted rooms are unsuitable, and unusual distractions should be avoided.

Group testing can be done satisfactorily and was employed in the standardization studies, but no more than eight to ten children or adults are to be tested with one Picture. More than ten can be tested simultaneously if additional pictures, space and supervision are available. It is necessary to arrange seating in close proximity because all testees must be able to view the test Picture and see the details portrayed in it. Picking up the Picture for close observation is permitted but it must be replaced in a central position so that all can see it and refer to it while writing their stories. The examiner makes certain that the Picture remains in position until the stories have been completed.

The writing paper and utensils are important. Young children are furnished the type of paper and pencils with which they are familiar. If accustomed to lined paper and large pencils, these are provided. When pens are used, care is taken so the proper paper is available. Moreover, standard sized writing paper is recommended because it affords the same potential for story length for all subjects and assures more ease of scoring. Though good handwriting to increase legibility is not mentioned, the examiner by his attitude and demeanor makes it clear that this is a test situation and careful work is expected.

When all arrangements have been made the examiner appears before the group, holds up the Picture so that all can see and says, "Look at this picture carefully." After a pause of about 20 seconds he says, "You are to write a story about it. You may look at it as much and as often as you care to. Be sure to write the best story you can. Begin writing whenever you are ready. " The Picture is then placed in a central position where it can be seen easily. Thereafter the examiner remains present and available, but in the background.

Questions are answered in a neutral manner indicating that neither help nor further suggestions will be given; the instructions are repeated until understood by all. For example, if the examiner is asked, "Should it have a title?" a typical reply is, "If you want to. Write the story the way *you* think is best." Infrequently a child or an adult may say, "I can't write a story." In this event encouragement is given through comments such as, "Try to write something—anything you can think of." The object is to secure the best sample of written language of which the individual is capable, even if it is only a few, poorly produced words or phrases.

Permission is given to use as much time as needed to complete the story. Writing rate, the number of words written per minute, correlates with chronological age especially at the lower age levels, the writing rate of the seven-year-olds being the slowest. Nonetheless, the age at which children achieve the rate of the average adult has not been established. Studies of rate and its relationship to factors such as chronological age might provide another parameter whereby facility with written language can be quantified. Evidence of the possibility is provided by Herrick.[17] In the standardization study it seemed that speed increased until approximately 13 years of age. In any event, use of the Picture Story Language Test assumes that the individual is given the time he needs to write the story and that he does not feel he must meet a time limit. All taking the test are made aware that they are to continue writing until they have completed their story, but they are not asked to hurry. Most children complete the story in 20 minutes and rarely does a child require more than 30 minutes.

REFERENCES

1. Anderson, C.: The new STEP Essay Test as a measure of composition ability. Educ. and Psychol. Measurement 20: 95, 1960.
2. Birch, H. G. and Lefford, A.: Two strategies for studying perception in "brain-damaged" children. *In* Brain Damage in Children, Herbert G. Birch (ed.). Baltimore, Williams & Wilkins Co., 1964.
3. Boder, D. P.: The adjective-verb quotient: A contribution to the psychology of language. Psychol. Record 3: 1940.
4. Braddock, R., Lloyd-Jones, R. and Schoer, L.: Research in Written Composition. Champaign, National Council of Teachers of English, 1963.
5. Brown, R.: Words and Things. Glencoe, The Free Press, 1958.
6. Cassirer, E.: The Philosophy of Symbolic Forms, Vol. I: Language. New Haven, Yale University Press, 1953.
7. Ceram, C. W.: The Secret of the Hittites. New York, Alfred A. Knopf, 1956.
8. Chomsky, Noan: Syntactic Structures. The Hague, Mouton, 1957.
9. Clodd, E.: The Story of the Alphabet. New York, D. Appleton, 1900.
10. Diederich, P. B., French, J. W. and Carlton, Sydell T.: Factors in Judgments of Writing Ability. Research Bulletin, RB–61–15, Princeton, Educational Testing Service, 1961.

11. Diringer, D.: Writing. New York, Frederick A. Praeger, 1962.
12. Fries, C. C.: The Structure of English. New York, Harcourt, Brace & Company, 1952.
13. Gelb, I. J.: A Study of Writing. Chicago, University of Chicago Press, 1963.
14. Goodman, J. H.: Growth in Punctuation and Capitalization Abilities. J. Educ. Research 18: 195, 1934.
15. Guiler, W. S.: Analysis of capitalization errors. English J. 20: 1931.
16. Heider, F. and Heider, G.: Studies in the psychology of the deaf. Psychol. Monog. 242: 1941.
17. Herrick, V. and Okada, Nora: Practices in the Teaching of Handwriting. *In* New Horizons for Research in Handwriting, Virgil E. Herrick (ed). Madison, University of Wisconsin Press, 1963.
18. Hillocks, G.: An analysis of some syntactical patterns in ninth grade themes. J. Educ. Res. 57: 8, 1964.
19. LaBrant, L. L.: A study of certain language developments of children in grades four to twelve, inclusive. Genetic Psychol. Monogr. 14: 1933.
20. McCarthy, Dorothea: Language development in children. *In* Manual of Child Psychology, 2nd Ed., Leonard Carmichael (ed). New York, John Wiley & Sons, 1954.
21. Miller, G. A.: Language and Communication. New York, McGraw-Hill, 1951.
22. Myklebust, H. R.: Development and Disorders of Written Language, Vol. II. New York and London, Grune & Stratton. In press.
23. ———: The Psychology of Deafness, 2nd Ed. New York and London, Grune & Stratton, 1964.
24. O'Connor, N. and Hermelin, B.: Speech and Thought in Severe Subnormality. New York, Macmillan, 1963.
25. Osgood, C. E., Suci, G. J. and Tannenbaum, P. H.: The Measurement of Meaning. Urbana, University of Illinois Press, 1957.
26. Pimsleur, P. and Bonkowski, R. J.: Transfer of verbal material across sense modalities. J. Educ. Psychol. 52: 104, 1961.
27. Pool, I. DeS., (ed): Trends in Content Analysis. Urbana, University of Illinois Press, 1959.
28. Stalnaker, J. M.: The construction and results of a twelve-hour test in English composition. School and Society 39: 218, 1934.
29. Stromzand, M. and O'Shea, M.: How Much English Grammar? Baltimore, Warwick & York, 1924.
30. Templin, Mildred C.: Certain Language Skills in Children. Minneapolis, University of Minnesota Press, 1957.
31. Thompson, W.: An analysis of errors in written composition by deaf children. Amer. Ann. Deaf, 81: 95, 1936.

PART TWO

DIRECTIONS FOR SCORING

Chapter IV

Productivity Scale

TOTAL WORDS (TW)

THE NUMBER OF WORDS expressed in either the spoken or written form has not been applied often as an indicator of verbal facility. Davis,[3] McCarthy,[7] and Templin,[11] however, included "length of remark" in studying the development of spoken language in young children. Johnson[6] and his associates used this measure to analyze the relationship between the number of different types of words and the total number of words written. He advisedly considered the ambiguity of the word "word." There is variation in the definition of this term, conveying the scholarly manner in which investigators have approached the study of verbal behavior.

Though it was necessary to evolve specific criteria for determining the number of words written, for our purpose it was not difficult to define what constituted a word. In fact, a common dictionary definition was employed: "a sound or combination of sounds, or its written or printed representation, used in a language as a sign of its conception; an element that can stand alone as an utterance."[12] On the basis of this definition all written units recognizable as elements that could stand alone and convey meaning were counted as words. They might be misspelled or even erroneously used, but if recognizable as words, they were so regarded. On the other hand, a series of letters joined together but unrecognizable as a word was excluded and omitted from the word count. Only moderate sophistication is required to determine the Total Word Score. A hand counter increases accuracy.

Principles for Scoring

Several special circumstances arise in determining Total Words, so principles were formulated in order that these be counted systematically and consistently. The following factors must be considered when the word count is being made; see also Illustrative Stories in the Scoring Guide.

Lists

Even though counting the number of words written is a simple mechanical task, certain problems are encountered. For example, a child might write a sentence consisting of a series of names of objects seen in the picture. Productions of this type have been designated as *Lists*. If all of the words are counted the Words per Sentence score becomes spuriously high inasmuch as the score is the result of the number of words written divided by the number of sentences. Such spurious effect derives from the fact that Lists do not entail structure, hence, cannot be considered a sentence. Therefore, Lists are a special circumstance when determining the word count.

Lists are defined as four or more words in a given series occurring within a sentence. When Lists appear, the rule is that not more than three units should be counted, the first two words and the last word written in the series. Those not counted are bracketed and recorded accordingly on the Record Form.

■ EXAMPLE

The boy is playing with blocks, toys, chairs, dolls, a mother, books, and some other things.

In this story the word count is denoted as follows:

The boy is playing with blocks, toys, [chairs, dolls, a mother, books,] and some other things.

The words falling within the brackets are not counted. The TW score, therefore, is 11; five words are not included. When recorded these results are shown as: TW = 11 (5). This reveals that 16 words were written but only 11 were counted, five of them being omitted because of the rule concerning Lists.

This procedure increases the reliability of the scores, but exceptions occur and must be scored differently. If the list consists of four units that are logically related and essential to the thought being expressed, four words in a series may be included in the word count. *In no instance are more than four counted.* In the following example the four words in the series are directly related to the concept of family, so they are all counted with the result that the TW score is 13.

■ EXAMPLE

The doll family is a mother, a father, a brother, and a sister.

Meaningless Language

There are four types of *Meaningless Language;* an example of each is given below. In Example (1) the writer has produced a series of scribbles which cannot be identified as words; hence, the Total Word score is *0.* Example (2) illustrates another type of zero score; letters have been written but there are no identifiable words. In stories as Example (3), though there is no relationship to the picture and they are designated as Meaningless Language, the words can be recognized and therefore must be counted. Example (4), because of its sophistication, is more difficult to score. Meaningless Language stories may be written by the mentally retarded, mentally ill, aphasic, dyslexic and others and thus are useful diagnostically. Whenever what is written can be recognized as words, the count is made in the conventional manner. Therefore, the TW scores for the examples given below are (1) *0,* (2) *0,* (3) *10,* (4) *170.*

■ **EXAMPLE**

(1)

(2)

(3)

Look Lookohohoh Com edn D See Dick
Dick

(4) The doctor came out of the surgery room. His eyes were serious. His hands were calm. The anxious family in the waiting room did not need to hear his words—they knew. He took off the surgical mask. And then to the family he handed a cross, a small silver cross which the child he had just operated on had held so tightly when he was taken into the room.

The doctor proceeded to take off his surgical wear. As he finished, he looked at the family, weaping and huddled together consoling each other. He walked to the door. As he grasped the knob he slowly turned around. His eyes were gray and his lips parted to utter three undistinct words.

He turned and walked slowly to the hospital chapel. He spoke not to any one, but fell on his knees inside the chapel door. He remained silent and motionless.

"Calling Dr. Brown, calling Dr. Brown. Report to surgery. Emergency. Report to surgery. Emergency."

The young doctor rose up. His steps hastened.

Naming Level

When there are no sentences, no subject-verb combinations but only a succession of words, usually identifying objects seen in the Picture, it is referred to as *Naming Level*. There may or may not be an article accompanying the noun. In these stories the words are counted in the usual manner so in the following example, the TW score is *five*.

■ EXAMPLE

boy, dog, a girl, chair

Hyphenated and Compound Words

Sometimes a word may be written incorrectly as two words, *million air* for *millionaire*. The reverse also occurs in that two words are erroneously combined and written as one word, *storybook* for *story book*, or *dollhouse* for *doll house*. These are regarded as spelling errors so they are counted as though written correctly, *million air* as one word and *storybook* as two words.

All hyphenated words are counted as one word. Hyphens often are incorrectly inserted in compound words, such as *playroom, playhouse,* and *plaything*. These also may be mistakenly written as two words.

Names, Initials, and Abbreviations

Frequently names are assigned to the characters in the story. When this occurs each name is counted as a word, as is each initial. Therefore, both

James Charles Smith and *James C. Smith* are counted as three words. *Jr.,* as well as all other abbreviations which replace a word, is also counted as a word.

Numbers

Numbers, whether written in the form of digits or as words, are counted as one word. Therefore, *27, 1027, twenty-seven,* and *one thousand twenty-seven* are all counted as one word. The symbol, #, sometimes used in place of the word number, also is so counted.

Signs and Symbols

Various types of signs and symbols may be used in a story. When required to convey the intended meaning, these are counted as words. Hence, dollar and cents signs ($, ¢) as well as @ are included in the Total Word count.

Contractions

To increase objectivity contractions are counted as one word, preventing confusion with abbreviations.

Titles

Story titles, or words used as *The End* or *Finale,* are not counted. Inasmuch as they are not a part of language structure, they were deliberately omitted from the test.

The Total Word score is highly revealing as a measure of facility with the written word, in that it clearly manifests developmental growth. As shown in Table 2, at seven years of age the average child writes only 22 words per story, whereas by 14 years of age the average length is 133 words, or six times greater. In addition this score is indicative diagnostically. The mean Total Word score for 11-year-old normal children was 106 words per story, whereas the mean for 11-year-old children with articulatory defects was 51 words, for 11-year-olds having a reading disability it was 49 words, and the 11-year-old educable mentally handicapped wrote only 17 words per story.[8] Such findings are beneficial when studying children with learning disabilities and can be helpful in making a differential diagnosis.

TOTAL SENTENCES (TS)

The number of sentences written seems to have been rarely used in the study of language behavior; sentence type has been investigated more frequently.[2,5] *Total Sentences* was included as a measure of Productivity in the Picture Story Language Test. Although there is a high correlation between Total Words and Total Sentences, so far as language study and clinical diagnosis are concerned each of these measures provides a different type of information and both are useful. Moreover, this score was necessary because the number of words and the number of sentences must be derived before the Words per Sentence score can be computed.

Superficially it seems that counting the number of sentences is a simple process, as indeed it is in most instances. However, when studying the written language of young children and of those having disorders of language, the problem often becomes complex. The sentence count is further complicated by the fact that a satisfactory, broadly applicable definition of a sentence is not available. This may be the reason that few workers who have studied sentence types report their criteria for defining a sentence.

For centuries a sentence has been defined as *a group of words expressing a complete thought*. A definition such as this attempts to establish *meaning* and *thought units* as criteria. Fries[4] reveals the inadequacy of content as the basis for defining a sentence because criteria are lacking for determining when a thought is complete. He and Bloomfield[1] stress that linguistic form must be used for this purpose. This reasoning or deduction leads to the conclusion that it is a type of utterance which can stand alone and as such varies from one language to another. These utterances, that is, sentences, characterize all languages. Bloomfield states that "each sentence is an independent linguistic form, not included by virtue of any grammatical construction in any larger linguistic form."

Perrin[9] also has furnished a valuable discussion, one which we found helpful in establishing criteria. He states that no one has evolved a completely satisfactory definition of a sentence and that "if we define it as an independent expression having a subject and a verb, we are faced with a number of obviously good sentences lacking one or the other of these elements . . . though most will have both." Also, again from Perrin, ". . . we know that there are certain small units of communication that stand by themselves, that at least grammatically are independent of each other. For their full meaning we may need sentences that come before or after, but their elements do not depend on other sentences for their grammatical standing. Spoken sentences are characterized by certain stresses and usually by a pause at their end, and written sentences are marked by periods, question marks, and exclamation marks. The words in a sentence also stand in some definable relation to each other, though sometimes it is slight. This relationship between words is the grammatical basis of a sentence."

Though these discussions and definitions were useful, even important to our purpose, noteworthy questions persisted. To some extent the definition in Webster's Dictionary[12] fulfilled more of our needs. It states that a sentence is "a grammatically self-contained unit consisting of a word or a syntactically related group of words that expresses an assertion, a question, a command, a wish, or an exclamation, that in writing usually begins with a capital letter and concludes with appropriate end punctuation, and that in speech is phonetically distinguished by various patterns of stress, pitch, and pauses."

This definition incorporates grammar, syntax, and punctuation as well as the typical types of content, or statements, which usually fall within a sentence. More inclusive considerations, such as those suggested by this definition, finally were used and served as the basis for determining the Total Sentence score. Criteria which are exclusively structural and grammatical often cannot be specifically or logically applied to the written language of young children, nor to the written expressions of individuals having language disorders. Under these circumstances often the structural form, grammar, punctuation, and other conventionalized aspects are lacking or greatly distorted. Therefore, in determining sentences we employed both the criteria of "grammatically a self-contained unit" as well as content, or meaning, by considering the ideas which the writer was intending to communicate. Stated differently, when there was a lack of punctuation, poor grammar, poor sentence structure, or sentences run together through undue use of connectives, the content, the idea units were used to assist in ascertaining the beginning and end of a sentence.

Ordinarily little difficulty occurs in deriving the sentence count. However, the scorer should be familiar with the problems and the procedures to follow when difficult compositions are encountered. He must divide the composition according to the most deducibly correct grammatical units on the basis of the established relationships among words, and also, according to the logical sequence of the ideas being expressed. Only on the basis of consistently used definitions can standards be evolved for rejecting or accepting a given language unit, and only on this basis could a scale of written language be devised. In the discussion below we present more specifically the procedures to be followed in determining the Total Sentence score; see also Illustrative Stories in the Scoring Guide.

Divide the Story into Sentences

The first step is to read the entire story to acquire an impression of the language structure, the ideas being expressed and the relationship of the words to each other. If the sentences are clearly indicated by the writer, the scorer simply inserts a bar at the *end* of each sentence, being careful not to obliterate the punctuation marks. The Total Sentence score is derived by counting the bars.

Style Is Not Scored

When dividing the story into sentences, the style of writing is not directly considered. Incorrect sentence structure is scored under Syntax. Stylistic peculiarities and deviations, however, indirectly enter into the scoring if they affect meaning and punctuation. This occurs infrequently when making the sentence count. In the following example the style is laborious and awkward but it is apparent that the writer intended two sentences, so the TS score is 2.

■ EXAMPLE

The teacher gave us a toy box with a lot of plastic figures and furniture to play with.\ I tried, that usually happens in the house, to act out a scene with the plastic figures.\

Meaningless Language

Meaningless Language has been discussed under Total Words. In stories of this type the Total Sentence score is determined by the conventional manner. The TS score in the following example is 6.

■ EXAMPLE

Naming Level

As discussed previously, when there are no sentences but only a succession of words, the production is referred to as *Naming Level*. In scoring such stories Total Words is tallied in the usual manner, but Total Sentences and Words per Sentence are given a score of *one*. It would be illogical to score each word as a sentence as it does not fulfill our definition of a sentence and to do so would result in an erroneous Total Sentence score. Thus the story is scored as having *one* sentence with *one* word per sentence. In this example the TS score is 1.

■ **EXAMPLE**

table, toys, a dog, boy, play\

Units Interpreted and Scored in Two Ways

When a word, phrase or sentence can be *interpreted* in more than one way, the scorer from context makes a deduction regarding what the writer intended to say. Usually the decision concerning the intended meaning can be made easily. In the following story the TS score is 5.

■ **EXAMPLE**

A boy has a book and he had a big ball and he do not go to school. and did had girl to play and do you no a good boy he was.

This story is divided into sentences as follows:

A boy has a book\and he had a big ball\and he do not go to school.\and did had girl to play\and do you no a good boy he was.\

Occasionally there are units that can be *scored* in two ways and the actual intent of the writer cannot be deduced from the context. To illustrate, in the following example there is no way to judge whether the child intended to write one or two sentences, so the unit is scored according to "least penalty" (see Syntax). It is scored as *one* sentence, not *two*; the TS score is 1.

■ **EXAMPLE**

The boy is playing and he is having fun.\

Run-on Sentences

Perrin[9] states that a "run-on sentence is made up of two or more grammatically complete sentences written as one, without a connective between

the statements and punctuated with a comma or with no mark at all."
A notation of Run-on Sentences is made on the Record Form. However,
the examiner must determine the logical beginning and end of such
sentences. In this example the TS score is 2.

■ **EXAMPLE**

The boy is playing house he has some toys.

This story is divided into sentences as follows:

The boy is playing house\he has some toys.\

In the example below the first two sentences are evident in that they
are independent grammatical units. The third sentence has an error to be
evaluated under Syntax. The fourth sentence is a fragment having no
relation to either the preceding or the succeeding unit, but as a frag-
mentary sentence it is counted. The last three sentences are clearly
indicated since they are independent units. With Run-on Sentences the
examiner must mentally punctuate the units and divide them into the
most logical sequence of ideas. He bears in mind that in a sentence the
words have a definable, grammatical relationship to each other, and that
typically there is a basic thought or idea which is being expressed in each.
In this story the TS score is 7.

■ **EXAMPLE**

That boy has toys he is playing he is having a good time what toys a
go time see the dog see the car do you see thing.

This story is divided into sentences as follows:

That boy has toys\he is playing\he is having a good time what toys\a
go time\see the dog\see the car\do you see thing.\

Undue Use of Connectives

Undue Use of Connectives is similar to Run-on Sentences except that
the connectives join independent clauses. The most excessively used connective is *and*, followed by *but* and *also*. In a Run-on Sentence the difficulty
is in dividing the units into sentences. This is true also in the Undue Use
of Connectives but the problem is more one of designating the appropriate
length of the sentence because the writer has joined independent units
through the improper use of conjunctions. In the example below each unit
as designated is complete and grammatically independent so is counted

as a separate sentence; the writer has made undue use of the connective *and*. In this case the unnecessary connective is included as a part of the sentence which follows it: the TS score is 4.

■ **EXAMPLE**

The boy has a dog and he is playing with dolls; and the father is coming home and there are toys on the shelf.

The sentence divisions are:

The boy has a dog\and he is playing with dolls;\and the father is coming home\and there are toys on the shelf.\

These errors must be differentiated from the proper use of compound and complex sentences. The following is a compound sentence in which the relationship between the parts is logical and evident as written, so it is scored as *one* sentence.

■ **EXAMPLE**

The boy has a chair in his hand and he will give it to the girl.

The Total Sentence score furnishes an indication of facility with the written word which differs from the other measures of Productivity. We have found that individuals might write fewer than the average number of words but show no difference in the number of sentences written. Because they are deficient in syntax, they write more but shorter, less complex sentences. To some extent this characterizes the written language of certain groups of handicapped children. Moreover, the developmental patterns for Total Words and Total Sentences are not identical.[8] For these and other reasons the proficient examiner will find the Total Sentence score a useful measure when making diagnostic studies as well as when evaluating the developmental level of normal children.

WORDS PER SENTENCE (WPS)

Sentence length or Words per Sentence has been used by a number of investigators as a measure of language facility.[5,10] Psychologists, specialists in linguistics, and educators have found it advantageous. According to our findings, it is a highly satisfactory measure of the development of written language in normal children. Moreover, it is sensitive to various types of impositions, as illustrated by the findings for the deaf, dyslexic, mentally retarded and socially-emotionally disturbed, as well as for those with articulatory defects and language deficiencies.[8]

The Words per Sentence score is readily derived after the Total Word and the Total Sentence scores have been determined. It is computed by dividing the number of words (TW) by the number of sentences (TS). This score is the average number of words written per sentence (WPS).

■ **EXAMPLE**

It is early in the afternoon and little Johnny is busy playing house. He has arranged the furniture just so and is now putting the toy people on their chairs around the table. The table is set with little dishes and play food. Everyone is called to eat, even the dog.

In this story the TW score is *51*, and the TS score is *4*. The WPS score is derived as follows:

$$WPS = \frac{TW}{TS} \quad or$$

$$WPS = \frac{51}{4} \quad or$$

$$WPS = 12.8$$

The normative studies disclosed an unusually even growth in Words per Sentence from seven through 17 years of age, the increment being between two and three words for each two-year interval; the average child seven years of age wrote six words per sentence and at nine years, he wrote nine words (see Table 2). The handicapped children wrote sentences of below average length. Of the five scores which can be derived from the Picture Story Language Test the Words per Sentence score may be one of the most stable and revealing.

SUMMARY

To derive the Productivity scores the procedure is as follows:

(1) Read the entire story noting the general level of expression, the relationship between words and sentences as well as the meaningfulness of the story. Make notations on the Record Form of the special types of language used.

(2) Count all the words written except those defined as Lists and Titles, and others as excluded under Principles for Scoring (TW).

(3) Divide the story into sentences by inserting a vertical bar at the end of each unit determined as a sentence, using the principles which have been established. Count the number of sentences (TS).

(4) Compute the Words per Sentence score by dividing Total Words by Total Sentences (WPS).

(5) Record all scores on the Record Form.

REFERENCES

1. Bloomfield, L.: Language. New York, Henry Holt, 1933.
2. Braddock, R., Lloyd-Jones, R. and Schoer, L.: Research of Written Composition. Champaign, National Council of Teachers of English, 1963.
3. Davis, Edythe A.: Mean sentence length compared with long and short sentences as a reliable measure of language development. Child Develop. 8: 69, 1937.
4. Fries, C. C.: The Structure of English. New York, Harcourt, Brace & Co., 1952.
5. Heider, F. and Heider, G.: Studies in the psychology of the deaf. Psychol. Monogr. 242: 1941.
6. Johnson, W.: Your Most Enchanted Listener. New York, Harper & Brothers, 1956.
7. McCarthy, Dorothea: Language development in children, *In* Manual of Child Psychology, 2nd Ed., Leonard Carmichael (ed). New York, John Wiley & Sons, 1954.
8. Myklebust, H. R.: Development and Disorders of Written Language, Vol. II. New York and London, Grune & Stratton. In press.
9. Perrin, P. G.: Writer's Guide and Index to English. Chicago, Scott, Foresman Co., 1942.
10. Stormzand, M. and O'Shea, M.: How Much English Grammar? Baltimore, Warwick & York, 1924.
11. Templin, Mildred C.: Certain Language Skills in Children. Minneapolis, University of Minnesota Press, 1957.
12. Webster's Third New International Dictionary. Springfield, G & C Merriam Company, 1963.

Chapter V

Syntax Scale

ONE OF THE MOST characteristic aspects of all verbal systems is uniformity, arbitrariness and conventionality. Inherent in the use of language is the need for the writer (speaker) and the reader (hearer) to be able to attach similar, if not identical, meanings to the words written (spoken). Effective communication can be achieved only when the verbal system has become highly conventionalized on the part of the community of users. It is this conventionality which constitutes the basis of most definitions of language. For example, in Webster's Dictionary[16] we find language is "a systematic means of communicating ideas or feelings by the use of conventionalized signs, sounds, gestures, or marks having understood meanings"; or, "any set or system of verbal systems as used in a more or less uniform fashion by a number of people, who are thus enabled to communicate intelligently with one another." The term *syntax* encompasses much of this characteristic of verbal systems, so essential to distinguishing between communication and language. Perhaps all forms of animal life communicate but when defined in terms of syntax, only Man has language.

Our theoretical formulation was that language can be measured only in three ways: in terms of the amount, or *Productivity*, *Correctness*, and meaning, or *Content*. From this point of view it is form, the conventionalized structure, the arbitrariness, which must be measured by a scale of correctness. It is this peculiarity which we have categorized under the rubric the *Syntax Scale*.

Problems arise in the development of such a scale. Yet all who are concerned with the effectiveness of communication, especially educators, cannot avoid the need for standards in both spoken and written language. Though the requirements for correctness cannot be stultified and rigid, communication can be successful only when at least minimal standards of usage are maintained. However, precisely because allowances must be made for change while simultaneously maintaining required levels of correctness, this aspect of language development presents obstacles to rigorous quantitative measurement.

Despite the complexities involved, a scale of correctness is required to advance the study of written language theoretically and scientifically as well as for meeting everyday practical clinical and educational needs. All concerned with language, developmentally or diagnostically, are aware that correct usage often presents a problem in terms of acquisition.

Incorrect usage has long been recognized as a characteristic of certain language disorders. In fact, the astute diagnostician makes deductions concerning the nature of certain language disturbances from both spoken and written expressions. For example, those deaf from early life use highly typical syntactical and grammatical distortions.[10] Moreover, diagnostic categories such as *dysnomia, semantic aphasia, syntactical aphasia* and *formulation aphasia* are based on symptomatic deficiencies in syntax accompanying certain dysfunctions in the brain.[11] It was deemed essential, therefore, to include a measure of correctness in the Picture Story Language Test.

Syntax

Comparatively there is substantial agreement regarding the facets of verbal behavior to be included under syntax. A common dictionary definition states that syntax is "the part of grammar that treats of the expression of predicative, qualifying, and other word relations according to established usage in the language under study", or, syntax pertains to "sentence structure—the arrangement of word forms to show their mutual relations in the sentence."[16] Syntax in these terms of reference was included in the Scale because ability to use a word in the correct relationship to other words is a significant indication of the extent to which an individual has mastered a given language.

On the other hand, syntax alone is inadequate as a comprehensive, inclusive measure of correct usage. It includes neither important aspects of vocabulary nor of punctuation. Moreover, morphological factors, also involved in correctness of expression, are not encompassed if syntax alone is employed as the standard of acceptance. Because our purpose was to include all facets consequent to accuracy of expression, it was necessary to develop a scale, which in addition to syntax, comprised other aspects.

Morphology

Pei and Gaynor[12] have defined *morphology* as "The science and study of the forms and formation of words, i.e., the study of the ways and methods of grouping sounds into sound-complexes, called *words*, of definite, distinct, conventional meanings." Bloomfield[1] states that "by the morphology of a language we mean the constructions in which bound forms appear among the constituents." In Webster's Dictionary[16] morphology is defined as "a study and description of word-formation in a language including inflection, derivation, and compounding—the system of word-forming elements and processes in language." Typically morphology is distinguished from syntax by indicating that as a term it refers to word formation rather than to the relationship of one word to another. Others have emphasized that morphology is the study of bound word forms, whereas syntax is the study of free forms.

Inasmuch as syntax as a category does not include word formation, it was necessary to include certain morphological aspects in the accuracy scale. This need arose because analysis of the errors of written language revealed that often the mistake was not one of the relationships among words but rather in the actual formation of words. In our scale these errors have been designated as Word-Ending Errors. The proper roots of the words have been chosen and they have been placed in the correct relationship to other words but an erroneous ending has been used, such as *playing* for *played*, and *knowed* for *knows*.

Word Choice

Another feature of the correctness of verbal expressions entails accuracy and precision of word selection. In this sense the Scale also measures vocabulary. It must be stressed, however, that this refers to the proper *choice* of words, not to the size or richness of the vocabulary. For example, the expression *I see father* for *I see a man* must be considered an error inasmuch as the two ideas being communicated are widely divergent. This is scored as a substitution error because a wrong word has been chosen in place of the correct one. In order that errors of this type not be overlooked or omitted, Word Choice was included in the measure of correctness.

Punctuation

Perhaps there is less agreement regarding requirements for accuracy of punctuation than for any other feature of language in the written form. Nevertheless, for most effective, meaningful communication certain standards must be met. Punctuation was defined as "a system of inserting various standardized marks or signs in written or printed matter in order to clarify the meaning and separate structural units."[16] Although included in the Scale, our approach was to allow considerable freedom and to penalize only obvious deviations from common practice, as discussed below under *Principles for Scoring*.

Summary

In summary, the Syntax Scale incorporates a measure of syntax, certain morphological aspects, correctness of word choice, and punctuation. Therefore, it cannot be compared with measures using only sentence structure, complexity or parts of speech. Our objective was to devise a scale which comprised all aspects pertinent to the accuracy with which the written word is used. Though referred to as the Syntax Scale because of the lack of a more appropriate term, not only syntax was included.

We justified this approach theoretically in that our interest was in studying the growth of language usage in general, not a single component or facet such as syntax, punctuation or morphology. For this reason we developed a generalized scale of correctness.

As a standard we adhered to the stringency level of Informal English as suggested especially by Perrin.[13] Basically, however, the error categories were drawn from the works of Thompson[15] and Hunt.[6] In devising an objective scale it is necessary to delineate and define in order to establish reference points, albeit these may be arbitrary in nature. Only when standard reference points are instituted and consistently adhered to can a correctness scale of written language be evolved. Other criteria for correctness might be developed but when the Picture Story Language Test is used, if our norms for children are to be applied, those established for this test must serve as the basis for deriving the Syntax Quotient.

As indicated by this discussion, four types of accuracy are included in the Syntax Scale: *Syntax, Word Formation, Word Choice* and *Punctuation.* When scored according to this scale, incorrect usage falls into three categories: *Word Usage, Word Endings* and *Punctuation.* Within each of these categories there are specified error types as follows: *Word Usage—* Additions, Omissions, Substitutions, Word Order; *Word Endings—*Additions, Omissions, Substitutions; *Punctuation—*Additions, Omissions, Substitutions.

This system for classification of accuracy errors is based on the assumption that *words,* the principal units of meaning, can be used erroneously in four basic ways. They can be incorrectly added, omitted, or substituted or they can be placed in the wrong order. Furthermore, it assumes that words consist of two parts, the root and the ending, and that both are involved in the communication of meaning. Hence, errors might be made in the root or in the ending. Inasmuch as an ending is a different type of error, it should be studied and scored as an error category. Because word endings are rarely placed in the wrong order, errors consist of their being incorrectly added, omitted, or substituted. Punctuation also conveys meaning, so its usage too should be appraised. As with word endings, marks of punctuation are not placed in the wrong order so incorrectness includes additions, omissions, and substitutions.

Further definition of the error categories and error types with examples is given below. First, general principles for scoring are considered; see also Illustrative Stories in the Scoring Guide.

PRINCIPLES FOR SCORING

The Stringency Level for scoring Syntax is Informal English, the same as for Total Sentences, referring to common, conventional usage. To score correctness adequately the examiner should be familiar with this level and when in doubt refer to the criteria given here, as well as to Perrin[13] or other references. As discussed previously and as shown on the Record Form, there are three error categories: Word Usage, Word Endings and Punctuation. Spelling was omitted because errors of this type are of a different order inasmuch as they are not involved in correct usage; the Syntax Scale was devised to measure only the accuracy of language usage.

Before beginning to score Syntax, the examiner determines Total Words, Total Sentences and Words per Sentence. While scoring Syntax, he inserts the designations indicating the type of error that has been made; see *Symbols for Designating Error Type.*

Stringency Level

We have indicated that everyone concerned with the objective evaluation of language usage must in some way appraise its correctness or its conformity with acceptable structure as experienced through common usage. Yet to do so assumes a norm, a standard of reference. Such a reference point is difficult to establish because patterns of usage vary greatly according to custom, tradition, intelligence, educational level, socioeconomic factors, and even on a geographic basis. Nevertheless, for research, educational and clinical purposes, though they may be arbitrary, acceptability standards must be utilized. These standards are referred to as the *Stringency Level.*

Perrin,[13] Fries,[5] Curme,[3] Jesperson,[7] and Bloomfield[1] have contributed notably to the intricacies involved in determining the correctness and incorrectness of language. In establishing our Stringency Level, we followed the standards for Informal English, primarily as indicated by Perrin[13] who states that in terms of rigor, it is that level of usage met "in ordinary life by people of good social standing, who are more or less concerned with public affairs." He defines this level of usage further as "the typical language of an educated person going about his everyday business. It lies between the uncultivated vulgate on one side and the more restricted formal level on the other."

To the extent possible it was this degree of correctness which was used in standardizing the Picture Story Language Test. We concluded that this allowed for reasonably strict grammatical standards without being oppressively dogmatic. The level of Informal English seemed particularly suitable for written narrative, the type required by our test. In order to quantify facility with the written word, it was necessary to formulate specific criteria for acceptable versus unacceptable form and structure. These criteria pertain principally to scoring Total Sentences and Syntax.

Intended Meaning

We have stressed that both meaning and grammatical-linguistic structure are relied upon to determine correctness. Here we emphasize the importance of appraising what the writer intended to say so that Syntax can be scored adequately. To some extent the intended meaning was noted while scoring Total Sentences. When not apparent the examiner deduces the intended meaning of a word, phrase or sentence from the total context and the sequence of events described in the story. With the intended meaning in mind he scores the correctness of the expression. The following example illustrates this procedure and may be used as a guide.

■ EXAMPLE

Once upon a time there live a boy who always plays toys. He puts the toys on the kitchen table. his toys wore all over the house. He would make a house. He would lamps and dogs a table on the table he a big box. he would put it on the chair. he has all kinds of toy in the box.

After the intended meaning had been determined, it was scored and corrected to read as follows:

Once upon a time there lived a boy who always played with toys. He put the toys on the kitchen table. His toys were all over the house. He would make a house. He would make lamps, dogs, and a table on the table. He had a big box. He would put it on the chair. He has all kinds of toys in the box.

Score Accuracy Only

Only conformity to correct usage should be scored. Although intended meaning often must be used adjunctively in determining correctness, meaning per se is not scored; the Abstract-Concrete Scale was devised for this purpose. Likewise, style per se is not to be scored. If style is deviate to the extent that it causes incorrect use of words, word endings or punctuation, then indirectly it is scored.

The Syntax Scale was designed to measure accuracy of usage only, not content or stylistic form. Common, acceptable colloquial expressions should not be scored as errors inasmuch as they fall within the stringency level of Informal English. The following example illustrates a style in written language which is inferior but which should *not* be scored; though stylistically inferior, the story contains no errors as measured by the Syntax Scale.

■ **EXAMPLE**

Our teacher, a man, gave us a box with a lot of figures and furniture of plastic. I tried to act out a scene with the plastic figures that usually happens in the house. My first day in kindergarten was very much fun.

Least Penalty Rule

When two possibilities are equally plausible, the rule of *least penalty* should be applied. However, usually the intended meaning is ascertained, so this rule is applied sparingly. Occasionally a circumstance occurs such as shown in the example below. The meaning of the first sentence is obscure because the writer may have intended, *This picture is of a boy playing*, but an equally satisfactory interpretation is, *This picture is of a playroom*. Applying the least penalty rule, this would be scored as a Substitution Error; the word *playful* being erroneously substituted for the word *playroom*. If scored according to the interpretation, *This picture is of a boy playing*, there is both an Omission and a Word Ending error, and hence a greater penalty; the word *boy* would have been omitted and the ending *ful* would have been substituted for *ing*.

■ **EXAMPLE**

This picture is of a playful. The boy is either in school or at home. He seems very happy playing with the plastic little people. It seems as if he is showing his home and family. Or someones he knew.

SCORING ERROR TYPES

Word Usage

Three broad categories of incorrect usage are scored: Word Usage, Word Endings and Punctuation. The most consequential errors, those that because of their influence on meaning impede communication most seriously, are the ones entailing the use of words. These may be Addition, Omission, Substitution or Word Order errors. The procedures for scoring each of these are discussed.

Additions

If an added word is superfluous, unnecessary and actually constitutes erroneous usage, it is scored as an *Addition* error. In this example, the word *be* has been added, comprising an error of Word Usage.

■ **EXAMPLE**

A boy is be playing.

Not all addition errors are this obvious. More common is the undue use of connectives, such as *and*. In the first example below, *and* is used to join three independent units, Addition errors in the undue use of connectives. In the second example there is another type of Addition error; the third *and* does not join independent units. It is scored as an error in the use of words because a comma should have been used after *girls* instead of the word *and* illustrating a misuse of a connective. In Example (3) the first *and* was inserted where a comma is required. Nevertheless, it is not assumed that the writer substituted *and* for the comma. Rather, the *and* is scored as an Addition, and the lack of a comma as a Punctuation Omission; one involves words and the other punctuation, and each is scored separately.

■ **EXAMPLES**

(1) The boy has a dog *and* he is playing with dolls *and* his father is coming home *and* there are toys on the shelf.

(2) The boy is playing with a playhouse and it has some boys and girls *and* a little dog and some dishes.

(3) He has a book *and* car and box.

Other examples of Addition errors showing the wrong use of words are given below. In Example (1) the word *the* causes an incorrect connotation; when omitted the sentence is correct. In the second example the word *the* has been added erroneously, causing an error in the use of words. The third illustrates a three word phrase that has been added and is unnecessary; when eliminated the sentence forms a unit. In this instance there is an Addition error of three words, *on the table*.

■ **EXAMPLES**

(1) There were some books in *the* back of him.

(2) He had some toys on *the* the chair.

(3) He has a table on which he puts his dolls *on the table*.

Omissions

Addition errors entail the use of words that are both unnecessary and erroneous. A sentence might be in error because of an opposite circumstance—the omission of words essential to correct structure. This is categorized as an *Omission* error in the use of words. When words essential to correct expression are omitted, it usually is obvious and can be readily scored.

In the first example it is apparent that the verb *is* has been omitted. The same type of error is seen in Example (2) in that *a* was omitted before the word *boy*, and *boy* was omitted before the word *playing*. Occasionally an Omission error involving Word Usage might be scored in two ways, either of which is correct. In Example (3) the story might have been written as one sentence by placing *and* after the word *dolls* and by omitting the words *also with*. Or there might have been a second sentence as *He is also playing with toys*. If this were scored according to the first possibility, inserting *and* and omitting *also with*, it could not be considered an Omission error because it would come under errors of Substitution and Additions. Because it seems more plausible that the writer intended to write, *He is also playing with toys*, it is scored as an Omission error of *three* words, *He is* and *playing*.

When two possibilities exist, it is beneficial to score the unit both ways to ascertain which is more plausible and to note the difference in penalty points; if both are equally plausible, the rule of *least penalty* is applied. Often the effect on the score is negligible. In Example (3) the difference was only *one* point in the total score. This, however, does not vitiate the need for careful scoring.

■ EXAMPLES

(1) A boy playing.

(2) He has a mother, a father and boy. This picture is of a playing.

(3) The boy is playing with dolls. Also with toys.

Substitutions

Incorrect usage other than Additions and Omissions might be manifested in the erroneous choice of words. When this occurs it is categorized as an error or *Substitution;* the incorrect word is substituted for the correct one. Usually these errors are apparent but diligent evaluation is required. Substitution errors often involve pronouns. In the first example, *they* was used in place of *them* and in Example (2), *himself* was substituted for *he*. To avoid the subjectivity in deducing that it is a mistake in spelling, whenever another word is used in place of the correct one, it is scored as a Word Usage Substitution error. Occasionally what appears to be a reversal forms another word, as shown in Example (3). Although it might be assumed that the writer wrote *saw* for *was*, it must be scored as incorrect.

■ EXAMPLES

(1) He gave the toys to *they*.

(2) His parents, relatives and even *himself* can always look back on the picture.

(3) He *saw* showing his house.

Word Order

An interesting aspect of language is that not only must the correct words be chosen but they must be arranged in the order that characterizes the language in question. The order of the words in a sentence determines much of what is signified by the term *structure*. Stated differently, sentence structure is comprised not only of the correct use of the parts of speech but also of word order. *Word Order* pertains directly to the phenomenon of the relationships between words when properly used.

In appraising correctness, therefore, it is necessary to evaluate the arrangement of the words within the sentence. As distinguished from the other categories in the Syntax Scale, errors of Addition, Omission and Substitution pertain to the selection of words, whereas Word Order pertains to the arrangement of these words after they have been selected. On this basis Word Order cannot overlap with the other error categories because inherently there can be a mistake in the arrangement of the words only if the proper words have been chosen; if the proper words are not present, the error falls into one of the other three categories. Hence, only when all the words necessary to form a sentence have been included but in the wrong order is it scored as an error of Word Order. Errors of this type are not as common as those discussed above, but they comprise a significant percent of all errors in written language, especially of those made by the deaf.[10]

In the first example the necessary words have been chosen but the order in which they have been placed is incorrect; *is* should fall between *boy* and *sitting*—*The boy is sitting*. The second example illustrates the misplacement of a phrase consisting of the two words, *of toys*; it should have appeared between *box* and *on*—*I saw a box of toys on a chair*. In the third illustration a phrase of four words has been placed incorrectly; *the dog and baby* should appear between *father* and *were*—*I saw the father, the dog and baby were in a car*. Although in Examples (2) and (3) phrases, not individual words have been misplaced, only *one* penalty is assigned to each because one error of sequence has been made; a Word Order penalty of one point is assessed for errors of this type.

When a word within a misplaced phrase is in the wrong order, two Word Order errors must be assessed. In Example (4) the phrase *a red car* has been misplaced, and in addition the word *red* within this phrase is out of order. The sentence should read, *The boy is playing with a red car. Two* errors have been made, the wrong placement of a phrase and a word in the wrong order.

Examples (5) and (6) are included to illustrate a difficult and sometimes controversial aspect of scoring Word Usage. It concerns split infinitives, misplaced modifiers, and other grammatical constructions of this type. The stringency level of Informal English permits considerable freedom so far as usage of these forms is concerned. On the other hand, errors, or even awkwardness of this type may confuse meaning, hence impede communication. Therefore, minimum standards are required. When such constructions influence meaning, they are scored as errors of Word Usage and treated in the same manner as other errors falling under this category.

Example (5) shows the use of a split infinitive scored as an error because meaning is confused by the position of the word *then* in the sentence. If this word had been placed at the beginning of the sentence or between *was* and *going*, the meaning would be clarified. Modifiers, when misplaced, often cause obvious distortions of meaning, as shown in Example (6). In this case the writer communicated a completely different meaning than was intended. He meant to say, *The boy's brown hair was too long.* These must be scored as errors in Word Order.

■ EXAMPLES

  (1) The boy sitting is.

  (2) I saw a box on a chair of toys.

  (3) I was the father were in a car the dog and baby.

  (4) The boy a car red is playing with.

  (5) He was going to then put the toys away.

  (6) The boy's hair was brown too long.

Word Endings

Word Ending errors were distinguished from errors of Word Usage because they do not concern the roots of words. The writer has chosen the correct word but used an incorrect ending. Because these constitute part-word errors and are less consequential to meaning, less in order of magnitude, they are scored separately and assigned a lower penalty. These errors are made up of Additions, Omissions or Substitutions.

Additions

Word Ending errors of *Addition* often involve verb tense and number. Example (1) concerns tense and use of the ending *ing;* it has been erroneously added to the verb; thus it must be scored as a Word Ending Error. Example (2) shows another tense error; the *ed* was added to *scold.* In

Example (3) the plural form is used incorrectly in that an *s* has been added to the word *furniture*. The fourth example illustrates two Word Ending errors of Addition in a single sentence, one of tense and the other of number. The ending *ed* has been incorrectly added to the word *know* and the letter *s* to the word *toy*. Both are scored; there are *two* Word Ending errors.

■ **EXAMPLES**

(1) He will playing with his toys.

(2) His father was wanting to scolded him.

(3) The boy is playing with some furnitures.

(4) He did not knowed that his mother had given him a new toys.

Omissions

Word Ending Omission errors are opposite from those of Addition because a necessary part of the word has been left off. Errors of this type are different in magnitude and must be distinguished from whole word errors. Often the incorrectness concerns tense and omission of the ending *ing*. Such errors, as shown in Example (1) below, must be scored. The ending *ing* was omitted from the word *play*.

Word Ending Omission errors also frequently involve the singular and plural form. These must be distinguished from spelling errors inasmuch as spelling is not scored on the Syntax Scale. Usually this can be done by noting the accuracy with which words are spelled throughout the story. The examiner makes a judgment accordingly and when spelling errors also are present, he differentiates them from an inability to use form as it pertains to number. As shown by the examples below, Omission errors of number frequently consist of leaving the letter *s* off words where it is required. In the second example it was omitted from the word *block* and in the third, from the word *thing*.

■ **EXAMPLES**

(1) The boy is play with his toys.

(2) The boy had some block.

(3) He did not know that his mother had given him so many thing.

Substitutions

Errors of Substitution also may comprise only the endings of words, not the whole word. An incorrect ending may be used in place of the correct one. Often the error is in substituting *ed* for *ing*, or *ing* for *ed* as illustrated by the examples below. As is the case in all Word Ending errors, the correct root has been chosen so only part of a word has been misused.

In Example (1) the ending *ed* has been substituted for the correct one, *ing*, whereas in the second we find the reverse, *ing* for *ed* on the word *calling*. A rare type of Word Ending error is illustrated in Example (3). By using the ending *ing* for the letter *y*, another word has been formed and therefore it cannot be treated as simply as an ending error. Actually an incorrect word has been used in place of the correct one so the error encompasses a whole word, not a word-part. To maintain objectivity and consistency, therefore, this must be scored as a Substitution error involving words, not Word Endings.

■ EXAMPLES

(1) He was played with toys.

(2) His mother told him he should not have calling the other boys.

(3) They are getting reading for supper.

Punctuation

Because punctuation influences meaning, it was included in the Syntax Scale. It is apparent that correctness of written verbal expression entails the use of punctuation marks, albeit its importance to the communication of meaning is less in comparison with whole words. In order of magnitude we equated it with word endings. Therefore, errors involving words were assigned the highest penalty, with endings and punctuation receiving less but equal value (see *Penalty Score Values*).

Punctuation is scored in accordance with the principles established for the other aspects of correctness measured by the Syntax Scale. Convention and practice as found in Informal English usage was the standard of acceptance. Moreover, the error categories previously used were applied because most errors of punctuation involve additions, omissions, or substitutions, as do errors of Word Usage or Word Endings. We first consider Punctuation Errors of Addition.

Additions.

The examples given serve as a guide for scoring Punctuation Errors of Addition. In the first example the writer has placed a comma after the word *house*, an error of placing a mark where it is not appropriate. The second shows the improper use of a period in that it is after the word *people* and before the end of the sentence. Example (3) illustrates the erroneous insertion of a hyphen. Apostrophes also may be inserted erroneously, such as in *toy's* in Example (4). A comma placed before the *and* that precedes the last unit in a series is optional and not considered an error, so the second comma in Example (5) is *not* scored as an error.

▪ EXAMPLES

(1) They play house, and dolls with the girls.

(2) I see a boy playing with doll people. on a table.

(3) Today he is a little boy of about six or seven playing with toys, but in years to come-he will be a grown man.

(4) The boy's toy's are on the table.

(5) The boy was playing with blocks, toys, and dolls.

Omissions.

One of the most common punctuation errors is the omission of marks where required. Commas, hyphens, periods, quotation marks, apostrophes, and question marks often are not used when convention and clarity of meaning do not permit their omission. These examples illustrate required uses of punctuation as scored on the Syntax Scale.

Example (1) shows good written language for a young child except that three periods have been omitted; *three* errors have been made. In Example (2) the writer failed to use a period to end a sentence; a period should have been placed after the word *from*. Though considerable freedom is permitted in the use of commas, when usage is in error, it must be so scored. Example (3) illustrates an error in omission of a comma because clarity of meaning requires that it be placed after the word *playroom*. In Example (4) an apostrophe has been omitted in the word *its*. An apostrophe must be inserted to indicate contractions and possession. Example (5) shows the omission of quotation marks. The writer specifically uses a phrase that is followed by *he said*. Correct form requires that the phrase be enclosed with quotation marks, and to be correct the marks must be used twice, preceding and following the quote. Because the writer failed to use quotation marks either before or after the phrase, he is assessed *two* errors. Each of the quotation marks is scored separately. The same procedure pertains to scoring a quote within a quote.

Hyphens must be inserted, especially in compound words. In Example (6) the writer has not used them in either the word *brother-in-law* or in the word *twenty-five*. Inasmuch as three hyphens are required he is assessed *three* punctuation errors.

▪ EXAMPLES

(1) He plays house He plays with toys A dog is in the picture

(2) He is given a box to chose from He is to pick out a set and make it look complete.

(3) He is in the playroom probably with the door shut.

(4) Its fun to play with toys.

(5) This is really fun he said, as he built his house on the table.

(6) His brother in law was twenty five years old.

Substitutions.

A Substitution Error of Punctuation consists of an incorrect mark being inserted in place of the correct one. In the first illustration a period instead of a question mark was placed after the word *different*. In Example (2) a comma has been used following the word *family* where a period is required. Another error would be assessed because when the period is inserted, the word *he* must be capitalized inasmuch as it is the first word in the sentence.

■ EXAMPLES

(1) "What makes this boy different". I asked.

(2) The little boy is pretending that he is the whole family, he is having so much fun.

Capitalization is considered a part of Punctuation and as having significance in the communication of meaning. However, in the development of the Syntax Scale scoring was limited to the omission of a capital at the beginning of a sentence. Errors entailing Capitalization, therefore, are scored only as Omissions, not as Additions or as Substitutions. Even the lack of capitals on proper nouns is not scored as errors, the rationale being that such incorrectness was more appropriately viewed as a mistake in spelling. On the other hand, a capital at the beginning of a sentence conveys meaning both in terms of sentence structure and in units of thought or expression.

Because only the omission of a capital at the beginning of a sentence is scored on the Syntax Scale, these errors can be readily identified. The examples given should be utilized as a guide. The only error scored is shown in the first illustration where the first word of the sentence was not capitalized. In Example (2) a proper noun was not capitalized and in Example (3) a capital was incorrectly used on a common noun. Neither of these are scored as errors. The last example shows a connective as the first word of a sentence but a capital was used so it too is not scored.

■ **EXAMPLES**

(1) he has some toys.

(2) The man is named bill.

(3) The boy had a Doll house.

(4) And he is having fun.

Special Situations

Occasionally there are special situations involving one or more error types. One of these pertains to words or units that have been bracketed. Under *Lists* we stated that only the first two and the last of the series are used in determining the word count. The words falling between the second and the last of the series are bracketed to indicate that they are not to be included in Total Words. The scorer should note that all which fall within the brackets also are disregarded when appraising the correctness of punctuation.

In the first example the unit enclosed by brackets is not included; only one error is scored because the article *a* was omitted before the word *dog*. In the second example there is a special circumstance in that one error has been superimposed on another; the pronoun *him* has been substituted for *he*, and the first word of the sentence has not been capitalized. In this instance there are *two* errors, one a Substitution involving words and one of Omission involving capital letters.

■ **EXAMPLES**

(1) The boy is reproducing a living room complete with a baby, dog, [chairs, tables, plates, spoons, fork, lamp, dresser,] and a stroller.

(2) I see a boy in the picture. him has black hair.

PENALTY SCORE VALUES

Errors encompassing two levels of magnitude are scored on the Syntax Scale. The rationale for using this method is that whole word errors are more consequent to meaning than part-word errors and errors in punctuation. In other words, we devised the Scale so that the more consequential errors, those that most basically distort meaning, were allotted the greater penalty.

The system of point values allocates one point to whole word errors and one-third point to both Word Ending and Punctuation errors. Therefore, the point value for each Error Type is as follows:

Word Usage

Additions	one point
Omissions	one point
Substitutions	one point
Word Order	one point

Word Endings

Additions	one-third point
Omissions	one-third point
Substitutions	one-third point

Punctuation

Additions	one-third point
Omissions	one-third point
Substitutions	one-third point

Designation of Syntax Errors

It is important diagnostically to maintain the individuality of the Error Categories and the Error Types measured by the Syntax Scale. Though the Syntax Quotient is a composite including scores for Word Usage, Word Ending and Punctuation, scores can be computed separately for each *Error Category* as well as for each *Error Type*, as shown on the Record Form. Scores can be derived individually for Word Usage, Word Order and Punctuation. Likewise, totals can be computed for Additions, Omissions, Substitutions and Word Order. These computations are useful in studying the incorrect usages that characterize individuals or groups. However, typically the total Syntax Quotient is computed inasmuch as this represents the individual's over-all proficiency in written language when measured in terms of correct usage.

Before considering the rationale and procedures for computing the Syntax Quotient, we present the symbols to be used to indicate both Error Category and Error Type.

ERROR TYPE SYMBOLS

Word Usage

Additions (╱)

The erroneous addition of a word is designated by placing a slash mark through the word that has been added incorrectly.

■ EXAMPLE

The boy was a̷n̷d̷ playing.

Omissions (∧)

Omission of a word is shown by inserting a carat at the point in the sentence where the word should have appeared.

■ **EXAMPLE**

The boy ∧ playing.

Substitutions (∿)

Word substitutions are indicated by drawing a wavy line under the word used erroneously.

■ **EXAMPLE**

The boy has playing.
　　　　∿

Word Order (↶⊃)

Errors of Word Order are designated by drawing a circle around the word, or words, that have been misplaced and an arrow from this unit to the point in the sentence where it should have been written.

■ **EXAMPLE**

The boy should ✔ in school (have been.)

Word Ending

Word Ending errors are designated by the same symbols used to indicate errors of Word Usage. When an ending has been added incorrectly, the mistake is shown by a slash mark (╱), when omitted it is shown by a carat (∧), and when incorrectly substituted the error is indicated by a wavy line (∿). However, an additional notation, the capital letter "E" designates it as a Word Ending error; the capital is less easily confused with other letters.

Additions ($\overset{E}{╱}$)

The slash mark designates that a Word Ending has been applied when not required. In this example, the slash is inserted through the *ed*, and the capital E is placed with it to specify that the error is at the end of the word, not a whole word and not one of Punctuation.

■ **EXAMPLE** 　$\overset{E}{╱}$

The boy will play*ed* with his toys.

Omissions ($\overset{E}{\wedge}$)

Omission of a required Word Ending is shown by the carat and the capital "E."

■ **EXAMPLE**

This picture is of a boy pla$\overset{E}{\underset{\wedge}{y}}$.

Substitutions ($\underset{\sim}{E}$)

An inappropriate Word Ending in place of the correct one is shown by drawing a wavy line under the one used erroneously and by inserting the capital "E."

■ **EXAMPLE**

He was pla$\overset{E}{\underset{\sim}{ye}}$d with toys.

Punctuation (p)

Errors of Punctuation are of three types: Additions, Omissions and Substitutions. Each carries a separate designation so that one can be differentiated from the other. Even though the same symbols are used to denote the Error Type, an additional designation, the letter "p," indicates that the error is one of Punctuation.

Additions ($\overset{p}{/}$)

A Punctuation Error of Addition, a mark used where it is not required, is shown by placing a slash mark through the error with the letter "p" above.

■ **EXAMPLE**

I see a boy$\overset{p}{/}$and a dog.

Omissions ($\overset{p}{\wedge}$)

Punctuation Omission Errors are designated by a carat with the letter "p." When indicated in this manner the mistake is easily recognized as one of omitting necessary punctuation marks, in this sentence the comma.

■ **EXAMPLE**

The boy has a dog$\overset{p}{\wedge}$a book and a chair.

Substitutions ($\underset{\sim}{p}$)

When incorrect marks are inserted in place of correct ones, a wavy line is drawn under the mark used erroneously and the letter "p" is placed above. In this example a period was used in place of the required question mark.

■ **EXAMPLE**

Do you think the boy is happy.

For analysis and diagnostic purposes it is possible to differentiate Capitalization errors from other punctuation errors. Thus to distinguish the omission of a capital from that of words or from other types of punctuation marks, the carat with a small "c" is inserted ($\overset{c}{\wedge}$). In this example the carat indicates that the error is one of Omission and the small "c," that a capital letter has been omitted.

■ **EXAMPLE**

c
he has some toys.
∧

SUMMARY

These illustrations manifest that by using the proper designations both Error Category and Error Type can be clearly indicated. It is not necessary to insert omitted or substituted words and punctuation marks, or to rewrite the sentences where errors of Word Order appear. In fact, to write in such corrections without the designating of symbols does not provide a record of the type of error made. But when individual errors are denoted and recorded on the Record Form, diagnosticians, research workers, and educators are in a position to analyze the specific nature of the deficiencies characterizing certain individuals or groups.

The symbols for designating incorrect usage can be summarized as follows:

ERROR CATEGORY

ERROR TYPE	Word Usage	Word Ending	Punctuation
Additions	(/)	($\overset{E}{/}$)	($\overset{P}{/}$)
Omissions	(∧)	($\overset{E}{\wedge}$)	($\overset{P}{\wedge}$)
Substitutions	(︵)	($\underset{︵}{E}$)	($\underset{︵}{P}$)
Word Order	(↶)		

RATIONALE FOR THE SYNTAX SCORE

We have presented the criteria for scoring correctness, as well as the symbols for designating each type of error. Here we consider the rationale and procedure for computing the *Syntax Score.* It is important that the scorer of the Picture Story Language Test be familiar with these procedures inasmuch as they constitute a departure from those commonly used for such purposes. From the discussion below it is apparent that raw scores alone seriously limit the significance of a score indicating correct usage. Only when computed as a ratio of correctness according to a given standard of acceptability does this score provide the type of information essential for developmental and diagnostic studies.

Review of the work pertinent to evaluation of correct language usage reveals many difficulties, though a number of systems have been attempted. The problem is that a segment of language on which to base the measurement of errors has neither been determined nor agreed upon. Accordingly McCarthy[8] states in this regard that LaBrant's study, " . . . uses the clause as the unit rather than the sentence, so again comparisons are impossible. It is indeed unfortunate that more direct comparisons cannot be made among these various studies." Braddock et al.[2] report that "Early frequency counts merely expressed the total number of errors found, regardless of the amount of writing examined, . . . results that were meaningless and confusing." Davis[4] refers to the methods as being "inaccurate and misleading, " and states that it is necessary to consider the frequency of occurrence in a given construction within a given sample before it can be adequately evaluated.

To achieve a common basis for determining language errors three primary proposals have been made: (1) those which consider the possibilities for an error to occur; (2) those based on language units, including errors per sentence, per clause, or per word; (3) those based on the total number of errors. Stormzand and O'Shea[14] utilized the first of these, the possibilities for an error to occur, or errors per chance for error. However, this procedure does not indicate the proportion of the material that is in error versus that which is correct. Hence, we do not know whether the productions were one-half, one-fourth or one-eighth incorrect.

Hunt[6] and others used the "number of prepositional phrase errors per number of total errors," distinguishing between the most important and the least important errors, a system effective for comparing the proportion of different types of errors made by various groups. It too is disadvantageous because it does not indicate the amount of language expressed correctly in comparison with that expressed incorrectly.

Instead of the parts of speech, the number of errors, etc., we chose to use *words* as the unit of measurement. For standardization and quantification, for purposes of a developmental scale of correct usage, *the word* seemed to be the most appropriate unit on which to base the accuracy score. We chose the *word* as the unit of measurement for other reasons, including that given by Bloomfield[1] when he defines it as the minimum free form of language. As a unit of language it is basic to grammar, morphology, and syntax. It is the only stable, constant entity in language and the foundation from which language originates and is formed. Moreover, as units, words are essentially uniform and equivalent. Other units, such as prepositional phrases and clauses are not uniform inasmuch as they are of varying lengths and include various grammatical types, structures, and forms.

Mention should be made also of the reason for not choosing the morpheme as the unit of measure because Miller[9] and others have defined it as "the smallest meaningful unit of language." Though it is the smallest meaningful unit, it is not necessarily independent. This can be demonstrated by the *s* in the word *girls*. The *s* has a meaning, more than one, but it has this meaning only when it appears at the end of a noun; it does not have this meaning when it appears in the word *small*. Because morphemes may be bound, not independent, they did not satisfy our objectives. In the example given, in comparison with the *s* the word *girl* can be placed in various word combinations and relationships and *retain* its meaning. For these reasons we concluded that the morpheme, as well as grammatical form and sentence structure, was unsuitable as a unit of measure for our purpose, that is, for a developmental scale of accuracy of language usage in the written form. With the *word* as the basis, the score obtained is stable and permits comparison from person to person so that patterns of normal language behavior can be described and deviations can be indicated diagnostically.

Syntax Quotient

The procedure devised for scoring Syntax allows for recording errors of usage by both category and type. Nevertheless, it seemed advantageous to provide a quotient that reflected correctness in a single score. Before considering the computation of the quotient more specifically, examples are given to illustrate the rationale for deriving this score in the manner indicated below. In each of the examples "correct" designates that which should have been written, whereas "incorrect" denotes what was written and under the assumed situation was erroneous.

■ EXAMPLES

(1)   Correct: He played
     Incorrect: He stood

(2)   Correct: He played there
     Incorrect: He played ∧

(3) Correct: He played
     Incorrect: He played ~~there~~

(4) Correct: He played in the room
     Incorrect: He played ∧ ∧ ∧

In the first example instead of *He played*, the writer wrote *He stood*; he substituted an incorrect word for one of the two words required. Hence we can state that 50 per cent of what was written was correct and 50 per cent of what should have been written was correct. Both formulations, what was written and what should have been written, consist of two words.

However, with Omissions, as shown by the second illustration, both formulations are not identical in the number of words used. The writer should have written *He played there* but he wrote only *He played*. If he is scored on the basis of the first formulation, the correctness of what was written, he scores 100 per cent; he wrote two words and both were used correctly. Only when scored on the basis of the second formulation, what should have been written, is the error revealed. This procedure manifests that out of the three words he should have written he wrote two correctly, obtaining a Syntax Quotient of 66.6.

When we consider this procedure as it pertains to Additions, illustrated by Example (3), another variation is apparent. Three words were written when there should have been only two. Applying the first formulation, the per cent correct out of the words written, the Syntax Quotient is 66.6; two out of the three words are correct. Applying the second formulation, the per cent correct out of what should have been written, we obtained a score of 100 per cent; he should have written two words correctly and he did so.

We observe, therefore, that the first process, the per cent correct from the words written, is unsuitable for scoring errors of Omission and that the second, the per cent correct from what should have been written, fails to identify Addition errors. On the other hand, either can be applied to Substitution errors when the number of words written and the number of words required is equal. Because neither formulation satisfied the requirements it was necessary to devise a method of scoring that encompassed both. *The Syntax Quotient as derived reflects all types of errors as well as correct usage.*

Our basic assumption was that an accuracy score should represent the ratio of what was written plus what should have been written minus the errors, to the number of words written plus what should have been written. Though this seems complex, it is simply the ratio of correctness to that required for total correctness (no errors as measured by the Scale). Important to this concept is the fact that Total Correct is not what was written minus the errors but rather, it is what was written *plus* what should have been written *minus* the errors. Likewise, Total Unit is not the number of words written but the number of words written *plus* what should have been written. This can be seen by the formulation:

$$\frac{\text{Number of Words (NW)} + \text{Total Omissions (TO)} - \text{Total Errors (TE)}}{\text{Number of Words (NW)} + \text{Total Omissions (TO)}}$$

or

$$\frac{\text{Total Correct (TC)}}{\text{Total Unit (TU)}}$$

or

$$\frac{\text{TC}}{\text{TU}} \times 100 = \text{Syntax Quotient}$$

Because scoring of Syntax is time consuming, studies were made to determine the number of sentences required to obtain a reliable score for correct usage. The results, presented in Tables 15 and 16, reveal that for certain purposes, only the first three sentences are needed. Nevertheless, often it is advantageous to score more than three sentences, if not the whole story.

The following résumé enumerates the steps for computing the Syntax Quotient, irrespective of the number of sentences scored.

(1) Count the number of words in the sentences that have been scored: (NW).

(2) Add Total Omissions (TO) to Number of Words (NW): Total Unit (TU).

(3) Substract Total Errors (TE) from Total Unit (TU): Total Correct (TC).

(4) Divide Total Correct by Total Unit: TC/TU.

(5) Convert this ratio into the Syntax Quotient by multiplying by 100.

REFERENCES

1. Bloomfield, L.: Language. New York, Henry Holt, 1933.
2. Braddock, R., Lloyd-Jones, R. and Schoer, L.: Research in Written Composition. Champaign, National Council of Teachers of English, 1963.
3. Curme, G. O.: English Grammar. New York, Barnes & Noble, 1947.
4. Davis, Edythe: Accuracy versus errors as a criterion in children's speech. J. Educ. Psychol. 30: 365, 1939.
5. Fries, C. C.: The Structure of English. New York, Harcourt, Brace & Company, 1952.
6. Hunt, J. F.: A study of errors in written language of deaf and hearing children. M.A. Thesis, Massachusetts State College, 1935.

7. Jesperson, O.: Language: Its Nature, Development and Origin. London, Allen & Unwin, 1922.
8. McCarthy, Dorothea: Child Development—Language. *In* Encyclopedia of Educational Research, Revised Ed., Walter S. Monroe (ed). New York, Macmillan, 1950.
9. Miller, G. A.: Language and Communication. New York, McGraw-Hill, 1951.
10. Myklebust, H. R.: The Psychology of Deafness, 2nd Ed. New York and London, Grune & Stratton, 1964.
11. Nielsen, J. M.: Agnosia, Apraxia, Aphasia. New York, Paul B. Hoeber, 1946.
12. Pei, M. and Gaynor, F.: Dictionary of Linguistics. New York, Philosophical Library, 1954.
13. Perrin, Porter G.: Writer's Guide and Index to English. Chicago, Scott, Foresman Co., 1942.
14. Stormzand, M. and O'Shea, M.: How Much English Grammar? Baltimore, Warwick & York, 1924.
15. Thompson, W.: An analysis of errors in written composition by deaf children. Amer. Ann. Deaf 81: 95, 1936.
16. Webster's Third New International Dictionary. Springfield, G & C Merriam Company, 1963.

Chapter VI

Abstract-Concrete Scale

As INDICATED PREVIOUSLY, the purpose of the Picture Story Language Test was to measure three aspects of language, all of which seem equally essential for effective communication. Two of these, Productivity, the length of the expression, and Syntax, the correctness of the production have been discussed. We come now to the third, the Abstract-Concrete Scale, designed for evaluating the quality of the ideas being expressed. To some extent this Scale parallels the attempts of others to measure meaning or content.[9,10]

The measurement of meaning, however, presented a number of obstacles, especially as we conceived of it. Our principal interest was the relationship between written verbal facility and the quality of the ideation being conveyed. We assumed that the unit of expression could be of adequate length and be appropriate syntactically but not necessarily effective in transmitting the fundamental ideas the writer was attempting to communicate.

Workers in the fields of Language Pathology and Learning Disabilities are familiar with the circumstance of a child or an adult who can utter or write words and sentences but who cannot convey what he has in mind. (See examples of Meaningless Language under Total Words.) When an individual speaks words or sentences *without* awareness of meaning, that is, meaninglessly, it is designated as echolalia. There is no equivalent term for this type of behavior when it appears in the written form. Therefore, we have categorized it as *Meaningless Language.*

Even though the individual who writes words and sentences without awareness of their meaning illustrates the need for a measure of *content,* this is an extreme circumstance and occurs infrequently. More common is the child or adult who has poor facility in the choice of words for expressing his ideas. If formulation aphasia, or "word-finding" aphasia is present he may even choose the word that is opposite from that intended. Again, we note the need for appraising meaning and content, especially as it relates to language disorders.

More generally, our purpose was to study the associations between written language and thought processes. Though scholars have been concerned with these associations for more than a century, scales for measuring such interrelationships have been slow in evolving. Our approach was to design a scale for evaluating the ideation being conveyed on a continuum from abstractness to concreteness. This dimension has a long history in psychology and education and seemed suitable as a criterion for manifesting the quality of the ideation being expressed.[2,3,5] The results as shown by the normative studies (Tables 2, 3, and 4) and the findings for various handicapped groups supported this presumption.[6]

The Abstract-Concrete Scale consists of a series of definitions, constituting criteria to be used in rating the level of abstract thought or the ideation being conveyed. Factors of language proficiency are ignored; only the content or quality of the ideation is evaluated. The story may be short and the syntax deficient but the content imaginative and abstract. The opposite also may occur. It must be noted, however, that a high correlation exists between Total Words and the use of abstraction as measured by the Picture Story Language Test.[6]

Abstract-Concrete behavior was viewed as falling on a continuum from marked concreteness to high degrees of abstraction. The definitions of this behavior, especially as provided by Goldstein,[2] Hinsie and Campbell,[4] and Oléron[7] were used in developing the Scale. The concept referred to by the term *stimulus-bound* was particularly relevant. The more the ideation was bound to the observable, the more it was considered as being concrete; the more it was detached from the stimulus, the more it was viewed as being abstract. Criteria were evolved accordingly with the most concrete level being defined as a list of the objects appearing in the picture, with the highest, most abstract level being represented by metaphor, allegory, and the use of concepts portraying a moral. It should be stressed that psychodynamically the process of abstraction involves both the *exclusion* of certain aspects of a situation or circumstance and the *inclusion* of others. In other words, the process of abstraction assumes that the more general aspects are distinguished in order that they can be associated with the broad commonalities of experience, so that which is different in detail can be related logically and categorized into patterns of similarity.

When we measure ability to abstract, therefore, we are appraising the capacity to inhibit some responses and to facilitate others; the more specific or concrete must be submerged into the background so that the more generalized can become foreground and be constituted as an abstraction. This frame of reference was used in the development of the five levels of abstraction comprising the Abstract-Concrete Scale. Because the criteria consist of a series of definitions to be applied to a given expression or type of behavior, it can be compared with the Vineland Social Maturity Scale[1] and the Oseretsky Motor Test.[8]

The Abstract-Concrete Scale was used in the standardization of the Picture Story Language Test; results for both normal and handicapped children have been obtained.[6] Even though the question of validity has not yet been studied extensively, reliability has been shown to be satisfactory. Abstraction as defined and measured shows a relationship to developmental age from seven through 17 years. At seven years the mean falls at the beginning of Level III, at nine years it is at the beginning of Level IV, at 11 years it is approximately in the middle of Level IV, at 13 years it is about two-thirds through this level, whereas at 15 years it falls at the top of this level. The mean for the 17-year-olds is in the second category of Level V. All of the handicapped groups, the deaf, mentally retarded, socially-emotionally disturbed, speech defective and those with reading disabilities and other types of learning disorders, were deficient in abstraction as compared with the normal, indicating that the Scale has usefulness as a diagnostic instrument.

DIRECTIONS FOR SCORING

The Abstract-Concrete Scale is divided into five levels, each representing an increment in the extent to which the content of the story manifests use of abstract ideas. With the exception of Level I, Meaningless Language, the levels are made up of several ranks or subcategories. The criteria for each of the levels with their subcategories and with illustrations are presented below; see also Illustrated Stories in the Scoring Guide. The score range is from 0 to 25, the higher scores designating greater use of abstraction.

The first step in scoring is to become thoroughly familiar with the scores and the levels they represent. It is necessary to study each criterion and the illustrative example, noting the succession and progression from one level to the next. Only after the examiner is apprised of both the categories and the subcategories is he ready to begin scoring.

LEVEL I: MEANINGLESS LANGUAGE

Score 0. The story shows a total lack of abstraction as here defined. The individual has attempted to write words but they consist only of unrelated letters, or he has written words which he can spell though they have no relevance to the Picture. This level also includes whole stories that are unrelated to the stimulus, however well written; such stories often have diagnostic value. Meaningless Language must be distinguished from that which is highly imaginative. (Note also the examples under Productivity.)

■ **EXAMPLE**

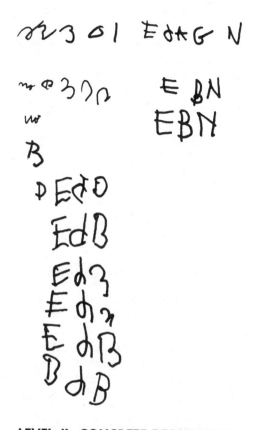

LEVEL II: CONCRETE-DESCRIPTIVE

There is abstraction even though purely descriptive, at least to the extent that names of the objects are given. The subject is not so bound to the stimulus that he is unable to relate it with his past experience. He recognizes that he has encountered similar situations and he has some appreciation for the generalities expressed by the concrete situation.

There are six subcategories, ranging from a list of the objects observed to ideas involving movement and quality, expressed through verbs and one or more adjectives. In other words, the range is from simple identification to the use and quality of the objects mentioned. Except for indicating color, size, or number the ideation is limited to the observable. Intransitive verbs do not raise the level of the story inasmuch as they are not considered to be action verbs.

Score 1. The lowest or most concrete level of ideation, represented by a score of *one*, is that in which there is only a list of objects seen in the

Picture, with no attempt at organization, or in which short, stereotyped sentences are used. The only difference in these expressions, as shown by the examples below, is that in one there is a carrier phrase followed by a noun, whereas in the other only the nouns are given (Naming Level).

■ **EXAMPLES**

boy, car, book, dog, mother

There is a boy.
There is a book
There is a baby and boy.

Score 2. The production consists of a List but words designating categories must be included. Inclusion of articles, *a, an, the,* or the use of *to be* or the word *some,* does not alter the scoring.

■ **EXAMPLES**

furniture, toys, people, animals.

Trist there are some Books.
There is a car.
There is a wooded sho
a ball.
and some more of toys.

Score 3. Action is indicated through verb-noun combinations; *to be* is not considered an action verb. Also, use of the personal pronoun *I* does not alter the scoring. Designation of category is not required.

■ **EXAMPLE**

I see a dog, a man, a car, some books and a baby.

Score 4. A single action and category are required although the form may be a List; more than one action with category receives a score of 5. The personal pronoun *I* does not alter the scoring.

■ **EXAMPLE**

I see toys.
I see a book.
I see a boy.
There is a toy.

Score 5.   Two or more actions are used in the story but only at the level of description. Category must be included.

■ **EXAMPLE**

I see a boy. He has toys. The ball is on the shelf.

Score 6.   In addition to the names of objects, actions, and category, a quality must be given. Descriptive words such as size, color or appearance are included.

■ **EXAMPLE**

There is a boy. He has some toys. There is a yellow ball on the table.

LEVEL III: CONCRETE-IMAGINATIVE

At this Level more of the concrete aspects of the stimulus are inhibited, whereas more of the refined aspects are discerned. Imaginary objects emerge in the sense that they are not portrayed in the Picture. The subject does not write, "He has some toys," which falls at Level II, but rather, "He is making a house with the toys." The later statement clearly specifies that the boy not only has the toys but that he has arranged them in some meaningful relationship in terms of past experience.

Level III encompasses six subcategories ranging from assigning a *role* to the boy in the Picture to expressing ideas which entail an *interaction* between the boy and the doll figures. Imaginative ideation must be manifested; the ideas are not only descriptive but are in terms of the observable. The situation portrayed has taken on meaning and the ideation reveals significance, relevance, and integration. To fall within the upper categories the ideation must be organized as shown by a story theme, with roles assigned to the participants. Interaction must be included but time and sequence are not.

Score 7.   The central figure in the Picture, the boy, is assigned a role; the elements of theme and organization are present. Mention is made of what the boy is doing and he is recognized as the focus of the activity which is portrayed. Some integration of the total situation must be manifested.

■ **EXAMPLE**

The boy is playing with his toys. He has some toy boys and girls and some fernicher. He is playing on the table.

Score 8. Not only what the boy is doing is included but mention is made of his feelings. In addition to a role with meaning, he is ascribed feelings that incorporate the setting.

■ **EXAMPLE**

The boy liked to play. I know a boy who liked to play with his toys. He had story books to read and cars to play with, but most of all he liked to play with toy furniture. He had a table, chairs, little dishes, cups and forks. He had a dresser, a cabinet and a few toy people. He had a very good time playing with his toys.

Score 9. The doll figures are assigned anthropomorphic characteristics and are referred to as mother, father, sister, brother, or other personages. Terms such as mother-doll and father-doll are not credited as these are not true characterizations. Likewise simple identifications, such as man, dog and baby, do not sufficiently indicate roles or characters, hence, do not score at this Level. A theme, a plan of relationships, also must be indicated.

■ **EXAMPLE**

In the picture I saw a boy playing with some dolls and some furniture from a doll house. He was playing on a table. He had five dolls and a dog. There was a father, a sister, a baby and two brothers. He had furniture from a living room. The boy looked like he would be about six or seven years old. In the background on a shelf there were some books, a car and some other things.

Score 10. The total scene takes on added significance and more complete organization with action assigned to the doll figures; activity may be ascribed to individual figures or to all of them as a group. Several independent actions or an action attributed to even one figure is credited. Stating that all of the figures are engaged in one activity, such as eating, also scores at this Level.

■ **EXAMPLE**

There was once a little boy playing in the korner. He was playing with some toys and some doll furnchair. He was playing house. He was brdinding the toys were real. He was playing with a baby and a lamp. And a sofue and a chair and a dog and a table and a dresser and a place where you keep dishes. And in the family there was a siter and a father and a mother and a brother and a strollr for the baby. They were eating brack fast.

Score 11. Action is projected to the figures and, in addition, interaction between them is expressed. This is the beginning of noting and stressing inter-relationships among the figures. Only one such interaction is necessary to receive credit.

■ **EXAMPLE**

> There is a boy playing with a doll house. There is a table, chairs, children and a dog too. There is a mother pushing a baby. There are two boys and one girl.

Score 12. Two or more interactions among the doll figures are required, representing the beginning of narrative form. There is a more consistent theme and more organization, with the story assuming roles on the part of the participants.

■ **EXAMPLE**

> This boy is depicting what his family life is like through dolls. He is pretending that they are actually living things and he is just watching them live their lives. One member of the family is playing with the dog, another taking care of the baby, and another getting up from the table after eating dinner. The man seems to be calling all of them to dinner as he stands by his chair.

LEVEL IV: ABSTRACTIVE-DESCRIPTIVE

Abstract-Descriptive, Level IV, assumes that the concepts of *time* and *sequence* have been introduced. The temporal relationships need not be consistent throughout the story. The Picture remains the focus of the ideation expressed but the story has greater continuity as manifested by true narrative form; there is portrayal of characters not appearing in the Picture. This Level consists of five steps or categories, ranging from narration relating to the central figure, the boy, including expression of sequence and time (such as reference to the future) to stories in which imaginative characters appear, but with the setting as portrayed being retained.

Score 13. There is a sequence of two or more consecutive events involving the central figure, the boy. There should not be reference to why he is there, how he came to be there, or what he will do in the future (see 18 and 19, below). The narration is in relation to what is indicated by the Picture, by the setting as portrayed. Reference to time as part of the setting is common but not required.

■ **EXAMPLE**

> Peter was puting up a seen on the table. He took out a chair a table and chairs for the table. He took out a boy and girl and a shelf. Then he took a father out and a chair and a dog and a baby and her mother and took a lamp. Here is the name of the family the boy Jack the girl cherry the mother Lorrine the father Earl the baby Vicky. The he put them in a group.

Score 14. A sequence of events involving the doll figures is clearly indicated. All participants are treated as a unit, necessitating the concept of a family, though not specifically stated.

■ **EXAMPLE**

One day Don was playing with some plastic furniture and people. The people were seated at the table. After they finished eating they began to read. It started to get dark so they turned on the light. After they finished reading they went to bed.

Score 15. The imaginary episode being constructed by the boy portrayed in the Picture is given a specific setting; the total scene need not be included to be credited.

■ **EXAMPLE**

The little boy is playing with some things. They are dollhouse characters. There are people, furniture and animals. He is playing with the objects on a table and they aren't in a doll house.

He looks very interested in what he is doing and it seems he's having a fine time arranging all the plastic people, furniture and animals.

The setting for his objects is in a dining room and the dollhouse characters are sitting down to eat a meal.

Score 16. The total scene portrayed in the Picture, including the boy and what he is doing, is given a specific and appropriate setting. In the narrative the entire situation is conceptualized into a given unit. Commonly ascribed settings are home, school, playroom, and dining room. Mere reference to objects indicative of a setting, such as dining room table or kitchen utensils, is not credited. The total situation must be mentally organized, structured as a whole and placed in perspective with the setting clearly indicated.

■ **EXAMPLE**

As I walked into the kindergarten classroom, I saw what you might expect to see in any average school. In the far corner of the room a boy was entertaining himself with doll house toys, which struck me odd, seeing how there were trucks and cars in the background on the shelf.

Score 17. Characters other than those depicted in the Picture, whether as doll figures or as human beings, are used in the story. A single descriptive reference to an imaginary character, however, does not qualify at this Level. Incorporation of the "outsider" is more than simple naming or description, such as *my sister's toys* or *his friend's dog*. He must be involved in the action, in the theme of the narration. The general setting which is portrayed can be retained. Imagining a different setting scores at a higher level (see 20 below).

■ **EXAMPLE**

Little Tommy has an interest in dolls, especially movable dolls. He likes to pretend that it is his family. Naturally he's the father. He started this when he was two years old. My aunt gave him one doll whose arms and legs could move. Tommy never left it out of his sight. Then my mother gave him a few more along with some furniture. When he was four he got a little statue of a white Cocker Spaniel. That's the dog of the family. He plays with it all the time.

LEVEL V: ABSTRACT-IMAGINATIVE

The Abstract-Imaginative represents the highest level of abstract thought measured on this Scale. The separate items pictured are unified meaningfully and significantly by expression of a relationship not given by the stimulus per se. At this Level the unifying relationship, or the plot, is imaginary. The story is characterized by ideation which is not bound to the observable. It encompasses plot, imaginative settings, metaphorical and allegorical reference, and connotation of moral values. Moreover, there is continuity from beginning to end. Level V consists of eight gradations, from the use of a plot with the setting taken at face value to an imaginary setting with use of allegory and moral connotation.

Score 18. A plot centering around either the boy or the toy figures is required. Plot, as interpreted here, means that the characters involved show foresight in planning and continuity of action; simple narration is not credited. The setting may be taken at face value. Reference to events which are imagined to have occurred prior to what is portrayed or the description of events leading up to the boy's presence in the picture is required, whereas reference to the future is not.

■ **EXAMPLE**

Today was the day I would spend my first day in kindergarten. I was happy when my mother left me alone in the room. I learned to say my teacher's name very fast. Our teacher told us where to sit. She then gave us a toy box with a lot of plastic figures and furniture to play with. I tried to act out a scene with the plastic figures, such as usually happens in a house. My first day in kindergarten was very enjoyable.

Score 19. The Picture serves as the point of reference, and some of what is portrayed is included in the story, but imaginary incidents occurring in the *future* are required; reference need not be made to events occurring in the past. In other words, the scene remains an integral part of the sequence which is imagined to have taken place but the writer goes beyond this by incorporating future events.

■ EXAMPLE

Once not very long ago there was a little boy who always used his imagination. One day he imagined that he had a dollhouse and that the people were real. They could walk, talk and eat so they should also be able to move, but they couldn't. That was the only trouble. One night they saw a fairy and she made it so they could move. When he woke up he heard his mother calling him. They were going to the land of the fairies. When they got there he saw the same fairy that he saw in his imagination. He was so surprised that he couldn't believe what he saw. They became very good friends and somehow got married and lived happily ever after.

Score 20. The setting portrayed in the Picture is incidental to the story and to the ideas expressed; in 19 it is an integral part of the imagined sequence. The emphasis of the story is removed from the stimulus itself. Although there may be mention of what the boy is doing, this is only incidental to the main theme which is beyond what is actually portrayed. The plot must have continuity.

■ EXAMPLE

A little boy who is sitting on the floor has his very good clothes on. The mother walks in and tells him, "You cannot play with toy cowboys with your good suit on." So the boy goes to his bedroom and changes his clothes. The mother is so glad to see that he is growing up.

Score 21. As in 20, the Picture serves only as a point of reference; it is incidental to the story itself. Unlike Category 20, the factor of *motivation* must be included. At this Level, therefore, it is required that the writer ascribe motives to the main character or characters consistent with the main theme of the narration. A complex plot is required but it need not be totally free of inconsistency.

■ EXAMPLE

There was a boy and his name was Tom. He liked to play with miniature dolls. He never went out during the day. He didn't know that there was any fun in playing with friends. He had all the toys he wanted and he never thought he could have anything else. He didn't know about having friends until one day he met a boy in his yard. The boy asked him if he wanted to play catch. He thought it was strange to play with someone else but he tried and much to his surprise, he liked it. For the first time he knew what friendship was.

Score 22.   The plot must be highly complex and inconsistencies are not permitted. The stimulus scene, although incidental to the story, usually is included in the plot in some way. Subplot(s) also are employed. Because of the complexity of the plot and the number of characters involved, the stories at this Level usually are greater in length and include many details, as well as descriptions of the characters and their feelings.

■ **EXAMPLE**

Ed was seven years old. This was his first day in school, in kindergarten that is. He was a couple of years older than the rest of the kids because he had a problem. His problem concerned his speech. Ed never said a word until he was five years old and then it was only yes and no. His problem affected his home life and his ability to get along with other people.

Ed had two brothers and a sister at home. His brothers looked upon him as a mistake made by their parents. However, Jane, his sister, was very kind to him. She spent many long hours trying to teach him to speak and to prepare him for this first day at school.

A big problem with Ed was friends. Most children at this age can be very cruel and they were. They constantly teased him about not being able to talk. From the first day at school he spent all his time in the doll corner. However, there were teachers who understood his problem and by their patient efforts, they were able to help Ed learn to talk. Although his speech is not perfect, Ed is now able to converse with his classmates, and he even gets along better at home.

Score 23.   To be credited as falling into this category the ideation must be highly abstract, widely removed from the Picture itself. In addition, the story must include a concern for the well-being of people through expressions which are philosophical in nature. For example, reference may be made to the boy's cleanliness, with a subtle inference that cleanliness "is next to Godliness," or the writer may state that the boy is mentally retarded and that it is incumbent upon us to be kind to such a child. Sometimes instead of a story an expository theme or an essay is written.

■ **EXAMPLE**

As I gaze upon said picture, I see a little boy with lots of toys. You say, "Oh, that's natural." But I want you to stop and think. Is it really so natural? See if you can visualize that little boy, say twenty-five years from now. What will he be doing then? Perhaps he will be an executive, or a steelworker, or even a space man! Think what that means! Today he is a little boy of about six or seven, playing with toys, but in the years to come he will be a grown man, and in those hands will be the future of our world. That is what I see in that picture—the future of the world—yours and mine!

Score 24. This category requires that the story be written allegorically. The plot, characters, and actions have significance beyond that conveyed by the usual meaning of the words as used in everyday life. This Level can be readily distinguished and recognized because it treats happenings figuratively, uses narration symbolically, and assumes metaphorical reasoning.

■ **EXAMPLE**

Billy Snear, the young son of Will Snear, prominent music and drama critic, had just started to school. He was playing one day with his new friend, Ready-for-Anything, when they noticed a big box in the corner cupboard. Their teacher, Miss Goahead, saw them looking at it and went over and told them they could look in if they liked. So they got it out and took it over to the table and opened it up. "Ha," said Billy Snear, "those are nothing but girls' toys. I don't want to play with girls' toys. Come on, Ready, let's go find something else." But Ready had spotted a toy dog in the box that looked just like his own dog, Nuisance, and he was already taking out the dog and the boy's family and beginning to set them up, paying no attention to Billy's disdainful remarks.

Twenty years later Billy and Ready, still friends even though much had happened to them, happened to meet Miss Goahead. Like all teachers Miss Goahead was interested in what had become of them. "I've been working for a company that manufactures children's toys," said Ready. "I'm just getting started as a sales representative. My job is to convince the stores that these are toys that children will want. I like my job." "And he's doing well too," said Bill. "I'm writing newspaper columns about crazy fads and games and recreation, but I can't find a thing to say about Ready's company."

Score 25. This category represents maximum use of abstract ideas as measured by this Scale and requires that both allegory and moral values be clearly manifested in the story.

■ **EXAMPLE**

Once upon a time there was a boy named Will B. Rough, whose mother and father gave him all the things he wanted. He was playing in the playroom one day with some new toys, when all of a sudden he thought he heard them talking to each other. "Oh Dear," said Mother Doll, "where did the baby go? I thought she was in the box with the rest of us, but I don't see her anywhere. You don't suppose that careless boy lost her somewhere?" "Now, now," said Father Doll, "I'm sure she'll turn up pretty soon." "But, Father, don't you remember hearing those things breaking yesterday when we were sitting over in the corner? Maybe the baby got in with those nice toys, and got broken." "No, dear, I looked later; she wasn't with them."

"I'll never forget the time our nice new red car was left out in the middle of the room and Mother Rough stumbled over it." said Mother Doll. "She fell down and broke the car and three nice new horses, not to speak of her own glasses. I do hope the baby hasn't been left right in the middle of the room."

Just then Will opened his eyes to find his sister, Bee, (her middle name was Knott) looking down at him. "You've been asleep," she said to him. "I was looking all over for you." "Come on, Bee, help me find the baby doll," said Will. Together they began to look around. Bee found the walker under Will's bed, and a little later Will found the baby, safe and sound, lying between the rollers of his roller skates. Will quickly put the baby in the walker and set her down near Mother Doll. He could almost imagine her saying how glad she was that he had learned something about being careful as well as about being thoughtful and kind to others.

REFERENCES

1. Doll, E. A.: The Measurement of Social Competence. Minneapolis, Educational Test Bureau, 1953.
2. Goldstein, K.: Language and Language Disturbances. New York and London, Grune & Stratton, 1948.
3. Flesch, Rudolf: Measuring the level of abstraction. J. Applied Psychol. 34: 384, 1950.
4. Hinsie, L. and Campbell, R.: Psychiatric Dictionary, 3rd Ed. New York, Oxford University Press, 1960.
5. Mowrer, O. H.: Learning Theory and the Symbolic Processes. New York, John Wiley & Sons, 1960.
6. Myklebust, H. R.: Development and Disorders of Written Language, Vol. II. New York and London, Grune & Stratton. In press.
7. Oléron, P.: Conceptual thinking of the deaf. Amer. Ann. Deaf 98: 304, 1953.
8. Oseretsky, N. I.: Psychomotorik: Methoden zur untersuchung der motoric. Beih. Zeitschrift Angewandte Psychol. 17: 162, 1931.
9. Osgood, C. E., Suci, G. J. and Tannebaum, P. H.: The Measurement of Meaning. Urbana, University of Illinois Press, 1957.
10. Pool, I. DeS.: Trends in Content Analysis. Urbana, University of Illinois Press, 1959.

PART THREE
NORMS FOR WRITTEN LANGUAGE

Chapter VII

Validity and Reliability

VALIDITY

IN APPRAISING VALIDITY the primary consideration is whether the test adequately serves the purpose for which it has been developed and for which it is intended. When defined in this manner, "validity has different connotations for various kinds of tests and, accordingly, different kinds of validity evidence are appropriate for them."[5] Actually, all tests of ability encompass aspects of behavior other than the one for which they were designed. Therefore, the basic question is, can it be demonstrated, under certain well-defined circumstances, that the test measures *principally* the characteristic for which it is intended? With the Picture Story Language Test this means, does it in fact measure written language or mainly some other behavioral characteristic, such as intelligence or motor ability? Though this question must be explored more fully, using given indicators and viewing validity broadly, it appears to be a valid test of facility with the written word.

Studies of predictive validity usually compare a given test with the results of other tests purportedly measuring the same function. Because comparable results were unavailable, this method could not be applied to Total Words, Total Sentences, Syntax or Abstract-Concrete scores but other findings could be compared with the Words per Sentence scores. Stormzand and O'Shea,[8] Heider and Heider,[3] and Hillocks[4] studied the sentence length of certain age groups. Although the "pool" of material from which they derived their scores was widely different from that utilized in the Picture Story Language Test, the agreement among the results is exceptional, as shown in Table 5.

Stormzand and O'Shea determined the average sentence length in compositions, Heider and Heider employed stories written about a short film, whereas Hillock used themes written by ninth graders. In comparison, the Words per Sentence score on the Picture Story Language Test seems to be remarkably valid.

The Test can be appraised further by considering its *face* validity.[5]

TABLE 5. Comparison of Picture Story Test results for Words per Sentence
with the findings of others.

Age	Stormzand-O'Shea	Heider-Heider	Hillock	Picture Story
9	11.1	10.9	—	9.7
11	12.0	11.1	—	11.5
13	15.2	13.7	—	14.0
15	17.8	—	15.0	15.1
17	19.8	—	—	16.1
Adult	20.9	—	—	—

Pertinent information accordingly can be gained from the results secured through its use with both normal and handicapped children. In regard to normal children, it is apparent from observation that their proficiency with written language gradually increases. The data presented in Chapter III disclose that the Picture Story Language Test reflects this maturational pattern for both Productivity and Syntax. Likewise, the results for the Abstract-Concrete Scale reveal that as age increases, the normal child is more capable of expressing abstract ideas by means of the written word. The results for normal children, therefore, indicate that the Test has validity.

Other evidence relevant to the assumption of validity is obtained from studies of handicapped children and from those who have language disorders. There is far-reaching documentation of the severe imposition of early life deafness on language acquisition.[7] Moreover, this handicapped group has been studied extensively, using the Picture Story Language Test, and it has clearly demonstrated their limited language ability. In addition, it has reflected differences in written verbal facility on the basis of the commonly accepted basic variables, such as degree of deafness, age of onset, intelligence and number of years of schooling.

Because an inability to acquire normal proficiency in written language has not been recognized as a type of learning disability requiring special education, groups of children having this specific type of disorder could not be studied. Nevertheless, for more than a decade we have employed the Picture Story Language Test in making diagnostic studies of both children and adults who have language disorders; comparative data on such populations is presented elsewhere.[6] These studies, covering large numbers of dyslexics, aphasics, and dysgraphics, signify that when the disorder either directly or indirectly influences written language proficiency, the Test denotes this limitation. A variety of illustrations have been provided in the Scoring Guide and in Chapter II.

In summary, though the data on validity are inadequate and further study of this important feature must be made, present results suggest that the Picture Story Language Test validly reflects facility with the written word in terms of maturational patterns, as well as in terms of the limitations commonly associated· with the diagnostic classifications used in special education.

RELIABILITY

The reliability of the Picture Story Language Test has been assessed in certain respects and these estimates have been highly positive, but because some of the traditional methods could not be applied, other appraisals had to be made. A complicating factor was the impracticability of developing a duplicate form to which the present test could be compared. The alternatives were to employ test-retest and/or the method of split-half.

The test-retest approach presented unusual difficulties when applied to a test that measures developmental aspects of behavior in children. For the data from the second administration to be comparable to the results from the original testing, the interim between the test and the retest should be only a few days. We followed this procedure in one of our evaluations, knowing that motivation for writing the second story would be more difficult to attain. Despite these limitations, the reliability coefficients for the total Sample included in this study were significant at the 1 per cent level of confidence. (N = 60, 10 at each age level.)

It is apparent, nevertheless, that readministration of the same standardized test, especially for purposes of appraising reliability, can be accomplished satisfactorily only after an interim of from six months to one year. Such delay introduces the problem of developmental change through maturation, so the scores obtained from the second administration are not directly comparable with those from the first, except perhaps in the case of quotients.

Our decision was to inaugurate a longitudinal study in which the Test is to be given to a large sample of school children once a year for three years. It is assumed that by comparing the results with the original norms, and through the use of various other types of statistical analyses, the data gained from this investigation will disclose the extent to which the Picture Story Language Test reliably measures growth of facility in use of the written word.

In addition to test-retest, the method of odd-even was employed to study the reliability of the Syntax and Words per Sentence scores. Because of their nature this procedure was not applicable to Total Word, Total Sentence and Abstract-Concrete scores. The odd-even correlation coefficients for Words per Sentence are given in Table 6 and for Syntax in Table 7.

TABLE 6. Odd-even reliability coefficients for Words per Sentence.

Age	N	Reliability Coefficient
7	33	.84*
9	37	.74*
11	47	.38*
13	47	.54*
15	44	.64*
Total	208	.82*

* Sig. at .01 level

TABLE 7. Odd-even reliability coefficients for Syntax.

Age	N	Reliability Coefficient
7	33	.90*
9	37	.92*
11	47	.56*
13	47	.52*
15	44	.74*
Total	208	.88*

* Sig. at .01 level

The Sample consisted of 208 stories selected randomly for the age range of seven through 15 years. The scores for Words per Sentence and Syntax for the odd numbered sentences were compared with the even numbered, using the Guttman Formula.[2] The reliability coefficients for all age levels and for the total group were significant at the 1 per cent level. The lowest coefficients occurred at the 11- and 13-year age levels, suggesting greater variability of performance at these ages. These data indicate that the Syntax and the Words per Sentence scores meet the typical standards for reliability.

Other information comes from having repeatedly administered the Test to children with language disorders. This has been done over a period of months to determine whether progress is being made while the child is enrolled for remedial training. Six examples are shown in Table 8. The scores on the second administration ordinarily reveal an increment in the aspect being measured. However, though some of the scores are higher, the similarity in pattern implies that the Test is a reliable measure.

TABLE 8. Results from repeated administration of the Picture Story Language Test to children with language disorders.

Test	Date	CA	TW	TS	WPS	Syntax	A-C
		Case One					
First	9/30/63	16–5	57	7	8.1	82	12
Second	4/29/64	17–0	97	13	7.5	95	12
		Case Two					
First	10/4/63	9–3	44	3	14.3	91	16
Second	9/21/64	10–3	86	7	12.3	96	16
		Case Three					
First	10/4/63	14–8	59	4	14.5	88	16
Second	4/2/64	15–2	74	5	14.8	97	19
		Case Four					
First	10/22/64	13–9	51	8	6.4	95	19
Second	2/13/65	14–1	97	11	8.8	93	18
		Case Five					
First	10/3/63	12–6	80	6	13.3	89	18
Second	4/25/64	13–1	119	11	10.8	87	19
		Case Six					
First	6/10/63	10–3	65	4	16.2	98	18
Second	10/1/63	10–7	89	5	17.8	90	21

INTERSCORER RELIABILITY

It has long been known that the objectivity with which a test can be scored is related to its reliability. For this reason in particular, but also because criteria for scoring written language had not been well established, the interscorer reliability of each of the five scores was investigated in detail.

In an attempt to make the Picture Story Language Test as widely applicable as possible, this type of reliability was analyzed both for trained and untrained scorers. There were three scorers in the trained group and seven in the untrained. Those who were trained and experienced in the administration and scoring of the Test also were highly skilled with other objective tests, theoretically and clinically; in background, they represented the Ph.D. level. The untrained consisted of students working toward the M.A. degree in Language Pathology, not sophisticated in the use of educational and psychological tests and not having had previous contact with the Picture Story Language Test.

Productivity Scale

Interscorer agreement was ascertained for the Productivity scores. Each worker scored 60 stories and the results were analyzed statistically using Ebel's Formula;[1] the distribution of the sample is given in Table 9. Two reliability coefficients were obtained, one showing the agreement between individual ratings and the other the average agreement among the ratings within each group of examiners. The results for the trained scorers are found in Table 10 and for the untrained in Table 11.

TABLE 9. Distribution of Stories used in determining interscorer reliability.

Age Group	7	9	11	13	15	17	Total
Number	10	10	10	10	10	10	60

TABLE 10. Interscorer reliability for Productivity scores as determined for three trained examiners.

Age	TOTAL WORDS		TOTAL SENTENCES		WORDS PER SENTENCE	
	Individual Ratings	Average Ratings	Individual Ratings	Average Ratings	Individual Ratings	Average Ratings
7	.99	.99	.98	.99	.93	.98
9	.99	.99	.99	.99	.88	.96
11	.99	.99	.99	.99	.92	.97
13	.99	.99	.91	.97	.95	.98
15	.99	.99	.97	.99	.94	.98
17	.99	.99	.98	.99	.98	.99
Total	.99	.99	.98	.99	.97	.99

TABLE 11. Interscorer reliability for Productivity scores as determined for seven untrained examiners.

Age	TOTAL WORDS		TOTAL SENTENCES		WORDS PER SENTENCE	
	Individual Ratings	Average Ratings	Individual Ratings	Average Ratings	Individual Ratings	Average Ratings
7	.99	.99	.97	.99	.78	.96
9	.99	.99	.73	.95	.52	.88
11	.99	.99	.97	.99	.86	.98
13	.99	.99	.93	.99	.77	.96
15	.99	.99	.97	.99	.91	.99
17	.99	.99	.96	.99	.90	.98
Total	.99	.99	.96	.99	.91	.99

These coefficients reveal that of the measures of Productivity, Total Words is highest in reliability, whether the examiner is trained or untrained. Next in order is Total Sentences, followed by Words per Sentence.

These findings conform to the order expected from experience. Moreover, as anticipated, the reliability of the scores is increased through training of the test users. On the other hand, with few exceptions there was a high degree of agreement among the untrained scorers. Although all of the coefficients were high, an individual rating for Total Sentences and Words per Sentence might vary from another at the lower age levels. The lowest coefficients for the trained examiners also were for stories written by the younger children.

There is a high degree of agreement in the scores obtained by different workers on the Productivity Scale. Nevertheless, the coefficients were influenced both by training and by the age of the child writing the story. The stories written by young school age children were the most difficult to score. As facility with written language stabilizes, there is greater agreement among scorers as to the number of sentences and the number of words written per sentence. However, these results clearly reveal that the interscorer reliability is satisfactory. Though the Words per Sentence scores as determined by untrained scorers must be interpreted with caution, a high degree of training apparently is not required so far as the Productivity Scale is concerned.

Syntax Scale

Of the three scales comprising the Picture Story Language Test, it was the Syntax Scale that presented the most difficulty in terms of objective criteria for scoring. The interscorer reliability coefficients disclose this fact inasmuch as the only relatively low levels of agreement among scorers occurred at certain age levels on this Scale. The reliability of the Syntax scores was appraised in the manner established for Productivity. Sixty stories, ten at each age level, were scored by the seven untrained and the three trained workers. The correlation among the scores was ascertained using Ebel's Formula; the coefficients for the trained are found in Table 12, and for the untrained in Table 13.

TABLE 12. Interscorer reliability for Syntax for three trained examiners.

Age	7	9	11	13	15	17	Total
Individual Ratings	.95	.85	.78	.65	.34	.80	.85
Average Ratings	.98	.94	.91	.85	.61	.92	.95

TABLE 13. Interscorer reliability for Syntax for seven untrained examiners.

Age	7	9	11	13	15	17	Total
Individual Ratings	.88	.45	.49	.49	.21	.45	.78
Average Ratings	.98	.85	.87	.79	.65	.85	.96

The agreement among scorers is less than that found for the measures of Productivity and Abstract-Concrete. The individual reliability coefficients for those with training range from .34 to .95, and for the entire group from .61 to .98. For those without training the individual ratings show correlations ranging from .21 to .88, and for the entire group from .65 to .98.

The least agreement among the scorers, whether trained or untrained, occurred for the stories written by the adolescents who were 15 years of age. Why more disagreement appeared for this age group is not clear. Other investigators have reported similar fluctuations at this age level, indicating a complex of factors, including maturational deviations. As shown by Figures 3 and 4, slight deviations in the growth curves appeared at this age for both Total Words and Total Sentences. Whatever the explanation, workers have found that stories written by 15-year-olds are more difficult to score than those written by any other age group. Excluding the 15-year-olds, the reliability coefficients for the individual ratings in the trained group fell above .65, and for the trained group as a whole above .85. For the untrained, when the 15-year age group is excluded, the individual ratings fell above .45 and for the group, above .79.

Another observation seems pertinent. In contrast to the reliability coefficients for Productivity, the highest degree of agreement among scorers for Syntax occurred at the lower age levels, specifically for the stories written by the seven-year-olds. Interscorer reliability increases with age for Total Sentences and Words per Sentences, but for Syntax it decreases. Though the pattern is not completely consistent, as written language matures and sentences are more clearly designated, Productivity can be scored more reliably. On the other hand, as sentences become longer, more intricate and complex, the factor of correctness becomes more difficult to score.

Albeit, these data concerning interscorer reliability reveal that the Syntax Scale can be used with confidence so far as the objectivity of scoring is concerned, training emerges as a critical factor. Further study must be made of the variables operative at the different age levels, especially at 15 years. In the hands of trained personnel, satisfactory agreement among scorers is obtained.

Number of Sentences Required for Reliabilty

Because scoring of Syntax is time consuming, studies were made to ascertain the number of sentences needed to attain a satisfactory level of reliability for this score. The statistical analysis was of two types. First, a correlated *t* test was made to indicate the degree of agreement between the Syntax Quotient derived from the first three sentences and the one derived from the total story. The analysis included 20 per cent of the population, representing an equal number selected randomly at each age level. The results are presented in Table 14. The correlated *t test* was applied because it provides a more stringent evaluation of the actual relationships between these quotients. Also, the sentences in a given story were written by one and the same subject and should be treated as dependent variables.

TABLE 14. Comparison between the Syntax Quotient for the first three sentences (Quo. 3) and the quotient for the total story (Quo. k) as determined by the correlated *t test* technique.

Age		df	Mean	SD	SE	Cor. t
7	Quo. 3	23	89.86	11.99	2.45	0.99
	Quo. k	23	89.29	12.11	2.47	
9	Quo. 3	25	92.65	8.90	1.75	2.09*
	Quo. k	25	90.85	9.80	1.92	
11	Quo. 3	25	96.77	3.70	0.74	2.40*
	Quo. k	25	95.50	3.23	0.63	
13	Quo. 3	25	95.58	4.46	0.88	0.69
	Quo. k	25	95.12	4.19	0.82	
15	Quo. 3	25	97.58	2.50	0.49	2.14*
	Quo. k	25	96.73	2.11	0.41	
17	Quo. 3	23	98.38	2.00	0.41	1.43
	Quo. k	23	97.58	2.02	0.41	

* Sig. at 5 per cent level: two-tailed test

The data in Table 14 disclose that the Syntax Quotients for the first three sentences and for the entire story failed to agree at the 5 per cent level of confidence at the nine-, 11-, and 15-year age levels. These quotients were in satisfactory agreement statistically at the ages of seven, 13, and 17 years. Therefore, at the ages of nine, 11, and 15 years the quotient for the first three sentences may not be an adequate indicator of the Syntax level of a given story. It should be noted, however, that the actual means, as shown in Table 14, are highly similar. Moreover, the means for the first three sentences are slightly higher than those obtained for the whole story at all age levels.

In view of these results it was deemed necessary to further evaluate the procedure of using only the first three sentences as a basis for the Syntax score. An analysis was made to determine the number of sentences required to attain a given level of reliability. The results as found in Table 15, provide the length of the confidence interval (L) and the approximate error in the estimate as compared with the true quotient—the quotient that would be obtained if it were based on an infinite number of sentences. For example, for the seven-year-olds a quotient based on only three sentences would be in error by 20.1 per cent. In other words, if a seven-year-old writes a great many stories and for each story the quotient is computed on the basis of the first three sentences, 95 per cent of the time the quotient will fall within the range of 20 per cent on either side of the true value.

Table 15 is useful in that it furnishes a means whereby one can ascertain, with a specified degree of accuracy, the number of sentences required to estimate the true Syntax Quotient. This can be done in two ways: by selecting the length of the confidence interval that one wishes to apply or by the acceptable per cent of error above or below the true quotient. By referring to the table, the required number of sentences (K) can be found that must be scored to obtain this specified degree of accuracy for the 95 per cent confidence level.

TABLE 15.   The approximate error in the Syntax Quotient when one up to 20 sentences are scored.

K	7 years		9 years		11 years		13 years		15 years		17 years	
	L	% Error	L	% Error	L	% Error	L	% Error	L	% Error	L	% Error
1	.58	32.7	.49	26.7	.26	13.7	.23	12.3	.20	10.5	.18	9.4
2	.43	24.2	.36	19.8	.19	10.2	.17	9.3	.15	7.8	.13	7.0
3	.35	20.1	.30	16.4	.13	8.4	.14	7.7	.12	6.5	.11	5.8
4	.31	17.5	.26	14.3	.14	7.3	.13	6.8	.11	5.6	.09	5.0
5	.27	15.7	.26	12.8	.12	6.6	.11	6.1	.09	5.1	.08	4.5
6	.25	14.4	.21	11.8	.11	6.0	.10	5.6	.09	4.6	.08	4.1
7	.23	13.3	.20	10.9	.10	5.6	.09	5.2	.08	4.3	.07	3.8
8	.22	12.5	.18	10.2	.10	5.2	.09	4.8	.07	4.0	.07	3.6
9	.21	11.8	.17	9.6	.09	4.9	.08	4.6	.07	3.8	.06	3.4
10	.19	11.2	.16	9.1	.09	4.7	.08	4.3	.07	3.6	.06	3.2
11	.19	10.7	.16	8.7	.08	4.5	.08	4.1	.06	3.4	.06	3.1
12	.18	10.2	.15	8.4	.08	4.3	.07	4.0	.06	3.3	.05	2.9
13	.17	9.8	.14	8.0	.08	4.1	.07	3.8	.06	3.2	.05	2.8
14	.16	9.5	.14	7.7	.07	4.0	.07	3.7	.05	3.0	.05	2.7
15	.16	9.2	.13	7.5	.07	3.8	.06	3.5	.05	2.9	.05	2.6
16	.15	8.9	.13	7.2	.07	3.7	.06	3.4	.05	2.8	.05	2.5
17	.15	8.6	.12	7.0	.07	3.6	.06	3.3	.05	2.8	.04	2.5
18	.14	8.4	.12	6.8	.06	3.5	.06	3.2	.05	2.7	.04	2.4
19	.14	8.1	.12	6.6	.06	3.4	.06	3.1	.05	2.6	.04	2.3
20	.14	7.9	.11	6.5	.06	3.3	.05	3.1	.05	2.5	.04	2.3

L = Length of Confidence Interval
K = Number of Sentences

To illustrate, suppose one desires to have an estimate of the number of sentences that must be scored to obtain a confidence interval of not more than .11 above or below the true quotient for seven-year-olds. In consulting Table 15 he finds that for not more than .22 error (.11 above and .11 below the true value), K is eight; eight sentences would be required to attain this level of accuracy. Similarly, suppose one desires to ascertain the number of sentences necessary to obtain a quotient that would be in error by only 10 per cent or less. For seven-year-olds, K for this estimate falls between 12 and 13 sentences.

Another manner should be mentioned in which Table 15 can be applied. After determining the number of sentences in a given story, one can find the number of these sentences that must be scored to attain a specified degree of reliability for the Syntax Quotient. For example, if the story has 20 sentences but only the first three are scored, we find that 95 per cent of the time the quotient error will not exceed 20.1 per cent for the seven-year-olds, 16.4 per cent for the nine-year-olds, 8.4 per cent for the 11-year-olds, 7.7 per cent for the 13-year-olds, 6.5 per cent for the 15-year-olds, and 5.8 per cent for the 17-year-olds. Or, suppose a story written by a 15-year-old consists of 30 sentences. Because scoring the whole story is time consuming (and according to our data, unnecessary), we wish to know the approximate error in the quotient if three sentences, only one-tenth of the story, is scored versus the approximate error if six sentences, one-fifth of the story, is scored. From the table we find that 95 per cent of the time the quotient for three sentences would be in error 6.5 per cent whereas for six sentences the comparable error is 4.6 per cent.

These results are of theoretical interest because the approximate error decreases as age increases. By 17 years of age the quotient for only one sentence would be in error 95 per cent of the time by no more than 9.4 per cent; for three sentences the error would be as low as 5.8 per cent, and for 20 sentences, 2.3 per cent. The implication is that as the child becomes older and syntax becomes stabilized, his sentence structure does not vary from one sentence to another and thereby his syntax ability can be judged reliably from shorter samples of written language.

A third type of evaluation was made of the relationship between the quotient for the first three sentences and the quotient for larger segments of the story. The quotients for the first three sentences were compared with those for the entire story using the correlation technique. The results by age are shown in Table 16. All of these correlations are significant at the .01 level of confidence, but they may be spuriously high because the quotient for the entire story includes the first three sentences. Nevertheless, the relationship shown to exist for Words per Sentence, as well as for Syntax, indicates a high reliability even when the quotient is based on only three sentences.

As shown previously, the reliability of the Syntax scores was analyzed also by the Odd-Even technique, using the same 208 subjects. These data were presented in Table 6. The reliability of the odd versus the even sentences was lowest at the ages of 11 and 13 years, with the coefficients for those above 11 years of age being lower than those for the younger age groups; the same pattern was found for the Product-Moment correlations.

Concerning the decrease in the correlations by age, it must be emphasized that there was no further growth in syntax after 11 years of age; at this age full maturity had been attained. It can be assumed, therefore, that the range of the Syntax scores above 11 years was exceedingly limited, causing these correlation coefficients to be spuriously reduced. At the seven- and nine-year age levels where a normal range of scores was found, the quotient for the first three sentences and the quotient for the remainder of the story, as well as the Odd-Even reliability coefficients, are in close agreement.

As a whole, these data reveal that for many purposes the quotient for the first three sentences can be taken as a reliable estimate of syntax ability. On the other hand, from experience it is clear that the written language of handicapped children, including those with learning disorders, is more difficult to score. Therefore, for diagnostic purposes it is usually advisable to score the whole story.

TABLE 16.   The Pearson Product-Moment correlations between scores for the first three sentences and for the total story.

Age	N	WPS	SQ
7	33	.86*	.97*
9	37	.70*	.91*
11	47	.75*	.87*
13	47	.79*	.73*
15	44	.65*	.84*
Total	208	.84*	.93*

* Sig. at .01 level.

Abstract-Concrete Scale

Three studies were made of the interscorer reliability of the Abstract-Concrete Scale. First, the degree of agreement was determined among the scores for three trained workers, the same group that participated in the reliability studies for Productivity and Syntax. Each participant scored the same 60 stories, ten at each age level. The results are given in Table 17; Ebel's Formula was employed. The agreement was excellent both for the individual ratings and for the group as a whole. These data indicate that trained scorers do not find the criteria for evaluating abstractness unduly subjective. Rather, they agree on the criteria to be applied.

TABLE 17. Interscorer reliability for Abstract-Concrete for three trained examiners.

Age	7	9	11	13	15	17	Total
Individual Ratings	.90	.97	.75	.85	.97	.92	.94
Average Ratings	.96	.99	.90	.94	.99	.97	.98

TABLE 18. Interscorer reliability for Abstract-Concrete for seven untrained and nine trained examiners.

Age	7	9	11	13	15	17	Total
Trained	.96	.90	.98	.92	.86	.85	.97
Untrained	.95	.88	.85	.80	.92	.91	.97

The second study concerned the extent to which training in the use of the Picture Story Language Test influenced the reliability of the scores on the Abstract-Concrete Scale. Seven untrained and nine trained scorers participated in this evaluation. The seven untrained participants had had no previous contact with the Scale but were familiar with objective tests and diagnostic procedures, especially in the areas of speech, hearing and language. The nine trained participants were moderately experienced and had received training in use of the Scale. However, they were not highly trained in comparison with the three examiners who participated in the study of reliability discussed above. Using the Ebel Formula, the reliability coefficients by age for the two groups were determined and the findings are given in Table 18.

These results reveal excellent agreement. The untrained group achieved a high degree of uniformity; in fact, the reliability of their scores is comparable to that obtained by those who had been trained. It is apparent that this Scale can be scored reliably by educators, guidance workers, psychologists, or by others not specifically trained. Whereas the untrained scorers were naive in regard to this test, they were not naive in the use of diagnostic procedures. It is our presumption that users should be sophisticated in the administration and scoring of objective tests. Given a degree of sophistication on the part of the examiner, we can say with confidence that the interscorer reliability is within the limits common to psychological and educational measures of this type.

A further analysis of the agreement among scores for trained workers was made by comparing the mean scores as derived by individual examiners. Three scorers participated; a different group from the one for which data have been reported above. Each participant scored 100 stories, 20 at each age level from seven through 15 years. The findings are given in Table 19; F-tests disclosed no significant differences in the variability of the scores as derived by any one examiner. In addition, the t-scores of the differences among the means were nonsignificant.

From these analyses of the reliability of the Abstract-Concrete Scale we concluded that: (1) the interscorer agreement is highly satisfactory; (2) interscorer reliability is not influenced significantly by training; (3) there is no difference in the means nor in the variability of the scores as determined by trained examiners.

TABLE 19. The mean Abstract-Concrete scores as derived by trained examiners.

Age	7	9	11	13	15	Total
Examiner 1	6.95	11.95	14.20	15.30	21.20	13.92
Examiner 2	8.10	12.65	14.30	16.15	21.10	14.46
Examiner 3	6.80	10.95	13.00	14.30	20.25	13.06
Total Group	7.28	11.85	13.77	15.25	20.85	13.81

SUMMARY

Though the validity of the Picture Story Language Test must be explored more fully, present indications are that it is a valid measure of proficiency in use of the written word. Odd-Even studies for Syntax and for Words per Sentence reflect that these measures attain a satisfactory level of reliability. In addition, repeated administrations of the test to children enrolled in a remedial training program indicate that the three scales, Productivity, Syntax, and Abstract-Concrete can be used with confidence.

Interscorer reliability was studied extensively and found to be excellent. However, previous training in scoring Syntax emerged as a critical factor. Significant differences between trained and untrained scores did not occur for the Productivity and Abstract-Concrete scales.

Because the scoring of Syntax is time consuming, an analysis was made to determine the number of sentences required to estimate the Syntax Quotient within certain levels of accuracy. It was found that for many purposes only the first three sentences are necessary. In the study of handicapped children and of those with language disorders, often it is advisable to score the whole story.

Though additional evaluation of the reliability of the Picture Story Language Test is anticipated, the Odd-Even coefficients, interscorer reliability and the agreement between the Syntax Quotients for the first three sentences and the total story signify that this test can be used with confidence so far as reliability is concerned.

REFERENCES

1. Guilford, J. P.: Psychometric Methods, 2nd Ed. New York, McGraw-Hill, 1956.
2. Guttman, L.: An approach for quantifying paired comparisons and rank order. Ann. Math. Stat. 17: 144, 1946.
3. Heider, F. and Heider G.: Studies in the psychology of the deaf. Psychol. Monog. 242: 1941.
4. Hillocks, G.: An analysis of some syntactical patterns in ninth grade themes. J. Educ. Res. 57: 8, 1964.
5. Lennon, R. T.: Test Service Notebook, Number 13. New York, Harcourt, Brace & World, Inc., 1965.
6. Myklebust, H. R.: Development and Disorders of Written Language, Vol. II. New York and London, Grune & Stratton. In press.
7. ———: The Psychology of Deafness, 2nd Ed. New York and London, Grune & Stratton, 1964.
8. Stormzand, M. and O'Shea, M.: How Much English Grammar? Baltimore, Warwick & York, 1924.

Chapter VIII

Interpretation of Scores

THE DIAGNOSTIC USEFULNESS of a test score depends upon the skill and the experience of the interpreter. Deviate scores can be indicative of one of several conditions, and at times even signify multiple involvement. Illustrative Stories written by normal, mentally retarded, socially-emotionally disturbed, speech defective, deaf, reading handicapped, dysgraphic, and aphasic children are shown in Chapter II and in the Scoring Guide. When interpreting scores, it is beneficial to study these illustrations carefully, noting the characteristics of each. Although there are similarities among the stories, each group varies qualitatively, and in certain respects statistically from the other.[1]

Each of the five scores derived from the Test reveals a diagnostically different type of deficiency in written language. For normal children the highest correlation is between Total Words and Total Sentences; the more words, the more sentences written. However, this correlation diminishes with age because of a greater variation in Words per Sentence at the higher age levels and, in part, because of variance in the number of words relative to variance in the number of sentences. It is interesting that Total Sentences shows no increment after 13 years of age (Table 2), whereas the number of words written per sentence continues to mature through 17 years of age.

The relationship between Total Words and Total Sentences as it exists for the normal does not characterize the written language of certain groups of handicapped children. For example, deaf children continue to write more and more sentences even into later school age. Though they gradually write longer stories, they do not simultaneously attain the verbal facility required to write more words per sentence. As their stories increase in length, because they do not write longer sentences, they must write more of them. This altered relationship of Total Words to Total Sentences in the written language of the deaf is shown by the fact that a deaf child at 11 years of age on the average writes only 40 per cent as many words per story but 60 per cent as many sentences as the hearing.

Nevertheless, significant association between Total Words and Total Sentences has been found for the handicapped groups studied to date. All were inferior in Total Words, the order from least to most deviate being Speech Defective, Deaf, Reading Disability, Socially-Emotionally Disturbed and Mentally Retarded. The order was essentially the same for Total Sentences.

The Words per Sentence score clearly manifests the importance of obtaining all three measures of Productivity if the most complete diagnostic information is to be secured. It is highly independent of both Total Words and Total Sentences and a remarkably stable indicator of facility with the written word. An individual or a group might show proficiency as measured by Total Words or by Total Sentences, yet be deficient as measured by Words per Sentence. Again, the Deaf serve as an illustration. Whereas at 11 years, in comparison with the hearing, they were third on Total Words and second on Total Sentences, they were fifth on Words per Sentence. On the other hand, the Reading Disability and Speech Defective children were distinctly more inferior on both Total Words and Total Sentences than on Words per Sentence, a pattern of performance opposite from that found for the Deaf.[2]

Results such as these led us to conclude that Productivity should be examined in the three ways indicated by the Test. A primary deficiency in Total Words reveals a generalized limitation in output, a problem which seems to characterize all handicapped groups. Relatively less retardation in Total Sentences suggests diagnostically that the individual is capable of more normal output than manifested by Total Words but he uses unduly short, simple sentences; his written language lacks complexity, variation, and spontaneity of structure. It is in this connection that the Words per Sentence score is especially revealing. As sentences increase in length, they increase in complexity. In the diagnosis of language disorders it often is this aspect of an individual's output that is strikingly deficient. He may be competent in emitting words and short simple sentences but be limited in the use of sentences of normal length.

Though inferences must be drawn cautiously, there are many diagnostic implications. Hence, the examiner must undertake basic interpretations. He views all three of the Productivity scores and analyzes the relationships among them. To illustrate, again using the results for 11-year-olds, the Speech Defective children attained a level of only 50 per cent of normal on Total Words and Total Sentences but a level of 90 per cent on Words per Sentence. A similar pattern appeared for the Reading Disability group. From these findings we conclude that the basic problem is one of a generalized lack of verbal proficiency rather than one of an inability to use sentences of average length and structure. These problems are not identical and denote different educational needs. In contrast, the Socially-Emotionally Disturbed and the Mentally Retarded showed uniform limitation on all of the language functions measured; all types of output, Total Works, Total Sentences, and Words per Sentence were more equally depressed.[1]

More than any other aspect measured, Syntax shows early maturation in normal children. Only slight growth occurs after nine years of age (Table 3). Deviate scores are most useful diagnostically in revealing specific disorders of language rather than generalized deficiencies. All of the handicapped groups showed greater proficiency on Syntax than on the measures of Productivity. For example, at 11 years of age the Mentally Retarded wrote only one-tenth the average number of words, but they scored 40 per cent accuracy on Syntax.

From the point of view of interpretation of scores, analysis is made of the differences between Productivity and correctness of usage, between output and grammatical construction. It is of interest that so far as *groups* of handicapped children are concerned, the greater problem is output, not accuracy. On the other hand, many children and adults with language disorders manifest specific and sometimes severe disturbances of Syntax; these may occur as Addition, Omission, Substitution and/or Word Order errors. The scoring procedure for the Picture Story Language Test makes it possible to derive separate scores for each type of error so that characteristic patterns can be identified. Diagnostically and educationally this profile is beneficial and should be determined. Our results indicate that children with learning disabilities such as dyslexia, dysgraphia and aphasia often have difficulty in acquiring normal use of Syntax. To illustrate, an intellectually above average boy 12 years of age wrote, *Father give I bike*, meaning *Father gave me a bike* (See Chapter II). Such a sentence contains many errors and each should be identified. This boy's problem, which had remained undiagnosed, was a severe formulation aphasia. Other evidence was required before this diagnosis could be made but an excellent clue was provided by his deviate Syntax score. As revealed by the Syntax Scale, these deficiencies often can be taken as an indication of a language disorder. Deviate scores should be interpreted accordingly.

At this stage in the development of the Picture Story Language Test, the Abstract-Concrete scores are the most difficult to interpret. The intercorrelation analysis revealed a highly significant correlation between Total Words and use of abstract ideas. There seems to be little question but that generalized verbal proficiency in written language and imaginative ideation are related. The mean scores for the handicapped groups, however, show that Productivity and abstraction are far from equivalent functions. For example, at 11 years the Speech Defective scored at 46 per cent of average on Total Words but attained a level of 67 per cent on abstraction. Similar patterns were found for other handicapped groups.

Though the results derived from the Abstract-Concrete Scale must be interpreted with caution inasmuch as the true nature of these scores need further study, they furnish information that is diagnostically provocative.

This is shown by the relationships between the scores for mentally retarded and deaf children. The Retarded at 11 years of age scored at 10 per cent of average on Total Words, 22 per cent on Words per Sentence, 43 per cent on Syntax and 13 per cent on Abstract-Concrete. Comparatively, the Deaf scored at a level of 40 per cent of average on Total Words, 43 per cent on Words per Sentence, 70 per cent on Syntax and 50 per cent on Abstract-Concrete. These results demonstrate that handicaps may have varying effects on facility with the written word as well as on use of abstraction. The intent of the Abstract-Concrete score is to provide a comparison between written language facility and ability to express meaning as indicated by the use of abstract ideas. It is in these terms that the Abstract-Concrete scores should be interpreted.

The five scores derived from the Picture Story Language Test provide information that is most useful diagnostically when interpreted as a whole, that is, as a profile. A certain relationship among these scores prevails for normal children denoting the maturational pattern for written language. Therefore, intepretation involves not only evaluating the level of ability on each of the five functions but also the relationships among them. The ratio of number of words to number of sentences or to the words in each sentence, etc. varies according to diagnostic condition and type of handicap. Only when the scores are analyzed in these terms can they be interpreted most meaningfully.

CONVERSION OF RAW SCORES

Only normal children were included in the standardization study; the norms presented are for such a population. Norms also are available for deaf children[2] and comparative studies have been made of children who are mentally retarded, socially-emotionally disturbed, defective in speech, as well as those who have reading disabilities.[1] Professional workers, students of language and others concerned with handicapped children will wish to avail themselves of these data. The differences between normal children, those having handicaps and those having deficiencies in learning, are illuminating in regard to their adjustment and educational needs.

The scores obtained on the Picture Story Language Test are interpreted in the same manner as are results derived from other standardized tests. Provision has been made for conversion of the raw scores in three ways. First, the *mean age scores* are presented. Because only alternate-year age groups were included in the standardization, the midpoint scores were computed by interpolation. The mean represents the average score by age group and the standard deviation shows the average variation of the scores from the mean. Although other evidence must be considered, the group to be included within the range of average is interpreted to comprise those falling one standard deviation above and one below the mean. The standard deviations for the age levels included in the standardization are found in Tables 2, 3 and 4.

Raw scores can also be converted into *percentile equivalents* and tables have been furnished for this purpose. The percentile score discloses valuable insights into an individual's relative position within a group because it reveals the per cent of the group which falls above and below a given raw score. This can be illustrated by a score of 108 for Total Words (Table 21). If obtained by a nine-year-old, he would have exceeded 80 per cent of the others falling at this age level, whereas if earned by an 11-year-old, he would be average in Total Words because his raw score is equivalent to the fiftieth percentile; he obtained an average score for his age group.

A third type of interpretation can be made. Raw scores can be converted into *stanine equivalents*. The stanine tables are computed by classifying the raw scores into nine categories of equal range. A certain per cent of the total scores, from lowest to highest, are assigned to each of these categories on the assumption that the scores represent a curve of normal distribution. The fifth stanine represents average, with a standard deviation of two. The stanine score has the advantage of showing the range of scores falling within a given category.

TOTAL WORDS

Mean Age Scores

The mean and midpoint scores for Total Words are shown in Table 20. The Total Word score for a given individual is converted into an equivalent by referring to these norms. (For convenience Conversion Tables also have been included in the Scoring Guide.) The growth pattern is not identical for males and females, a fact that must be considered when converting raw scores.

There is a plateau for Total Words at 14, 15 and 16 years causing it to be difficult to convert certain raw scores into age equivalents. Though estimates are possible, actual interpretation must be made on the basis of other factors, such as chronological age. Moreover, use of the percentile and stanine tables is suggested whenever the age equivalent is in doubt. For example, a score of 124 is average for a 12-year-old male and 123 is average for a male of 15 years. By consulting Table 21, we find that 124 falls essentially at the midpoint between the fiftieth percentile for the ages of 11 and 13 years and at the fifty-fifth percentile for 15 year olds. Similarly, the stanine ranks should be used to assist in the interpretation of such scores.

TABLE 20

TOTAL WORDS

Mean and Midpoint Scores by Age and Sex

Age	7	8	9	10	11	12	13	14	15	16	17
Male	22	52	83	94	106	124	143	133	123	140	158
Female	33	65	97	111	125	140	156	154	153	158	164

A question arises concerning the range to be included within that which is considered average. As shown in Table 2, the standard deviations for Total Words are high which in itself cautions us not to take these scores too literally. In addition, no single score should be used as the basis for classification. All five of the scores for written language, reading, mental test results, etc., are required when making a specific diagnosis. On the other hand, a significant deficiency in written language may be indicated by scores falling one or more years below average. Usually such scores will place the individual below the forty-fifth percentile and outside of the average stanine range for his age group.

Percentile Scores

In making diagnostic evaluations, as well as in the study of groups, it is advantageous to be able to interpret findings in terms of the percentile equivalents of the raw scores. The data in Tables 21, 22 and 23 have been furnished for this purpose.

Total Word scores can be converted into their percentile equivalents by referring to these tables. For example, a Total Word score of 106 for males falls at the eightieth percentile for nine-year-olds, at the fiftieth percentile for 11-year-olds, at the thirtieth percentile for 13-year-olds, at the fortieth percentile for 15-year-olds and at the twenty-fifth percentile for 17-year-olds.

TABLE 21

TOTAL WORDS

Percentile Equivalents for Males

	Age					
Percentile	7	9	11	13	15	17
98	61	184	280	430	308	340
95	50	162	272	366	288	336
90	42	124	178	246	190	268
85	36	115	168	225	177	232

TABLE 21—Continued.

Percentile	Age					
	7	9	11	13	15	17
80	31	106	162	203	173	214
75	28	102	144	188	168	199
70	26	95	136	175	159	196
65	24	90	128	162	146	189
60	22	86	122	155	133	180
55	21	82	115	148	124	174
50	19	77	106	132	118	159
45	18	70	92	121	113	140
40	15	67	83	113	106	125
35	14	63	78	108	102	121
30	12	60	77	105	96	113
25	11	54	67	100	91	105
20	10	48	62	86	87	97
15	9	44	53	81	73	92
10	6	40	44	73	66	83
5	4	28	35	54	50	75
2	1	10	22	37	40	65

TABLE 22

TOTAL WORDS

Percentile Equivalents for Females

Percentile	Age					
	7	9	11	13	15	17
98	97	286	308	354	248	348
95	84	208	276	276	228	340
90	64	174	228	264	205	304
85	49	156	204	234	192	252
80	45	143	180	216	185	215
75	41	128	172	198	179	202
70	38	120	160	192	175	196
65	36	96	146	186	172	180
60	35	84	139	168	160	170
55	34	80	129	162	152	162
50	32	76	110	149	148	158
45	30	70	100	138	144	155
40	28	68	94	126	140	144
35	27	65	88	114	137	134
30	25	62	81	100	132	130
25	24	58	78	87	126	124
20	19	54	74	80	122	116
15	14	50	69	76	118	98
10	11	44	60	66	96	84
5	4	31	48	58	80	70
2	1	29	42	42	57	56

TABLE 23

TOTAL WORDS
Percentile Equivalents for Total Group—Males and Females Combined

Percentile	Age					
	7	9	11	13	15	17
98	76	292	272	330	248	324
95	63	202	237	273	216	300
90	48	162	192	240	194	252
85	44	144	173	225	186	224
80	38	126	164	202	179	208
75	36	115	150	194	173	198
70	33	104	142	186	165	192
65	31	93	135	168	158	181
60	29	86	125	160	147	172
55	27	82	116	150	141	162
50	25	77	107	138	134	156
45	23	72	98	126	130	150
40	22	68	88	117	123	132
35	20	64	82	109	118	128
30	16	62	79	102	112	121
25	14	56	74	91	102	112
20	12	52	67	84	93	104
15	11	48	61	78	86	94
10	10	42	50	69	72	88
5	5	32	44	57	59	75
2	3	21	36	40	50	65

Stanine Ranks

The stanine rank is useful in the interpretation of scores because it provides the range of scores falling at equal intervals; the stanine ranks for Total Words are presented in Tables 24, 25 and 26. A deviation of one stanine is less than the standard deviations for Total Sentences as presented in Table 2. However, a deviation of two stanine ranks exceeds most of these standard deviations, so a score that deviates only one stanine can be viewed as falling within the normal range, whereas one that deviates two ranks must be considered significantly different from average.

TABLE 24
TOTAL WORDS
Stanine Ranks for Males

Stanine	7	9	11	13	15	17
			Age			
9	55–up	172–up	276–up	366–up	280–up	336–up
8	42–54	118–171	176–275	237–365	188–279	256–335
7	29–41	104–117	150–175	195–236	170–187	204–255
6	22–28	86–103	122–149	155–194	133–169	180–203
5	15–21	67–85	84–121	113–154	106–132	125–179
4	11–14	52–66	65–83	93–112	90–105	102–124
3	8–10	41–51	45–64	75–92	67–89	84–101
2	3–7	24–40	32–44	48–74	48–66	72–83
1	0–2	0 –23	0–31	0–47	0–47	0–71

TABLE 25
TOTAL WORDS
Stanine Ranks for Females

Stanine	7	9	11	13	15	17
			Age			
9	97–up	218–up	294–up	282–up	232–up	338–up
8	63–96	168–217	222–293	252–281	200–231	294–337
7	43–62	134–167	176–221	204–251	182–199	208–293
6	34–42	85–133	138–175	168–203	160–181	170–207
5	29–33	68–84	94–137	126–167	140–159	144–169
4	23–28	57–67	76–93	85–125	124–139	120–143
3	12–22	44–56	64–75	67–84	100–123	85–119
2	10–11	30–43	45–63	54–66	79–99	68–84
1	0–9	0–29	0–44	0–53	0–78	0–67

TABLE 26
TOTAL WORDS
Stanine Ranks for Total Group—Males and Females Combined

Stanine	7	9	11	13	15	17
			Age			
9	68–up	216–up	236–up	282–up	228–up	304–up
8	48–67	158–215	184–235	237–281	192–227	244–303
7	37–47	117–157	156–183	198–236	175–191	202–243
6	29–36	86–116	124–155	161–197	147–174	172–201
5	22–28	68–85	88–123	116–160	124–146	132–171
4	13–21	56–67	72–87	87–115	100–123	110–131
3	10–12	44–55	51–71	72–86	75–99	88–109
2	4–9	30–43	42–50	54–71	60–74	72–87
1	0–3	0–29	0–41	0–53	0–59	0–71

TOTAL SENTENCES

Mean Age Scores

The mean scores by age for Total Sentences are presented in Table 27; a raw score is converted into an age-level equivalent by referring to this table; see also Conversion Tables in the Scoring Guide. Again, there are variations by sex, the males reaching a plateau at 13 years of age and the females at 11 years. These plateaus can be explained by the fact that though they wrote longer stories as they became older, they wrote sentences of greater length. Therefore, the Total Sentence score did not continue to increase by age.

Comparatively, the Total Sentence scores were less variable than those for Total Words but more variable than the Words per Sentence scores (Table 2). Interpretation should consider the standard deviations which range from five to six sentences for most of the age levels above seven years. Moreover, the fact that above 11 years the means usually fall at ten to 11 sentences causes some difficulty in converting raw scores into age equivalents. As suggested for Total Words, frequently it is necessary to base the interpretation on the percentile and stanine scores for individuals above 11 years of age. A variation from average of more than one to two years may indicate a significant deviation. Final interpretation is made on the basis of the relationship of Total Sentences to the other written language scores and pertinent psychometric and educational achievement data.

TABLE 27

TOTAL SENTENCES

Mean and Midpoint Scores by Age and Sex

Age	7	8	9	10	11	12	13	14	15	16	17
Male	3.6	6.1	8.6	9.3	10.1	10.6	11.1	9.7	8.4	9.1	9.9
Female	5.0	7.7	10.5	11.0	11.5	11.5	11.5	11.2	10.9	11.2	11.5

Percentile Scores

The percentile equivalents of the Total Sentence raw scores are given in Tables 28, 29 and 30. In referring to these we find that a Total Sentence score of 11 for a female falls at the ninetieth percentile for seven-year-olds, at the sixty-fifth percentile for nine-year-olds, the fifty-fifth percentile for 11-year-olds, the sixtieth percentile for 13-year-olds, the sixty-fifth percentile for 15-year-olds and at the sixtieth percentile for 17-year-olds.

TABLE 28

TOTAL SENTENCES

Percentile Equivalents for Males

Percentile	Age					
	7	9	11	13	15	17
98	9	27	27	39	25	28
95	8	18	24	33	21	23
90	7	13	19	24	17	18
85	5	11	18	19	14	16
80	5	10	16	14	11	15
75	4	10	15	13	10	14
70	3	9	13	12	9	12
65	3	9	12	12	9	11
60	3	8	10	11	8	10
55	3	8	10	10	7	9
50	2	8	9	9	7	8
45	2	7	8	9	6	8
40	2	7	8	8	6	7
35	1	6	7	7	6	6
30	1	6	6	7	6	6
25	1	6	6	6	5	6
20	1	5	5	6	5	6
15	0	4	4	5	4	5
10	0	3	4	4	4	4
5	0	2	3	3	3	3
2	0	1	1	2	2	2

TABLE 29

TOTAL SENTENCES

Percentile Equivalents for Females

Percentile	Age					
	7	9	11	13	15	17
98	11	30	34	33	28	42
95	10	20	27	24	25	40
90	9	18	25	19	16	21
85	8	17	18	18	15	18
80	7	15	16	16	13	16
75	6	13	15	15	12	15
70	5	12	14	14	11	13
65	5	11	13	12	11	12
60	4	9	12	11	10	11
55	4	9	11	10	10	10
50	4	8	10	9	10	9

TABLE 29—Continued.

Percentile	Age					
	7	9	11	13	15	17
45	3	8	9	9	9	9
40	3	7	9	8	9	9
35	3	7	8	7	9	8
30	3	6	7	7	9	8
25	2	6	6	6	8	7
20	2	5	5	6	7	7
15	1	5	4	5	6	5
10	1	4	4	4	6	4
5	0	3	3	3	5	3
2	0	2	1	2	5	2

TABLE 30

TOTAL SENTENCES

Percentile Equivalents for Total Group—Males and Females Combined

Percentile	Age					
	7	9	11	13	15	17
98	11	31	27	30	26	30
95	10	21	25	21	17	19
90	9	17	21	18	16	18
85	8	13	18	15	14	16
80	7	12	16	15	12	15
75	6	11	15	14	11	14
70	5	10	13	12	11	13
65	5	9	12	12	10	11
60	4	9	11	11	9	10
55	4	9	10	10	9	9
50	3	8	9	9	8	9
45	3	8	8	9	8	9
40	3	7	8	8	7	8
35	2	6	7	7	7	7
30	2	6	6	7	6	7
25	2	5	6	6	6	6
20	1	5	5	6	6	6
15	1	4	4	5	5	5
10	0	4	4	4	4	4
5	0	3	3	3	4	3
2	0	2	1	2	3	2

Stanine Ranks

The stanine ranks for the Total Sentence raw scores are found in Tables 31, 32 and 33. The scores falling at the fifth stanine, representing average, are in close agreement with the means and the scores falling at the fiftieth percentile. The most satisfactory interpretation can be made by referring to all three of the conversion tables, the means, the percentiles and the stanines. But a score falling more than one stanine below average is indicative of a deficiency.

TABLE 31

TOTAL SENTENCES

Stanine Ranks for Males

Stanine	Age					
	7	9	11	13	15	17
9	8–up	25–up	25–up	33–up	21–up	27–up
8	6–7	13–24	19–24	23–32	16–20	18–26
7	4–5	10–12	15–18	13–22	10–15	14–17
6	3	8–9	11–14	11–12	8–9	9–13
5	2	7	8–10	9–10	6–7	8
4	1	6	6–7	6–8	5	6–7
3	0	4–5	4–5	4–5	4	5
2	0	2–3	2–3	3	2–3	4
1	0	0–1	0–1	0–2	0–1	0–3

TABLE 32

TOTAL SENTENCES

Stanine Ranks for Females

Stanine	Age					
	7	9	11	13	15	17
9	11–up	22–up	33–up	24–up	25–up	32–up
8	9–10	18–21	23–32	18–23	16–24	21–31
7	7–8	13–17	16–22	15–17	12–15	15–20
6	5–6	9–12	12–15	11–14	10–11	12–14
5	4	8	9–11	8–10	9	9–11
4	3	6–7	6–8	6–7	8	7–8
3	1–2	4–5	4–5	4–5	6–7	5–6
2	0	3	3	3	5	3–4
1	0	0–2	0–2	0–2	0–4	0–2

TABLE 33

TOTAL SENTENCES

Stanine Ranks for Total Groups—Males and Females Combined

Stanine	7	9	11	13	15	17
			Age			
9	11–up	25–up	25–up	22–up	17–up	21–up
8	9–10	16–24	21–24	17–21	15–16	18–20
7	7–8	12–15	15–20	14–16	12–14	14–17
6	5–6	9–11	11–14	11–13	9–11	10–13
5	3–4	7–8	8–10	8–10	7–8	8–9
4	2	6	6–7	6–7	6	6–7
3	1	4–5	4–5	4–5	5	5
2	0	3	3	3	4	4
1	0	0–2	0–2	0–2	0–3	0–3

WORDS PER SENTENCE

Mean Age Scores

Of the three Productivity measures, the Words per Sentence scores were the least variable. The standard deviations, as shown in Table 2, are stable and in magnitude fall between one-fourth and one-fifth of the mean. The mean and midpoint scores are presented in Table 34; see also Conversion Tables in Scoring Guide. Though the increment from one age to the next is slight, especially after 13 years of age, gradual growth is made throughout the age range studied (Figure 5). Females wrote sentences of slightly greater length than the males but the difference was not statistically significant.

There is excellent agreement among the mean, percentile and stanine scores. However, because the differences between the means from one age level to the next are slight, one must be cautious when converting raw scores into age equivalents. Clinically significant variations can be determined only from relating Words per Sentence scores with other relevant data. It appears that a deviation of two or more years should be considered a deficiency. Words per Sentence matures in a manner that is highly

TABLE 34

WORDS PER SENTENCE

Mean and Midpoint Scores by Age and Sex

Age	7	8	9	10	11	12	13	14	15	16	17
Male	6.7	8.1	9.5	10.6	11.8	13.0	14.2	14.5	14.8	15.1	15.4
Female	6.3	8.1	9.9	10.5	11.2	12.5	13.8	14.6	15.4	16.1	16.8

linear, emphasizing the importance of scores that vary from the growth curves presented in Figure 5.

Percentile Scores

The percentile equivalents for the Words per Sentence raw scores are presented in Tables 35, 36 and 37. These scores are converted into per-

TABLE 35

WORDS PER SENTENCE

Percentile Equivalents for Males

Percentile	Age					
	7	9	11	13	15	17
98	10.8	16.0	20.4	29.0	34.0	25.4
95	10.2	15.5	19.7	27.0	33.0	24.8
90	9.1	13.4	16.3	20.0	22.4	22.4
85	8.7	13.0	14.5	17.8	19.0	21.4
80	7.8	11.5	14.1	16.8	18.2	20.8
75	7.6	11.4	13.6	15.9	17.5	20.0
70	7.3	11.0	12.4	15.4	17.1	19.0
65	7.1	10.7	11.6	15.0	16.6	18.2
60	6.8	10.5	11.3	14.8	16.0	17.6
55	6.5	10.2	11.0	14.1	15.7	16.5
50	6.2	9.7	10.7	13.9	15.4	16.0
45	5.9	9.4	10.5	13.4	14.6	15.8
40	5.8	9.1	10.1	12.6	14.4	15.4
35	5.4	8.5	9.8	12.0	14.2	15.0
30	5.0	8.3	9.4	11.4	13.4	14.4
25	4.6	8.1	9.2	11.1	13.0	13.4
20	4.3	7.7	8.9	10.8	12.4	12.8
15	3.9	7.4	8.4	10.2	11.8	12.4
10	3.7	7.0	8.0	9.6	10.9	11.9
5	3.0	5.8	7.2	8.6	9.1	10.4
2	0.3	5.3	7.0	7.1	6.4	9.4

TABLE 36

WORDS PER SENTENCE

Percentile Equivalents for Females

Percentile	Age					
	7	9	11	13	15	17
98	13.0	14.4	23.4	22.0	22.1	28.4
95	11.4	13.5	20.8	19.0	20.5	27.2
90	9.7	12.8	18.2	18.2	18.6	21.6
85	8.6	11.6	14.7	17.6	18.0	19.6

TABLE 36—Continued.

Percentile	7	9	11	13	15	17
80	8.3	10.9	14.3	16.8	17.6	19.0
75	8.0	10.5	14.0	16.2	16.9	18.0
70	7.7	10.4	13.2	15.9	16.2	17.3
65	7.5	10.1	12.5	15.6	15.8	16.8
60	7.2	9.8	12.2	14.9	15.4	16.5
55	7.0	9.6	11.6	14.3	15.0	16.0
50	6.9	9.2	11.1	13.9	14.5	15.6
45	6.8	8.9	10.8	13.6	14.2	15.2
40	6.2	8.7	10.6	13.4	14.0	14.6
35	6.0	8.4	10.2	13.0	13.6	14.2
30	5.6	8.2	9.8	12.2	13.0	13.4
25	4.9	7.8	9.7	12.0	12.5	12.6
20	4.5	7.5	9.4	11.4	12.2	12.1
15	4.1	7.2	9.0	10.6	11.3	11.6
10	3.8	6.7	8.6	10.2	9.8	10.4
5	2.8	6.2	6.4	8.9	8.9	9.0
2	2.4	6.1	5.2	8.4	8.4	8.3

TABLE 37

WORDS PER SENTENCE

Percentile Equivalents for Total Group—Males and Females Combined

| Percentile | Age | | | | | |
	7	9	11	13	15	17
98	12.4	15.8	20.8	25.0	22.8	27.0
95	10.8	14.8	19.0	19.8	21.0	23.9
90	9.6	13.2	15.4	17.8	19.2	21.4
85	8.8	12.4	14.4	17.5	18.2	20.6
80	8.2	11.5	14.2	16.6	17.7	19.6
75	7.8	11.1	13.2	16.0	17.0	18.4
70	7.5	10.6	12.5	15.0	16.6	17.8
65	7.2	10.4	12.2	14.8	16.0	17.0
60	7.0	10.0	11.6	14.7	15.6	16.5
55	6.9	9.8	11.3	14.2	15.3	16.2
50	6.6	9.5	11.0	13.9	14.8	15.8
45	6.3	9.2	10.7	13.5	14.4	15.5
40	6.0	8.8	10.3	13.0	14.2	15.0
35	5.8	8.4	9.9	12.6	13.8	14.2
30	5.4	8.2	9.6	12.0	13.2	13.8
25	4.9	8.1	9.4	11.6	12.7	13.0
20	4.5	7.6	9.2	11.0	12.3	12.4
15	3.9	7.2	8.8	10.4	11.7	12.0
10	3.8	6.8	8.2	9.8	10.6	11.4
5	3.2	6.2	7.1	8.9	9.2	10.0
2	1.1	5.6	6.4	7.9	8.0	8.8

centile equivalents by referring to these tables. To illustrate, a raw score of 11.0 for males falls at the seventieth percentile for nine-year-olds, at the fifty-fifth percentile for 11-year-olds, at the twenty-fifth percentile for 13-year-olds, just about the tenth percentile for 15-year-olds, and between the fifth and tenth percentile for 17-year-olds.

Stanine Ranks

The stanine ranks of the Words per Sentence raw scores are found in Tables 38, 39 and 40. According to the standard deviations, a variation from average of less than one stanine should be considered as falling within the normal range. A variation of two stanines corresponds closely to one standard deviation from the mean and furnishes a valuable guide for the interpretation of raw scores.

TABLE 38

WORDS PER SENTENCE

Stanine Ranks for Males

Stanine	Age					
	7	9	11	13	15	17
9	10.5–up	15.7–up	19.8–up	28.8–up	33.0–up	24.8–up
8	9.0–10.4	13.3–15.6	15.9–19.7	19.2–28.7	21.6–32.9	21.9–24.7
7	7.6–8.9	11.4–13.2	13.9–15.8	16.2–19.1	17.6–21.5	20.4–21.8
6	6.8–7.5	10.4–11.3	11.3–13.8	14.5–16.1	16.0–17.5	17.6–20.3
5	5.8–6.7	9.1–10.3	10.1–11.2	12.5–14.4	14.4–15.9	15.4–17.5
4	4.5–5.7	8.0–9.0	9.2–10.0	11.0–12.4	12.7–14.3	12.2–15.3
3	3.8–4.4	7.1–7.9	8.1–9.1	9.6–10.9	11.2–12.6	12.0–12.1
2	2.3–3.7	5.6–7.0	7.1–8.0	8.4–9.5	8.4–11.1	10.4–11.9
1	0–2.2	0–5.5	0–7.0	0–8.3	0–8.3	0–10.3

TABLE 39

WORDS PER SENTENCE

Stanine Ranks for Females

Stanine	Age					
	7	9	11	13	15	17
9	12.0–up	13.6–up	21.8–up	19.3–up	21.0–up	27.0–up
8	9.5–11.9	12.8–13.5	17.0–21.7	18.0–19.2	18.2–20.9	20.0–26.9
7	8.1–9.4	10.8–12.7	14.1–16.9	16.4–17.9	17.2–18.1	18.4–19.9
6	7.2–8.0	9.8–10.7	12.1–14.0	14.8–16.3	15.4–17.1	16.6–18.3
5	6.2–7.1	8.7–9.7	10.5–12.0	13.3–14.7	14.0–15.3	14.6–16.5
4	4.7–6.1	7.7–8.6	9.6–10.4	11.9–13.2	12.4–13.9	12.4–14.5
3	3.8–4.6	6.8–7.6	8.6–9.5	10.2–11.8	10.2–12.3	10.6–12.3
2	2.5–3.7	6.2–6.7	6.4–8.5	8.8–10.1	8.8–10.1	8.8–10.5
1	0–2.4	0–6.1	0–6.3	0–8.7	0–8.7	0–8.7

TABLE 40

WORDS PER SENTENCE

Stanine Ranks for Total Group—Males and Females Combined

Stanine	Age 7	9	11	13	15	17
9	10.9–up	15.4–up	19.0–up	20.4–up	22.8–up	24.4–up
8	9.4–10.8	13.1–15.3	15.0–18.9	17.6–20.3	18.8–22.7	21.2–24.3
7	7.9–9.3	11.2–13.0	13.8–14.9	16.3–17.5	17.2–18.7	18.8–21.1
6	7.0–7.8	10.0–11.1	11.6–13.7	14.5–16.2	15.6–17.1	16.6–18.7
5	6.0–6.9	8.8–9.9	10.3–11.5	13.0–14.4	14.2–15.5	15.0–16.5
4	4.7–5.9	7.8–8.7	9.4–10.2	11.3–12.9	12.5–14.1	12.7–14.9
3	3.8–4.6	7.0–7.7	8.4–9.3	9.8–11.2	10.8–12.4	11.4–12.6
2	3.0–3.7	6.1–6.9	6.8–8.3	8.8–9.7	8.8–10.7	8.4–11.3
1	0–2.9	0–6.0	0–6.7	0–8.7	0–8.7	0–8.3

SYNTAX

Mean Age Scores

The means and standard deviations for Syntax are presented in Table 3 and the growth curve in Figure 6. We have stressed that this maturational aspect of written language is acquired early in life with the result that a plateau appears at 11 years of age.

The Syntax score is a ratio of the extent to which the language produced conforms to the criterion of correctness, a quotient of 100 representing no errors. The mean Syntax Quotients by age are presented in Table 41; see also Conversion Tables in the Scoring Guide. In using this table it should be noted that the standard deviations for the age groups above seven years are small (see Table 3). Therefore, although the increments are slight the mean age scores are useful. Nevertheless, it is the quotients that fall below 90 that are most suggestive diagnostically, a quotient below 80 being indicative of a language disorder. Scores falling above 95 represent the level of correctness attained by the average adult.

TABLE 41

SYNTAX

Mean and Midpoint Scores by Age and Sex

Age	7	8	9	10	11	12	13	14	15	16	17
Male	85	89	94	95	97	97	97	97	97	97	98
Female	89	92	96	97	98	98	98	98	99	99	99

Percentile Scores

The percentile equivalents of the Syntax Quotients are shown in Tables 42, 43 and 44. The quotients are converted into percentile scores by referring to these tables. To illustrate: a female who earns a score of 93

TABLE 42

SYNTAX

Percentile Equivalents for Males

	Age					
Percentile	7	9	11	13	15	17
98	99	100	100	100	100	100
95	99	100	100	100	100	100
90	99	99	99	100	99	100
85	98	99	99	100	99	99
80	97	99	99	99	99	99
75	96	99	99	99	99	99
70	96	98	99	99	99	99
65	94	98	98	99	99	99
60	94	98	98	99	99	99
55	93	97	98	98	98	99
50	92	97	98	98	97	99
45	91	97	98	98	97	99
40	89	96	97	97	97	99
35	87	95	97	97	97	98
30	84	94	96	96	96	98
25	80	93	95	96	96	97
20	76	90	94	95	95	96
15	72	88	92	94	93	94
10	68	85	90	93	91	93
5	12	79	87	92	89	90
2	2	62	84	90	84	86

TABLE 43

SYNTAX

Percentile Equivalents for Females

	Age					
Percentile	7	9	11	13	15	17
98	100	100	100	100	100	100
95	99	100	100	100	100	100
90	99	100	99	100	99	100
85	98	100	99	100	99	99

TABLE 43—Continued.

Percentile	7	9	11	13	15	17
			Age			
80	98	99	99	99	99	99
75	98	99	99	99	99	99
70	98	99	99	99	99	99
65	97	98	99	99	99	99
60	96	98	99	99	99	99
55	95	98	99	99	99	99
50	95	98	99	99	98	99
45	94	97	98	98	98	99
40	93	96	98	98	98	99
35	92	96	98	97	98	98
30	90	95	96	97	98	98
25	84	94	96	97	98	98
20	84	93	95	96	97	97
15	80	92	95	95	97	96
10	73	88	94	93	96	94
5	30	85	91	92	95	92
2	17	79	86	84	88	86

TABLE 44

SYNTAX

Percentile Equivalents for Total Group—Males and Females Combined

Percentile	7	9	11	13	15	17
			Age			
98	99	100	100	100	100	100
95	99	100	100	100	100	100
90	99	100	99	100	99	100
85	98	99	99	100	99	99
80	98	99	99	99	99	99
75	97	99	99	99	99	99
70	97	99	99	99	99	99
65	96	98	98	99	99	99
60	95	98	98	99	99	99
55	94	98	98	98	98	99
50	93	97	98	98	98	99
45	93	97	98	98	97	99
40	92	96	97	97	97	99
35	90	95	97	97	97	98
30	88	95	97	96	97	98
25	83	94	95	96	97	97
20	80	92	94	95	96	96
15	76	89	93	94	95	95
10	69	87	92	93	94	93
5	16	83	88	92	90	90
2	4	66	85	88	86	86

falls at the fortieth percentile for seven-year-olds, at the twentieth percentile for nine-year-olds, between the fifth and tenth percentiles for 11-year-olds, at the tenth percentile for 13-year-olds, between the second and fifth percentile for 15-year-olds and between the fifth and tenth percentile for 17-year-olds.

Stanine Ranks

Reference to Tables 45, 46 and 47 reveals the marked plateauing of these scores. Above nine years of age the means for each of the age groups are essentially equal. Despite this circumstance it is not uncommon to find youths of high school age who score below the fourth or even the third stanine rank. Usually they are found to have a language disorder.

TABLE 45

SYNTAX

Stanine Ranks for Males

			Age			
Stanine	7	9	11	13	15	17
9	99–100	100	100	100	100	100
8	99	100	100	100	100	99
7	97–98	99	99	99	99	99
6	94–96	97–98	98	99	99	99
5	89–93	96	97	98	97–98	99
4	79–88	91–95	94–96	95–97	96	96–98
3	69–78	86–90	90–93	93–94	92–95	93–95
2	7–68	74–85	86–89	91–92	88–91	89–92
1	0–6	0–73	0–85	0–90	0–87	0–88

TABLE 46

SYNTAX

Stanine Ranks for Females

			Age			
Stanine	7	9	11	13	15	17
9	99–100	100	100	100	100	100
8	99	100	100	100	100	100
7	98	99	99	99	99	99
6	96–97	98	99	99	99	99
5	93–95	97	98	99	99	99
4	87–92	94–96	96–97	97–98	98	97–98
3	76–86	89–93	95	93–96	96–97	95–96
2	16–75	84–88	91–94	91–92	95	90–94
1	0–15	0–83	0–90	0–90	0–94	0–89

TABLE 47

SYNTAX
Stanine Ranks for Total Group—Males and Females Combined

Stanine	7	9	11	13	15	17
				Age		
9	99–100	100	100	100	100	100
8	99	100	100	100	100	99
7	98	99	99	99	99	99
6	95–97	98	98	99	99	99
5	92–94	96–97	97	98	98	99
4	82–91	93–95	95–96	96–97	97	97–98
3	71–81	87–92	92–94	93–95	94–96	93–96
2	12–70	82–86	88–91	91–92	90–93	90–92
1	0–11	0–81	0–87	0–90	0–89	0–89

ABSTRACT-CONCRETE

Mean Age Scores

From the results found in Table 4 we note that the standard deviations for the Abstract-Concrete scores are not large; the mean scores are not highly variable. The mean and midpoint scores by age are presented in Table 48; see also Conversion Tables in the Scoring Guide. Although the use of abstraction increases developmentally through 15 years for the

TABLE 48

ABSTRACT-CONCRETE
Mean and Midpoint Scores by Age and Sex

Age	7	8	9	10	11	12	13	14	15	16	17
Male	7	10	13	14	15	16	16	17	17	18	19
Female	8	11	14	15	16	16	17	18	19	19	18

females and 17 years for the males, most of the differences are slight from one age level to the next. Hence minor score differences must be interpreted with caution. Conservatively, deviations of less than two years without other evidence usually should be considered as falling within the average range. On the other hand, children such as an 11-year-old boy who scores below 13 or a girl of the same age who scores below 14 would be considered inferior. Adults scoring below 16 or 17 should be suspected of being deficient in ability to convey abstract meaning, though they may show normal competence in both Productivity and Syntax.

Percentile Scores

The percentile equivalents for the Abstract-Concrete raw scores are presented in Tables 49, 50 and 51. Because of the limited range, special problems arise in the conversion of some scores. For example, a score of 17 for a 13-year-old male covers a range from the fortieth to the fifty-fifth

TABLE 49

ABSTRACT-CONCRETE

Percentile Equivalents for Males

			Age			
Percentile	7	9	11	13	15	17
98	19	22	24	23	25	24
95	13	20	23	22	24	23
90	10	19	21	21	23	23
85	9	19	20	20	22	22
80	8	18	19	20	22	22
75	8	18	19	19	20	21
70	8	17	18	19	20	21
65	7	16	18	18	20	21
60	7	15	18	18	19	20
55	7	14	17	17	18	20
50	6	12	17	17	18	20
45	6	11	16	17	18	20
40	6	10	14	17	17	19
35	6	9	12	16	17	19
30	6	8	11	16	16	18
25	5	8	9	15	15	18
20	4	7	8	13	14	18
15	3	7	7	10	11	17
10	2	6	7	8	8	15
5	1	6	6	7	7	8
2	0	3	6	6	6	4

TABLE 50

ABSTRACT-CONCRETE

Percentile Equivalents for Females

			Age			
Percentile	7	9	11	13	15	17
98	17	21	24	22	24	25
95	16	20	22	21	23	24
90	11	20	21	21	23	23
85	10	19	20	20	22	22
80	10	19	19	20	21	22

TABLE 50—Continued.

Percentile	Age 7	9	11	13	15	17
75	9	18	19	20	21	21
70	9	18	18	19	21	21
65	8	17	18	19	21	21
60	8	16	18	18	20	20
55	8	14	18	18	20	19
50	8	12	17	18	19	18
45	7	12	16	17	19	18
40	7	11	16	17	18	18
35	7	10	15	16	18	17
30	6	10	13	16	18	17
25	6	9	12	15	18	16
20	6	8	11	13	17	15
15	6	8	10	10	16	14
10	5	7	8	8	13	11
5	2	6	7	7	10	8
2	1	5	6	6	7	4

TABLE 51

ABSTRACT-CONCRETE

Percentile Equivalents for Total Group—Males and Females Combined

Percentile	Age 7	9	11	13	15	17
98	19	22	24	22	24	24
95	16	20	22	21	23	23
90	11	19	21	21	23	23
85	10	19	20	20	22	22
80	9	18	19	20	21	22
75	9	18	19	19	21	21
70	8	17	18	19	20	21
65	8	16	18	18	20	21
60	8	16	18	18	20	20
55	7	14	17	17	19	20
50	7	13	17	17	19	19
45	7	12	16	17	18	19
40	7	11	15	17	18	18
35	6	10	13	16	17	18
30	6	9	12	16	17	17
25	6	8	11	15	16	17
20	6	8	9	13	15	17
15	5	7	8	10	14	16
10	4	7	7	8	11	12
5	1	6	7	7	8	8
2	0	5	6	6	6	4

percentile. Typically, a boy of this age earning this score would be said to be average in the use of abstraction. A helpful guide under these circumstances is the midpoint of the percentile range. By this standard a score of 18 for a female would be interpreted as falling at the 72.5 percentile for nine-year-olds, at the 62.5 percentile for 11-year-olds, at the 55th percentile for 13-year-olds, at the 32.5 percentile for 15-year-olds and at the 45th percentile for 17-year-olds.

TABLE 52
ABSTRACT-CONCRETE
Stanine Ranks for Males

Stanine	Age					
	7	9	11	13	15	17
9	16–up	20–up	24–up	23–up	24–up	23–up
8	9–15	19	21–23	21–22	23	22
7	8	18	19–20	20	21–22	21
6	7	16–17	18	18–19	19–20	20
5	6	11–15	14–17	17	17–18	19
4	5	7–10	8–13	15–16	15–16	18
3	3–4	6	7	8–14	8–14	16–17
2	1–2	5	6	7	7	7–15
1	0	0–4	0–5	0–6	0–6	0–6

TABLE 53
ABSTRACT-CONCRETE
Stanine Ranks for Females

Stanine	Age					
	7	9	11	13	15	17
9	16–up	20–up	23–up	22–up	23–up	24–up
8	10–15	19	21–22	21	23	22–23
7	9	18	19–20	20	22	21
6	8	16–17	18	18–19	21	20
5	7	11–15	16–17	17	19–20	18–19
4	6	8–10	12–15	15–16	17–18	16–17
3	5	7	8–11	8–14	14–16	11–15
2	2–4	6	6–7	7	9–13	7–10
1	0–1	0–5	0–5	0–6	0–8	0–6

Stanine Ranks

The stanine ranks for the Abstract-Concrete raw scores are found in Tables 52, 53 and 54. The 5th stanine ranks are in close agreement with the means and provide further insight into these scores. Moreover, a deviation of more than two ranks coincides with the standard deviations and indicates the variations that might be expected to fall within the range of average.

TABLE 54

ABSTRACT-CONCRETE

Stanine Ranks for Total Group—Males and Females Combined

Stanine	Age					
	7	9	11	13	15	17
9	16–up	20–up	23–up	21–up	23–up	23–up
8	10–15	19	20–22	20	23	22
7	8–9	18	19	19	21–22	21
6	7	16–17	18	18	20	20
5	6	11–15	16–17	17	18–19	18–19
4	5	8–10	11–15	15–16	16–17	17
3	4	7	7–10	8–14	11–15	13–16
2	1–3	6	6	7	7–10	7–12
1	0	0–5	0–5	0–6	0–6	0–6

SUMMARY

Interpretation of test results is most meaningful when the total relationships of the scores are considered. Three types of conversions can be made of the raw scores, permitting broad insights into the written language facility of a given individual. These conversions are the mean age scores, percentile and stanine ranks. Specific diagnoses and classifications are made by relating these scores to each other and to other diagnostic findings, such as psychometric and educational achievement test data.

REFERENCES

1. Myklebust, H. R.: Development and Disorders of Written Language, Vol. II. New York and London, Grune & Stratton. In press.
2. ———: The Psychology of Deafness, 2nd Ed. New York and London, Grune & Stratton, 1964.

PART FOUR
SCORING GUIDE

Productivity and Syntax

THE SCORING GUIDE has been included not only as a convenient reference but as a means whereby the examiner may acquire facility in scoring more quickly. Illustrative Stories are presented first in their original form as written by normal children, speech defective, those having reading disabilities, the socially-emotionally disturbed, educable mentally retarded and deaf children. Immediately following, by age, the story is reproduced with the scoring symbols inserted and with each of the scores listed. (Scoring is based on first three sentences.)

Stories written by normal children and by five types of handicapped children have been included for two reasons. First, those responsible for the diagnosis and classification of children with handicaps and learning disabilities might benefit from seeing a variety of scored stories. Second, the sample of stories by age for normal and handicapped children provides ready illustrative material relative to the acquisition of written language. These stories were selected as being representative—as falling as close as possible to the mean by age, sex and type of imposition on learning; because five scores are involved, certain of these are not always illustrative of average function by a given group.

Students of language will recognize both similarities and differences among the groups and it is these that the diagnostician is especially interested in revealing through his study of individuals. Only by careful, painstaking identification of the specific deficits that characterize each child or adult can we expect to be most helpful in alleviating his deficiency. Furthermore, only through such identification can the special psychology of learning that accompanies each type of disability be further understood and applied with maximum benefits.

ILLUSTRATION 20. Illustrative scored stories written by normal children.

▶ **7-YEAR-OLD MALE**

ORIGINAL

Tom likes to go to school. It is fun. and he likes It. he Went to Play.

SCORED

Tom likes to go to school. It, is fun.\ and he likes It.\ he Went to Play.\

	Score	Age Equivalent	Percentile	Stanine
TW	17	7	45	5
TS	4	7	75	7
WPS	4.3	−7	20	3
SQ	88	8	40	4
A/C	8	7	70	7

ILLUSTRATION 20—Continued.

▶ 7-YEAR-OLD FEMALE

ORIGINAL

SCORED

	Score	Age Equivalent	Percentile	Stanine
TW	23	—7	25	4
TS	3	7	45	5
WPS	7.7	7	70	6
SQ	94	8	45	5
A/C	9	7	70	7

ILLUSTRATION 20—Continued.

▶ 9-YEAR-OLD MALE

ORIGINAL

The Little House Maker

Once there was a little boy
who liked to play with toys
he had a house with people
in it the house had many
things in it he was working
on the table. The little boy and put a
table down a few chairs and put a
lamp down. The little boys
put father down and two children
when the little boy finished
he showed his mother and
everybody else in the famally
and they were proud of him.

SCORED

The Little House Maker

Once there was a little boy
who liked to play with toys: \
•he had a house with people
in it \ •the house had many
things in it: \ he was working
on the table. \ The little boy and put a
table down a few chairs and put a
lamp down. \ The little boys
put father down and two children \
when the little boy finished
he showed his mother and
everybody else in the famally
and they were proud of him. \

	Score	Age Equivalent	Percentile	Stanine
TW	79	9	50	5
TS	7	8	45	5
WPS	11.3	11	75	6
SQ	94	9	30	4
A/C	17	14	70	6

(Run-on Sentences)

ILLUSTRATION 20—Continued.

▶ **9-YEAR-OLD FEMALE**

ORIGINAL

One day a boy wanted to play with toy's. And never played with any thing els. And he played with toy's on the kitcien table. And he played with books, and car's and mostlie with girl's stuff. He has lots of fun with he's toy's. He works in offic and he learn's how to read and do other thing. He just had fun in he's life. And he played with furniture of a doll house. And played with toy' shoe's. He away's stayed in a suit

SCORED

*One day a boy wanted to play with toy's. \ And never played with any thing els \ And he played with toy's on the kitcien table. \ And he played with books, and car's and mostlie with girl's stuff \ He has lots of fun with he's toy's \ He works in offic and he learn's how to read and do other thing \ He just had fun in he's life \ And he played with furniture of a doll house. \ And played with toy' shoe's. \ He away's stayed in a suit *

	Score	Age Equivalent	Percentile	Stanine
TW	85	9	60	6
TS	10	9	60	5
WPS	8.5	8	35	7
SQ	88	7	30	4
A/C	8	7	55	6

ILLUSTRATION 20—Continued.

▶ **11-YEAR-OLD MALE**

ORIGINAL

Frank and his playtime
Frank went to his first
day in kintergarden and he
was looking for something to do.
All the boys and girls had all
the games except one it was
a dall house so he got it out.
Everyone laughed at him for play
with a girls toy but he did
care.
Frank made a dinningroom
look very nice and he went
from one room to another
and arranged and rearranged
the rooms and he thought he
made the doll house perect
in aranging his rooms
then he was admiring his
rooms when someone bumped
the house and he had to
start all over again but
he could never make it
the same.
The End

ILLUSTRATION 20—Continued.

SCORED

Frank and his playtime
Frank went to his first
day in kintergarden and he
was looking for something to do.
All the boys and girls had all
the games except one, it was
a doll house so he got it out.
Everyone laughed at him for play
with a girls toy but he didn't
care.
Frank made a dinning room
look very nice and he went
from one room to another
and arranged and rearranged
the rooms and he thought the
made the doll-house perect
en draanging his rooms,
then he was admiring his
rooms when someo a bumpe
the house and he had to
start all over again but
he could never make it
the same
The End

	Score	Age Equivalent	Percentile	Stanine
TW	113	11	55	5
TS	9	10	50	5
WPS	12.6	12	70	6
SQ	98	14	65	6
A/C	19	17	80	7

ILLUSTRATION 20—Continued.

▶ 11-YEAR-OLD FEMALE

ORIGINAL

Tommy my 5 year old brother was in the basement one day. He got out his toy people and furniture to play with. He loved to play with them. He would have them get up eat breakfast go to school and so on. He thought they were just swell.

When he started to school he never play with them again. I bet they are still down in the big box where he left them.

SCORED

Tommy? my 5 year old brother ? was in the basement one day.\ He got out his toy people and furniture to play with.\ He loved to play with them.\ He would have them get up eat breakfast go to school and so on.\ He thought they were just swell.\

When he started to school he never play with them again.\ I bet they are still down in the big box where he left them.\

	Score	Age Equivalent	Percentile	Stanine
TW	74	8	20	3
TS	7	8	30	4
WPS	10.6	10	45	5
SQ	98	12	45	5
A/C	19	5	75	7

ILLUSTRATION 20—Continued.

▶ 13-YEAR-OLD MALE

ORIGINAL

The picture tells of a boy around seven years old who seems to be setting doll furniture on a table arranging it around to look like a dining room where a family is beginning to eat dinner. There is a table, three chairs which matches the table, a high chair, a chair which looks like it is meant to be in the living room, a bouffet, china cabinet, light, a stroller with a baby in it, a dog, food and plates on the table, and four older occupants who are older than the baby.

The boy seems to be doing this in a room with other various toys. Some of the toys are doll furniture and the rest are books, a car, ball and other objects.

The boy seems to be absorbed in what he's doing by the expression on his face.

He is neatly dressed and looks happy.

The room in which he is in is sort of difficult to tell though it looks like a playroom or some room in school which is meant to be used as a playroom. Of course it can be of anything else too.

ILLUSTRATION 20—Continued.

SCORED

The picture tells of a boy around seven years old who seems to be setting doll furniture on a table; arranging it around to look like a dining room where a family is beginning to eat dinner. There is a table, three chairs which matches the table, [a high chair, a chair which looks like it is meant to be in the living room, a bouffet, china cabinet, light, a stroller with a baby in it, a dog, food and plates on the table,] and four older occupants who are older than the baby.

The boy seems to be doing this in a room with other (various) toys. Some of the toys are doll furniture and the rest are books, a car, [ball] and other objects.

The boy seems to be absorbed in what he's doing by the expression on his face.

He is neatly dressed and looks happy.

The room in which he is in is sort of difficult to tell though it looks like a playroom or some room in school which is meant to be used as a playroom. Of course it can be of anything else too.

	Score	Age Equivalent	Percentile	Stanine
TW	107	11	30	4
TS	7	8	35	4
WPS	15.3	16	65	6
SQ	96	11	30	4
A/C	18	16	65	6

ILLUSTRATION 20—Continued.

▶ 13-YEAR-OLD FEMALE

ORIGINAL

One day in school I was taken into a new room with some of my classmates. It was a real pretty room. All kinds of toy. The teacher said we could play with anything we wanted to. I looked around and in a box I saw some plastic figerines and furnishings. I took the box over to a little table and sat down and started to make a little house. I put a table chairs dishes hichair. I sat a little girl down in a chair, had a boy chaiseing a dog, the father getting ready to sit down, the mother taking the baby out of its carrige.

ILLUSTRATION 20—Continued.

SCORED

One day in school I was taken into a new room with some of my classmates.\ It was a real pretty room; all kinds of toy.\ The teacher said we could play with anything we wanted to.\ I looked around and in a box I saw some plastic figurines and furnishings.\ I took the box over to a little table and sat down and started to make a little house.\ I put a table chairs [dishes] &chair \I sat a little girl down in a chair, had a boy chasing a dog, the father getting ready to sit down, the mother taking the baby out of its carriage.\

	Score	Age Equivalent	Percentile	Stanine
TW	153 (38)	13	50	5
TS	8	8	40	7
WPS	19.1	17	95	9
SQ	95	9	15	3
A/C	16	12	35	4

ILLUSTRATION 20—Continued.

▶ 15-YEAR-OLD MALE

ORIGINAL

I was allowed to play in this part of the room all by my self. I enjoyed playing in the room. There was miniature toy furniture and little toy dolls to play with. I set the box on a chair and took the pieces out one by one. After I had enough pieces to start with I began to play. I used the top of the table to play on because I did not want to get my pants dirty.

I took the dresser, table, chair, and cabinet and pretended it was a dinning room. I put the dolls over all over the room and made them look busy. For a while it was fun but then I got tired of it I did not want to tell anyone I was tired because I asked to play here. Well, I guess I'll just have to sit here and play around with these toys until they tell me its time to leave.

ILLUSTRATION 20—Continued.

SCORED

I was allowed to play in this part of the room all by my self. I enjoyed playing in the room. There was miniature toy furniture and little toy dolls to play with. I set the box on a chair and took the pieces out one by one. After I had enough pieces to start with I began to play. I used the top of the table to play on because I did not want to get my pants dirty.

I took the dresser, table, chair, and cabinet and pretended it was a dinning room. I put the dolls over all over the room and made them look busy. For a while it was fun but then I got tired of it. I did not want to tell anyone I was tired because I asked to play here. Well, I guess I'll just have to sit here and play around with those toys until they tell me its time to leave.

	Score	Age Equivalent	Percentile	Stanine
TW	160	17	70	6
TS	11	13	80	7
WPS	14.5	14	45	5
SQ	97	16	50	5
A/C	19	17	60	6

ILLUSTRATION 20—Continued.

▶ 15-YEAR-OLD FEMALE

ORIGINAL

My little brother Jerry was in his room one day playing with some of his toys. These certain toys he was playing with were toy people from a make believe world. The story he told me later about the make believe people is as follows

"There was this little dog who had many owners. A father, some boys and a baby and more. The people were rearranging their furniture in the house when the little dog let out a yelp! The father, boys and even the little baby looked all over for the dog. They could not find him. When they did find him he was running all over the place. Later they noticed that some of the furniture was gone. A couple of years later the people found out that the dog had taken the furniture out the door and one time his tail got caught in the door and he let out the yelp for his little dog friend to come and open the door so he could get his tail out of the door. The dog was setting up a house of his own with his masters furniture.

ILLUSTRATION 20—Continued.

SCORED

My little brother "Jerry" was in his room one day playing with some of his toys. These certain toys he was playing with were toy people from a make believe world. The story he told me later about the make believe people is as follows: "There was this little dog who had many owners a father, some boys and a baby and more. The people were rearranging their furniture in the house when the little dog let out a yelp! The father, boys and even the little baby looked all over for the dog. They could not find him. When they did find him he was running all over the place. Later they noticed that some of the furniture was gone. A couple of years later the people found out that the dog had taken the furniture out the door and one time his tail got caught in the door and he let out the yelp for his little friend to come and open the door so he could get his tail out of the door. The dog was setting up a house of his own with his masters furniture.

	Score	Age Equivalent	Percentile	Stanine
TW	191	17	85	7
TS	12	17	75	7
WPS	15.9	16	65	6
SQ	93	8	5	1
A/C	20	17	60	5

ILLUSTRATION 20—Continued.

▶ **17-YEAR-OLD MALE**

ORIGINAL

Tommy is six years old but is not an ordinary child for he is physically handicapped. The disease he has affects the nervous system and he cannot control his hands or legs completely. The disease as far as we know is incurable but scientists all over the country are searching for a cure to this dread disease. In the picture you see Tommy playing with different toys. It helps Tommy in learning how to control his limbs. The docters have found that this physical therapy has done some good but it is still not a cure. This is where you come in for the docter and scientists need your contribution to carry on their fight against the disease.

ILLUSTRATION 20—Continued.

SCORED

Tommy is six years old but is not an ordinary child for he is physically handicapped the disease he has affects the nervous system and he cannot control his hands or legs completely. The disease as far as we know is incurable but scientist all over the country are searching for a cure to this dread disease. In the picture you see Tommy playing with different toys. It helps Tommy in learning how to control his limbs. The docters have found that this physical therapy has done some good but it is still not a cure. This is where you come in for the docters and scientists need your contribution to carry on their fight against the disease

	Score	Age Equivalent	Percentile	Stanine
TW	108	11	25	4
TS	7	8	40	4
WPS	15.4	17	40	5
SQ	98	17	35	4
A/C	23	17	90	9

ILLUSTRATION 20—Continued.

▶ 17-YEAR-OLD FEMALE

ORIGINAL

The first day of school, and I must admit I was a little nervous about how things would go for me. This was my big day as a kindergarten teacher.

The children began to come in the room with their mothers. At first they were timid and afraid, but as I began to talk to them their were more at home. There was one boy who for some reason caught my attention from the very beginning. As I talked to Johnny and his mother, Mrs. Fielding, I discovery Johnny was a shy quiet boy. When the children went to play with the toys, I noticed most all of the children playing in groups except for Johnny. He sat in one corner with some doll furniture and dolls and began to arrange the furniture, when he looked up and saw the other children in their groups a look came over him like he truely felt left out.

A few weeks passed and with a little prodding Johnny became one of the outgoing people in my class.

ILLUSTRATION 20—Continued.

SCORED

The first day of school, and I must admit I was a little nervous about how things would go for me. \ This was my big day as a kindergarten teacher. \

The children ea began to come in the room with their mothers \ At first they were timid and afraid, but as I began to talk to them they were more at home. \ there was one boy who for some reason caught my attention from the very beginning. \ As I talked to Johnny and his mother, mrs. Fielding, I discovery Johnny was a shy quiet boy. \ When the children went to play with the toys, I noticed most all of the children playing in groups except for Johnny. \ He sat in an corner with some doll furniture and dolls and began to arrange the furniture, \ when he looked up and saw the other children in their groups a look came over him like he truely felt left out. \

A few weeks passed and with a little prodding Johnny became one of the outgoing people in my class. \

	Score	Age Equivalent	Percentile	Stanine
TW	175	17	60	6
TS	10	10	55	5
WPS	17.5	17	70	6
SQ	95	9	15	3
A/C	21	17	70	7

ILLUSTRATION 21.   Illustrative scored stories written by speech defective children.

▶ 7-YEAR-OLD FEMALE

ORIGINAL

SCORED

	Score	Age Equivalent	Percentile	Stanine
TW	19	−7	20	3
TS	3	−7	40	4
WPS	6.3	7	40	5
SQ	66	−7	10	2
A/C	7	7	40	5

ILLUSTRATION 21—Continued.

▶ 9-YEAR-OLD FEMALE

ORIGINAL

The boy is playing with the toy in his house. He have book and game to play with it to. He have ~~so~~ somuch fun with it he like to ~~p lay~~ play with it. He love to ~~play~~ with it.

SCORED

The boy is playing with the toy in his house. He have book and game to play with it to. He have ~~so~~ somuch fun with it he like to ~~p lay~~ play with it. He love to ~~play~~ with it.

	Score	Age Equivalent	Percentile	Stanine
TW	39	7	10	2
TS	5	7	20	3
WPS	7.8	8	25	4
SQ	81	7	5	1
A/C	8	7	20	4

ILLUSTRATION 21—Continued.

▶ 11-YEAR-OLD FEMALE

ORIGINAL

There is a boy playing with a doll. there is some story Books. and a (chure) bas with toys. there is a showe an a shilf. the boy has brown eyes blue suit. and beawn (heary) hary, and he is playing (with) on a table.

SCORED

*There is a boy playing with a doll. \ there is some story Books; and a (chure) bas with toys. \ there is a showe an a shilf. \ the boy has brown eyes blue suit and beawn (heary) hary, \ and he is playing (with) on a table. *

	Score	Age Equivalent	Percentile	Stanine
TW	45	7	5	2
TS	5	7	20	3
WPS	9	8	15	3
SQ	92	8	5	2
A/C	7	7	5	2

(Undue Use of Connectives)

ILLUSTRATION 21—Continued.

▶ **13-YEAR-OLD MALE**

ORIGINAL

A boy is sitting down at a table it looks as though if hes making up a home with tiny dolls In the picture he has five statues of people al guess he supposes to be the Father the Mother children and a table a couch some chairs and other furniture

The boy is wearing a suit and is putting the tiny people in the way he wants to and he even as a dog in the picture

SCORED

A boy is sitting down at a table: it looks as though if hes making up a home with tiny dolls. In the picture he has five statues of people: al guess he supposes to be the Father the Mother children and a table a couch some chairs and other furniture

The boy is wearing a suit and is putting the tiny people in the way he wants to and he even as a dog in the picture

	Score	Age Equivalent	Percentile	Stanine
TW	71 (7)	9	10	2
TS	7	8	35	4
WPS	10.1	10	15	3
SQ	93	9	10	3
A/C	9	8	15	3
(Lists)		(Undue Use of Connectives)		

ILLUSTRATION 22.   Illustrative scored stories written by reading disability children.

▶ **9-YEAR-OLD FEMALE**

ORIGINAL

One day a little boy name allan saw playing whit some toys. Boll house things there are gurls, boy, and mother, and father, and furniture. He had some book, cars, and a Big Ball, and some blocks.

SCORED

One day a little boy name allan saw playing whit some toys : Boll house things there are gurls, boy, and mother, and father, and furniture. He had come book, cars, and a Big Ball and some blocks.

	Score	Age Equivalent	Percentile	Stanine
TW	29 (8)	7	2	1
TS	4	7	10	3
WPS	7.3	8	15	3
SQ	80	7	2	1
A/C	9	7	25	4
	(Lists)			

ILLUSTRATION 22—Continued.

▶ **11-YEAR-OLD FEMALE**

ORIGINAL

In this picture a boy is playing with with plastic toys that look like people and furchair. He is playing on a table with some toys on the selves in back of him. And a couple books. This boy lookes like he is having a lot of fun.

SCORED

In this picture a boy is playing with with plastic toys that look like people and furchair. \ He is playing on a table with some toys on the selves in back of him. And a couple books. \ This boy lookes like he is having a lot of fun. \

	Score	Age Equivalent	Percentile	Stanine
TW	48	7	5	2
TS	4	7	15	3
WPS	12	12	60	5
SQ	85	7	2	1
A/C	8	7	10	3

ILLUSTRATION 22—Continued.

▶ 13-YEAR-OLD MALE

ORIGINAL

This story is about a little boy playing with little toy funter its about a family with a man a women and two boys and al dog and furter uie They were siting down at the table and were eating diner at home and the baby was playing and one ob the boys were playing with the dog and the father wers earing is diner.

The Eend

SCORED

This story is about a little boy playing with little toy funter ᵃ its about a family with a man ? a women [and two boys and al dog] and furter uie They were siting down at the table and were eating diner at home ? and the baby was playing and one ob the boys were playing with the dog and the father wers earing is diner.

The Eend

	Score	Age Equivalent	Percentile	Stanine
TW	58 (6)	8	5	2
TS	4	7	10	3
WPS	14.5	14	60	6
SQ	92	9	5	2
A/C	15	11	25	4

(Run-on Sentences)   (Undue Use of Connectives)

ILLUSTRATION 22—Continued.

▶ 15-YEAR-OLD MALE

ORIGINAL

Tom is a boy but a crazy doy he plays with grils things. An uther doy wood play with boys things not girls things. ~~their is not mutch things to rite~~ When boys smil they should not play with girls things. the tops in the back is the toys that he should play with.

SCORED

Tom is a boy? but a crazy doy?\ the plays with grils? things.\An uther doy wood play with boys? things? not girls? things.\ ~~their is not mutch things to rite~~ When boys smil they should not play with girls things.\ the tops in the back is the toys that he should play with.\

	Score	Age Equivalent	Percentile	Stanine
TW	48	8	5	2
TS	5	8	20	4
WPS	9.6	9	5	2
SQ	90	8	10	2
A/C	23	17	90	8

(Run-on Sentences)

ILLUSTRATION 23.   Scored illustrative stories written by socially-emotionally disturbed children.

▶ **7-YEAR-OLD MALE**

ORIGINAL

There wasaboy
howewas playing
Whithe boles with
was vare Silly to me,

SCORED

There wasaboy
howewas playing
Whithe boles, with
was vare Silly to me.

	Score	Age Equivalent	Percentile	Stanine
TW	15	−7	40	5
TS	2	−7	45	5
WPS	7.5	8	75	6
SQ	89	8	40	5
A/C	7	7	60	6

ILLUSTRATION 23—Continued.

▶ 9-YEAR-OLD MALE

ORIGINAL

He play in the house Toy
He is got Book
He got a car
He gota Toy box

SCORED

He play in the house toy
He is got Book
He got a car
He gota toy box

	Score	Age Equivalent	Percentile	Stanine
TW	19	7	5	1
TS	4	7	15	3
WPS	4.8	—7	2	1
SQ	62	—7	2	1
A/C	7	7	20	4

ILLUSTRATION 23—Continued.

▶ 11-YEAR-OLD MALE

ORIGINAL

The boy is play house and he put every Body the table and he thave a good time

SCORED

The boy is play^E house and he put every Body, the table and he ^thave^E a good time ^P

	Score	Age Equivalent	Percentile	Stanine
TW	18	7	2	1
TS	2	−7	5	2
WPS	9	9	20	3
SQ	82	7	2	1
A/C	8	7	20	4

ILLUSTRATION 23—Continued.

▶ 13-YEAR-OLD MALE

ORIGINAL

There was a boy who had a lot of
toys and he made a dineingroon
out of doll house finuter and popll
he also had sone book and a ball
this boy was very happy because
he was content with his toys
he had a lot of fun playing with
his toys.

SCORED

There was a boy who had a lot of
toys.ᴾ\and he made a dineingroon
out of doll house finuter and popllᴾ\
he also had sone bookᴱ; and a ball\
this boy was very happy because
he was content with his toys\
he had a lot of fun playing with
his toys.\

	Score	Age Equivalent	Percentile	Stanine
TW	53	8	5	2
TS	4	7	10	3
WPS	14	13	55	5
SQ	96	11	30	4
A/C	15	11	25	4

(Run-on Sentences)

ILLUSTRATION 23—Continued.

▶ **15-YEAR-OLD MALE**

ORIGINAL

> A boy is playing with some doll house toys he is seting them up on the table the mother is playing the boy is playing with the dog the girl is sitting at the table the father is going to the table this picture shows a boy having fun with his toys

SCORED

> A boy is playing with some doll house toys \ he is seting them up on the table \ the mother is playing \ the boy is playing with the dog \ the girl is sitting at the table \ the father is going to the table \ this picture shows a boy having fun with his toys \

	Score	Age Equivalent	Percentile	Stanine
TW	52	8	5	2
TS	7	8	55	5
WPS	7.5	8	2	1
SQ	91	9	10	2
A/C	12	9	15	3

(Run-on Sentences)

ILLUSTRATION 24. Scored illustrative stories written by educable
mentally retarded children.

▶ **9-YEAR-OLD FEMALE**

ORIGINAL

an boy was playe wits his toy

SCORED

an boy was playe wits his toy

	Score	Age Equivalent	Percentile	Stanine
TW	7	−7	2	1
TS	1	−7	2	1
WPS	7	7	15	3
SQ	82	7	5	1
A/C	7	7	10	3

ILLUSTRATION 24—Continued.

▶ 11-YEAR-OLD MALE

ORIGINAL

There is a boy and
some toys he is haveing
fun there is some books
to and a car.

SCORED

There is a boy and
some toys. he is haveing
fun. there is some books.
to and a car.

	Score	Age Equivalent	Percentile	Stanine
TW	19	7	2	1
TS	3	7	5	2
WPS	6.3	7	2	1
SQ	87	8	5	2
A/C	8	7	20	4

(Run-on Sentences)

ILLUSTRATION 24—Continued.

▶ 13-YEAR-OLD MALE

ORIGINAL

The boy was playing a game with toys. I saw the father and the dog the baby was in a car. I saw a box of toys on a chair.

SCORED

*The boy was playing a game with toys. \ I saw the father and the dog the baby was in a car. \ I saw a box of toys on a chair. *

	Score	Age Equivalent	Percentile	Stanine
TW	30	7	2	1
TS	4	7	10	3
WPS	7.5	8	2	1
SQ	97	13	40	4
A/C	7	7	5	2

(Run-on Sentences)

ILLUSTRATION 24—Continued.

▶ 15-YEAR-OLD MALE

ORIGINAL

the boy is ~~shit~~ sit at a teabel
boy and and gvild out of plastic
the by is playing house with chaee
play furniture and in his roon
he has a car book ball that my
storry

SCORED

	Score	Age Equivalent	Percentile	Stanine
TW	36	8	2	1
TS	5	8	5	4
WPS	7.2	7	2	1
SQ	77	−7	2	1
A/C	7	7	5	2

ILLUSTRATION 25. Scored illustrative stories written by deaf children.

▶ **7-YEAR-OLD FEMALE**

ORIGINAL

I see four books a car. I see two chirs.

I see sleepy box milk. Mother man.

and girl baby boy

SCORED

I see four books, a car. I see two chirs.

I see, sleepy box, milk. Mother man

and girl baby. boy.

	Score	Age Equivalent	Percentile	Stanine
TW	16 (5)	−7	15	3
TS	3	−7	40	4
WPS	5.3	7	30	4
SQ	66	−7	10	2
A/C	3	−7	5	2

(Lists)

ILLUSTRATION 25—Continued.

▶ 9-YEAR-OLD MALE

ORIGINAL

1) The girl is on chair.
2) The box is in box.
3) The boy like a play.
4) The man is walking.
5) The light is read book.
6) The book is words.
7) The dog is walked the town
8) The car is go to town.

SCORED

1) The girl is on chair.
2) The box is in box.
3) The boy like a play.
4) The man is walking.
5) The light is read book.
6) The book is words.
7) The dog is walked the town
8) The car is go to town.

	Score	Age Equivalent	Percentile	Stanine
TW	40	8	10	2
TS	8	9	55	6
WPS	5	−7	2	1
SQ	69	−7	2	1
A/C	10	8	40	4

ILLUSTRATION 25—Continued.

▶ 11-YEAR-OLD MALE

ORIGINAL

A boy learn to nice the house. He can to try help her house. He put on the tables with something to use. He can to sweep the floor I can to learn the house. I think so a boy wash the dishes every day. a boy's mother is nice to her house.

SCORED

A boy learn to (nice) the house. \ He can to try help her house. \ He put on the tables with (something to use). \ He can to sweep the floor I can to learn the house. \ I think so a boy wash the dishes every day. \ a boy's mother is nice to her house. \

	Score	Age Equivalent	Percentile	Stanine
TW	54	8	15	3
TS	7	8	35	4
WPS	7.7	8	10	2
SQ	65	−7	2	1
A/C	9	8	25	4

ILLUSTRATION 25—Continued.

▶ 13-YEAR-OLD FEMALE

ORIGINAL

Ireey is a little boy. Doe like to play game.

Ireey like to read other story and he like best of all was play home.

Ireep think play people was real plays. He like to tell me soom about how to live.

He has a car name biby.

Biby drive to the home were the peopl live.

The peopl will go soon plase.

Ireey peopl has a dog name lizzy. Lizzy is a lizzy dog he is brown & white.

ILLUSTRATION 25—Continued.

SCORED

Jeey is a little boy. We like to play games. Jeey like to read other storys and he like best of all was play home. Jeep think play people was real plays. He like to tell me soom about how to live. He has a ear name biby. Biby drive to the home were the peopl live. The peopl will go soon place. Jeey peopl has a dog name lizzy. Lizzy is a lizzy dog he is brown a white.

	Score	Age Equivalent	Percentile	Stanine
TW	80	8	20	3
TS	10	9	55	5
WPS	8	8	2	1
SQ	78	−7	2	1
A/C	10	8	15	3

ILLUSTRATION 25—Continued.

▶ 15-YEAR-OLD MALE

ORIGINAL

"Jimmy's Toy Things"

Jimmy had some toy things and he played with the toy things and he put the toy thing on the table and he put the toy girl on the chair and the toy mother tried to care the toy baby and the toy boy tried to pet the toy dog and the toy boy stood on the floor near the closet and Jim enjoyed to play with the toy things and he held the chair up his hand.

The books, toy car, ball and shoe house, setted on the closet.

ILLUSTRATION 25—Continued.

SCORED

"Jimmy's Toy Things"

Jimmy had some toy things, and he played with the toy things, and he put the toy thing on the table, and he put the toy girl on the chair and the toy mother tried to care the toy baby and the toy boy tried to pet the toy dog and the toy boy stood on the floor near the closet and Jim enjoyed to play with the toy things and he hold the chair up his hand.

The books, toy car, ball and shoe house, setted on the closet.

	Score	Age Equivalent	Percentile	Stanine
TW	90	10	25	4
TS	10	11	75	7
WPS	9	9	5	2
SQ	83	7	2	1
A/C	13	9	20	3

(Run-on Sentences)

ILLUSTRATION 25—Continued.

▶ 17-YEAR-OLD MALE

ORIGINAL

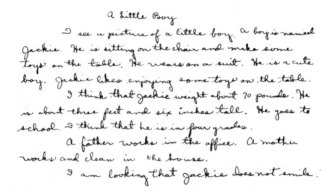

A Little Boy

    I see a picture of a little boy. A boy is named Jackie. He is sitting on the chair and make some toys on the table. He wears on a suit. He is a cute boy. Jackie likes enjoying some toys on the table.

    I think that Jackie weight about 70 pounds. He is about three feet and six inches tall. He goes to school. I think that he is in four grades.

    A father works in the office. A mother works and clean in the house.

    I am looking that Jackie does not smile.

SCORED

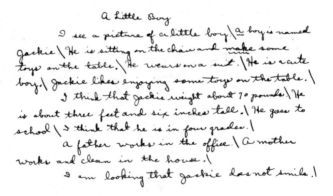

A Little Boy

    I see a picture of a little boy. \ A boy is named Jackie. \ He is sitting on the chair and make some toys on the table. \ He wears on a suit. \ He is a cute boy. \ Jackie likes enjoying some toys on the table. \

    I think that Jackie weight about 70 pounds. \ He is about three feet and six inches tall. \ He goes to school \ I think that he is in four grades. \

    A father works in the office. \ A mother works and clean in the house. \

    I am looking that Jackie does not smile. \

	Score	Age Equivalent	Percentile	Stanine
TW	95	10	20	3
TS	13	17	70	6
WPS	7.3	7	2	1
SQ	92	9	10	2
A/C	17	15	15	3

Abstract-Concrete

THE RANGE OF SCORES for the Abstract-Concrete Scale is from 0 to 25. To provide additional illustrations two stories representative of each score have been included in the Scoring Guide. These should be studied carefully.

To further portray the diagnostic implications of this Scale, the writer of each story has been identified. Because children within each of the handicapped groups rarely attain high scores, the stories illustrating the upper levels were written by normal children. To date we have not encountered an individual who attained a score of 25; hence, these stories were improvised.

LEVEL I: MEANINGLESS LANGUAGE

Score 0

Mentally Retarded: 9-year-old male

Look Look oh oh oh Come and see Dick
Dick

Age Equivalent	0
Percentile	0
Stanine	0

Mentally Retarded: 9-year-old male

P A l o E b L F N M K H U

Age Equivalent	0
Percentile	0
Stanine	0

LEVEL II: CONCRETE-DESCRIPTIVE

Score 1

Mentally Retarded: 11-year-old male

man car tren dog ball bolk baby girl boy brx

Age Equivalent	−7
Percentile	2
Stanine	1

Mentally Retarded: 11-year-old male

car   boy

Age Equivalent	−7
Percentile	2
Stanine	1

Score 2

Normal: 7-year-old male

books a box bol toys
shoe

Age Equivalent	−7
Percentile	10
Stanine	2

Speech Defective: 7-year-old male

Boy Toys kane dog man

Age Equivalent	7
Percentile	10
Stanine	2

Score 3

Speech Defective: 7-year-old male

I see a doll on the table?
A doll father is on the table.
I see a doll baby?
I see a chair?
I see a big boy?

Age Equivalent	−7
Percentile	15
Stanine	3

Mentally Retarded: 11-year-old male

I see a Boy
I see a DoG
I see a quilt
I see a Book
I see a a

Age Equivalent	−7
Percentile	2
Stanine	1

Score 4

Normal: 7-year-old female

He has toys.
There are books on the shelf.

Age Equivalent	−7
Percentile	10
Stanine	2

Deaf: 7-year-old female

I see books. I see car. I see furnitute. I see ball.

Age Equivalent	−7
Percentile	10
Stanine	2

Score 5

Speech Defective: 11-year-old male

In this story I can see a boy. With some toys. He has some books a car
and a shoe. The toys look like dogs, peple and furture.

Age Equivalent	−7
Percentile	2
Stanine	1

Reading Disability: 7-year-old female

I saw a boy with his dog. He has a box of toy.

Age Equivalent	−7
Percentile	10
Stanine	3

Score 6

Reading Disability: 9-year-old female

The littl a hole box of was toys and nany nore He has a doll and four stoy book and a toys man and toys dog and four Toys car and for toys baby doll a Toys tale and chairs a toys and a toys ball

Age Equivalent	−7
Percentile	5
Stanine	2

Speech Defective: 9-year-old male

The toy Rome

Once that was a boy he had many toy he had a mans made of wood and woman and child he had a lot of books in the toy rome he had many many toy

Age Equivalent	7
Percentile	5
Stanine	3

LEVEL III: CONCRETE-IMAGINATIVE

Score 7

Normal: 9-year-old male

A boy in the picher is playing with a doll house and he picked up a girl doll. In the back ground there is some books and a car, with a tree or a ring thing. And there is a shose house or a thing we put blocks we put in it. The little boy has brown hari. And a round ball in the picher with a glay coat or jachte. And has brown eyes. And a table with a dog and a man.

Age Equivalent	7
Percentile	20
Stanine	4

Normal: 7-year-old female

There was a little boy.
He played with toys all day.
The toys was in a box.
There was a show in the house.

Age Equivalent	7
Percentile	40
Stanine	5

Score 8

Speech Defective: 7-year-old male

A boy is playing alone with his toys. He does not look happy. The boy is dressed up. He looks like he is going some where. There is a clock on the shelf. There is a car on the shelf. There is also a book named words.

Age Equivalent	7
Percentile	75
Stanine	7

Speech Defective: 7-year-old male

The boy is play with his toy and he is have lots of fun.

Age Equivalent	7
Percentile	75
Stanine	7

Score 9

Normal: 7-year-old female

A boy is playing with his toys. There is a man wife and children. There is some more toys on the chair   There are books on the shef.

Age Equivalent	7
Percentile	75
Stanine	7

Normal: 7-year-old female

A little boy is playing a game that has a man and a girl. Then it has a boy a father and a mother.

Age Equivalent	7
Percentile	75
Stanine	7

Score 10

Normal: 9-year-old male

Toys

Will it looks like he is playing with toys. He looks like he is making a house with furniture of grils. On the shelf there is some books and a car a shoe. On the chair there is a box of toys. He is putting gril at a table and there is a man walking to the table. Will there is a dog and a man. He has a chair in his hand. He has a suit coat on he has black hair. Will there is a bouling ball on the shelf. There is a table with dishes and glasses. He is going to make a house.

That is the End

Age Equivalent	8
Percentile	40
Stanine	4

Speech Defective: 11-year-old female

He has ben play with toys to day   he sat the gril down on the chire   she was goeat   eat her denner.

Age Equivalent	8
Percentile	15
Stanine	3

Score 11

Normal: 9-year-old female

Jim's Toys

One day a little boy had been playing with a farm set. He was playing with cowboys. Their were books on the shelf. Some cowboys were standing up on the table. Their were some games on the shelf. Their is a little pole on the shelf with some round things on it. Jim was sitting on a chair and their was another chair pulled out. On the shelf their was a car.

On one of the chair their was a big box with toys in the big box. Their was a cowboy trying to cauth a dog. Their were serrial chairs on the table also. Their was a big shoe on the table. The shoe was a big shoe and it was black and it was also white.

The little boy hair was black. Their was a white thing on the table. Their was a black thing also. It look like a fence.

Age Equivalent	**8**
Percentile	**40**
Stanine	**3**

Normal: 9-year-old female

Little Man in the Corner

I was a little boy and I lived in a big white house. I had freacles and brown hair.

I was playing on the kitchen table, with my toys. I was playing with plastic toys: I had a man, wife, baby, dog, table, chest, dishes, and food. On my shelf I had a book, it was the book of Words. I had many other toys too!

I was playing that a little boy was eating lunch. I was just setting him down. He had roast beef and gravy for lunch! Just think Roast Beef for lunch!

That boy must have been lucky. His father was chasing the dog, and the baby was playing with her toys.

The End

Age Equivalent	**8**
Percentile	**40**
Stanine	**3**

Score 12

Normal: 9-year-old female

I see a boy at a table with a playhouse. He is playing dolls and furachure. Their are plats with food on the table. A boy and a dog are playing. The mother is caring for baby. The father is walking to the table to have lunch. the little boy is putting a doll in a chair.

The End

Age Equivalent	**8**
Percentile	**50**
Stanine	**5**

Normal: 9-year-old male

The Boy and His Toys

The little boy was playing with his toy people.

There were five people and one dog.

One girl was eating her lunch. A boy was playing with the dog. Another boy was playing with the baby. The father was walking around the room. There was a chair, a desk and a table.

He had a car on the cuborad. He had someother toys 'n the box

Age Equivalent	**9**
Percentile	**50**
Stanine	**5**

LEVEL IV: ABSTRACT-DESCRIPTIVE

Score 13

Reading Disability: 9-year-old male

I see a boy whit some little people and he well play house and well read a book mame words and we will go to the house and then he will go and play some more of the house.

Age Equivalent	**9**
Percentile	**55**
Stanine	**5**

Reading Disability: 13-year-old male

This is a story about a boy in a room.

He had meney thing to play with, pictures to look at, book read, and toy to play with.

He always sets up a little room on a table. He has dolls in it, tables, chears, and meney other peaces of furnature. And when he is all throw he starts to make a nother room. By the end of the day he may have put to-gether about ten room for a little dool house.

Age Equivalent	9
Percentile	20
Stanine	3

Score 14

Normal: 11-year-old male

The Makeup Store

This boy's name is Roger. He is playing house. He is putting Jean, Bob, Larry, and Billy at the table to eat denner. After denner Billy went for a walk to the park with his dog. When Billy came home he saw Larry had ate all the cookies. Mother and Roger were in bed slepping. Soon it was time for sapper. Jean helped mother set the table. When sapper was ready thay all sat down an ate sapper an wasded the ders and went to bed.

Age Equivalent	10
Percentile	40
Stanine	5

Normal: 9-year-old male

A Bise Home

It is a boy seting up peaple, furnecher, Peter is playing with his dog. Sally is siting at the table. Mother is getting tim out of the stroler. Father is coming home from work, Father kises mother and eats suppe so dos Peter, Sally and Mother

Age Equivalent	**10**
Percentile	**55**
Stanine	**5**

Score 15

Normal: 11-year-old female

Playing Alone with Imagination

This is a picture showing a boy and his toys. He is setting a room in a home out of his toy furniture. He has a table setting ready for a family of plastic dolls. It shows an infant in a stroller holding his hands to his mother. A man that has pulled out a chair for a lady. Their is boy stooping over and following a dog. He is consentrating where to place a chair. His imagination is on a home. It is a dining room, perhaps like his. Really imagination is important to him now, its his friend

Age Equivalent	**10**
Percentile	**35**
Stanine	**4**

Speech Defective: 11-year-old male

This is a boy doll furnichure he has then in dinning room sitting down for dinner. He is putting the girl in her seet mother is getting the baby.

Age Equivalent	**11**
Percentile	**40**
Stanine	**5**

Score 16

Normal: 9-year-old male

The Boy and His Toys

The boy is in a nursery. He is making a sean. He has the little girl eating her dinner. Mother is trying to make the baby to come to her. The little boy is playing with his little dog. Father got up from his chair and went to the dinner table. Baby finally got out of his storrel and into his chair. And they all got up to the table and ate. And that is the end.

Age Equivalent	**12**
Percentile	**65**
Stanine	**6**

Normal: 13-year-old male

A Young Boy At Work

This looks like a boy of five or six. He looks like he would be play with some kind of they look like they are toys that any nomal child would play with. He is all dressed up like he came back from church or some place such as church. He had little toy men and looks like he might be playing house or something of the sort. He also looks like he is in the kitchen play on the kitchen table. He has other toys near the table in a box on the chair to the left of the table. He is holding a chair in his hand as if he is going to put it some place on the table. He had a immmpression on his face that he is content He looks as if he is in first grade because of all the work books that have new words in them. He has some toys and some book on a self in back of him. There are some toy women an chairs and a toy table and stuff like that in the picture

Age Equivalent	**12**
Percentile	**35**
Stanine	**4**

Score 17

Normal: 9-year-old female

My Doll House

This little boy is having fun making a little doll house. He has a big box of furniture and toy dolls. He is making it for a friend who is in the hospital. He is a good friend to everyone. His mother helps the poor people. His father is a judge. This little boy is in second grade. He's making a scene of his home He saves little things like this. He said he thinks it is fun. And his mothey and father say,

It's Your little Doll House

The
End

Age Equivalent	13
Percentile	98
Stanine	9

Normal: 9-year-old male

One time there was a boy named John. He was five years old. He was playing at his friends house. His friends names wer David and Doug. They were bothe five years old to. They wer playing with some toys. They wer playing in David's room. The toys were David's. They were called Tinker Toyes. They were having fun until There friend came in he was nine years old. He wanted them to let him play he played. And they had lots of fun.

The End

Age Equivalent	14
Percentile	70
Stanine	6

LEVEL V: ABSTRACT-IMAGINATIVE

Score 18

Normal: 9-year-old female

They Are Real Too!

"My birthday," thought Jimmy Crape "I'm 5 years old at last." Then he heard mother and daddy say: "Happy birthday son." Now it's time for breakfast. Some waffles please and pass the surup was all Jimmy said. He wanted his present! After breakfast father said, come down to the basement. "There's a surprise waiting." Jimmy hurried down. Then his face drooped. I don't see anything but a carton full of broken toys, Jimmy wailed. Those toys aren't broken, Jimmy. They are pieces of a doll house that you can snap together. Here, like this. Now, the house is finished you can make the furniture and family too. Then you can play house. Thank you daddy and mommy Jimmy said with feeling. Then he sat down and played with the toys.

Age Equivalent	14
Percentile	75
Stanine	7

Normal: 9-year-old male

One day I went down to the basment to play with my dolls. I took the box off the cabinet and emptied it. I pretended that I was a father and I had a family. And then I put my furniture where I wanted it. My son was riding a bike. I just got home from work and dinner was on the table. So I went to the head of the table and we ate dinner.

But one thing is wrong you do not have any food for my dog.

Age Equivalent	16
Percentile	80
Stanine	7

Score 19

Normal: 11-year-old male

Perry is sitting in his playroom with all his toys. Perry has his suit on. He has a toy living room set. One of the toy boys has a dog with him. Perry is having fun. He had just come home from church. Perry liked his toy boys and girls very much.

Perry had just got his toy set three months before for his birthday. He had another huge box of toys. He liked his toy set more than any other toy he had. He decided to read one of his books. The book that Perry wanted to read was "The Golden Book of the World. After Perry read part of his book he wanted to do something else. Perry couldn't decide what to do then. Finally he decided to play with his little blue car. After a little while his mother called him for supper. After supper Perry played with his toys. At nine o'clock he washed and went to bed.

Age Equivalent	17
Percentile	90
Stanine	7

Normal: 11-year-old male

One day John Peters was at school. He was setting up a doll house. He had the table set for dinner. There were five people and one dog. John was putting a girl down at the table. He had furniture around. He had a lot more people and pieces of furniture in a box beside him.

It took him a hour to set up all the people and pieces of furniture. He went to ask the teacher to see it. It was very hot in the room so the windows were open. When he went in the door a sudden gust of wind shot through the windows. When he got to the place where the set up was it was all bloun down.

Age Equivalent	17
Percentile	80
Stanine	8

Score 20

Normal: 13-year-old male

Mental Health

This is the story of a boy who was born with a damaged brain. When he was five his parents put him in a clinic for mentally retarded children. Here he was taught to create things with his hands and to use simple machines.

As he grew he learned to do things he liked better and soon became very skillful in these things. The boy in the picture may some day be a furniture arranger.

When he became old enough he took Industrial Arts and was very good in leatherwork. After some time he began selling his work and is earning enough money to support himself.

Age Equivalent	**17**
Percentile	**85**
Stanine	**7**

Normal: 13-year-old male

Little children have very imaginative minds as we all know. A Joe Schmo believs that he can make dolls come to life and maybe this is true because just a few months ago some very strange things were seen. One of Joe's freinds saw him pour some kind of chemical on a little wooden doll. He wasn't sure but he thought he saw the doll move. Later many huge 75 feet high wooden structures that resembled people were seen all over town. These monsters were controled by a little swith in the *Little Golden Book of Words.*

Joe enlarge a plastic car to the height of 74 feet. Little Joe later woke up to find that he gladly had just been dreeming.

Age Equivalent	**17**
Percentile	**85**
Stanine	**7**

Score 21

Normal: 11-year-old female

One day Jim was playing with his toys. His Friend Bob rang the bell. Jim was so busy with his toys that he didn't hear the bell. Then he herd his mother say, "Jim, Bob is at the door and wants to play with you."

"All right send him in." screamed Jim. through the doors raced Bob, but Jim was too busy playing with his toys to notice anything.

Bob said, "Aren't you even going to say hello to me, Jim." But there was know answer. So Bob sat there for about a half in hour, But still no answer came from Jim. Bob became unpatint, and screamed, "You and your toys that's all you care about." this was true Jim had no scocell life. All he did was play with his toys. Then Bob push Jim's toys off the table and ran out. Most of the toys were brocken. Jim begain to cry. When his walked in.

"Why don't you apolagies to him," she said."

"But it was his falt," Jim replied.

"Think it over it was really both you falts wasn't it." Then his mother left and he thought it over. He decided to make up with him.

Jim was half way out the door when Bob came in. Bob replied, "I came to apolishgise."

"I was just going over to your house to appolisize. After that the two boys made up and they were friends.

Age Equivalent	+17
Percentile	90
Stanine	8

Normal: 9-year-old male

Once upon a time there was little boy who was crippled but he was very smart and could do many things with his hands.

His mother and father were poor and couldn't pay for his operation.

This boy was always trying to think of a way he could raise the money to pay for the operation. One day he finally thought of a way he could help pay for it. He asked his father to go out side and get a few pieces of wood and a certain kind of rock. His father brought in the wood and the rock. Next he asked his father to bring him a knife. He sharpend the knife on the rock and began to carve the wood his father brought. He carved little people and cars and other things. Next his father sold them and with the other money they had saved up they had enough money to pay for the operation.

He had and payed for his operation and he was the happiest boy in the world

Age Equivalent	**+17**
Percentile	**98**
Stanine	**9**

Score 22

Normal: 11-year-old female

Tommy was at home. He was in the play room playing with his sisters doll house. He was having fun too. Tommy sat a woman in a chair. Tommy didn't like her there so he put her on the couch. He thought she looked more comfortable there. Tommy was pretending that this family came for a visit at the Jones. They were staying here for Christmas. The people brought their little boy, who is one year old along. They wanted their little boy to have a nice Christmas. Days past and it was getting nearer to Christmas. On Christmas Eve they had some friends over and their friends stayed till 3 o'clock. The Jones and their visitors went to bed. In the morning there were presents. Finally it was time for the visitors to start back. They were glad their visitors had a nice Christmas.

Age Equivalent	**+17**
Percentile	**95**
Stanine	**8**

Normal: 11-year-old male

One day Bobby Smith was sitting in his playroom looking out the window in dismay. It was raining, and Bobby wanted something to do, but it was easy to see he couldn't go out.

While he was sitting there he was thinking that he would like to be the host of a party. He just sat there thinking for about five minutes and began to get sleepy. Then he remembered the little people that were in his sisters dollhouse. Before he new it he was back with all of the furniture and people.

Then all of a sudden he was in his dress suit. All of the people were dancing and drinking punch and eating on the treats that were placed on the table. One of the little men was talking to Bobby. He was talking about such an interesting subject that he never noticed some of the little men climb off the table.

While he was talking the little men climbed on his desk and crawled in his little safe. They took all the money with them.

Soon Bobby decided to get his money and show the man how rich he was. The little men who robbed the safe had put a bomb in the safe so if Bobby opened it it would go off. Bobby started to turn the dial on the safe to the first number of the combination. He was about on the last one when he heard his mother call.

Then Bobby woke up. It was all a dream and it had stopped raining. He then decided to go out and play.

Age Equivalent	+17
Percentile	95
Stanine	9

Score 23

Normal: 11-year-old male

Kindergarten is the place for little kids from ages 5 to 6. There you can learn some numbers and how to print your name. The little ones enjoy playing games and working with clay. Sometimes you can send boys and girls to kindergarten for $3 a week. They supply the crayons and books, scissors, paper, and toys. The boys and girls will really like kindergarten. It also gives mother a chance to get her work done. It will last maybe all morning or a couple hours in the afternoon.

The children might also get a glass of fruit juice and some cookies. Kindergarten also helps children learn manners and associate with other children.

The End

Age Equivalent	+17
Percentile	95
Stanine	8

Normal: 13-year-old female

Ronnie Monroe was one of those people who are among the unfortunate ones. He was born with polio but he is trying to make the best of it. He learns new things everyday. This picture shows his learnings. He has learned how normal people live and is striving to become one of them. He practices walking up and down stairs, walking without crutches, and exercising his arms. As you see he has already learned how to move his arms without trouble. He has learned to walk without crutches, and someday this little boy will walk and run with the wind just like other people. What does it take? Courage and determination. He is a small boy considering the other ones just like him. But so many of us don't realize how lucky we are until we see someone like Ronnie or a million others just like him.

These children never have had a home life but they play with such toys as the little boy in the picture is playing with. In this way he learns how other people live and their home life.

Age Equivalent	+17
Percentile	98
Stanine	9

Score 24

Normal: 17-year-old female

Once upon a time there lived a family of four, their nurse, and their dog on a table in the playroom of a huge doll. They lived in a world of three dimensions, and their knowledge of the world in which they lived extended to a strong, but proof-less belief in an inexorable, omnipotent, and omnipresent force they called "God." They lived, laughed, and loved, content enough to carry on with the mundane actions of living, such as eating, sleeping, and playing; yet they were forever haunted by a feeling of predestination and sometimes dissatisfaction with the knowledge of their little universe. They were actually blind to anything beyond the universe of their comprehension.

Without, the doll played childishly with the family. Though young, he was somewhat aware of his dimensional superiority to these toys. They were his, and their actions were determined by his young whim. Later, he would leave the toys and move into the mature dimensions of his own universe. This too, was only what existed within his comprehension. But this was truth.

Age Equivalent	+17
Percentile	95
Stanine	9

Normal: 17-year-old female

This is a picture of my little brother. He always plays with my doll house toys. He seems to like to play with people and move them around. He told me about a dream he had the other night. He started out playing with toy dolls, but suddenly they came alive. They grew to his size and began to act exactly as humans—disregarding each other, being discourteous and thinking themselves geniuses. Now, if you knew my brother you would know that he doesn't like to be ignored. He wants everyone only looking after him. So he yelled loudly, "There will be a nuclear attack and only I can save you." Of course upon the words "nuclear attack" everyone went into hysteria and, of course, prayer. But my brother shouted, "Forget your God! If he had the power to create it, man now has the power to destroy it, and so is his equal." The people of course were so confused that they would have accepted anything even this faulty logic. The people then clustered at his feet and begged to be saved, and he again had them in his power as he wished.

But then a person, who stilled retained some control over himself yelled,

"But can you recreate the world once it is destroyed?" Luckily my brother woke up at this point, for he would not know what to do.

Age Equivalent	+17
Percentile	95
Stanine	9

Score 25

Improvised

The giant peered down from his lofty height and spied a group of midgets on the plateau in front of him. A flick of the finger would remove the lot of them from his sight. Why not? They had been a lot of bother to him, almost always under foot or cluttering his ambitious plans in some manner. Often they had been a source of friction between him and the super-giants whose presence could mean trouble to him. Lurking midgets like to trip supergiants and cause sore vexations. After these reflections, the giant reconsidered. He didn't want to incur the wrath of the supergiants nor did he wish to be snared by the midgets. The better part of wisdom, he thought, lay in caution.

Improvised

Boy had been asked to demonstrate his budding design talents in the local school exhibits. Boy was an able lad.

In the first exhibit Boy constructed a flashy scene which he thought would impress the visitors. Many people came to Boy's table but left feeling he was a charlatan. In the second exhibit Boy constructed an even more elaborate scene. Many people stopped to see it but word was getting around that his work was phony and irrelevant. Boy tried a different approach for Exhibit Three. This time only a few came and went away equally unimpressed.

Boy decided it was time to do something really significant. Up out of his depths he created the scene most essential to his very being. Here was surely the culmination of Boy's talents expressed in the best of all possible ways. It was in the last exhibit, but no one came to see it. Despite his disappointment, he knew his life would now be different.

Use of Record Form

THE RECORD FORM provides a means whereby pertinent background information and the five scores from the Picture Story Language Test can be recorded and computed. As shown below, the first page permits a summary of these scores so they can be analyzed diagnostically. In the case of Billy, we note that each of the scores—Age Equivalent, Percentile and Stanine—shows him to be seriously deficient in all aspects of written language. Though the Age Equivalents do not vary substantially the Percentile and Stanine scores reveal that his best performance is on Total Sentences and on Abstract-Concrete, whereas his poorest performance is on Syntax. Billy will require considerable assistance so far as remedial training and special education are concerned. However, his greatest need is for improvement in Syntax and in expressive language, as manifested by the scores for Total Words and Words per Sentence. Ideation—content and meaning—appears to be above his level of ability expressively. It is in judgments, that is, in clinical interpretations such as these, that the summary of the test scores can be of greatest benefit.

After the scores have been derived for Productivity and for Abstract-Concrete, they are recorded on page two. Space is also provided for indicating the level of Abstract-Concrete ideation attained. Page three comprises the procedures necessary for recording and computing the Syntax Quotient. These procedures make it possible to ascertain the various types of scores that are useful in studying both children and adults. For example, Billy's scores show that his errors are: Word Usage, 22; Word Ending, 1⅓; Punctuation, ⅓—his Total Error score is 23⅔ (one point for each Word Usage error and ⅓ point for each of the Word Ending and Punctuation errors). It is obvious that Billy's low Syntax score can be attributed to his inferior facility in Word Usage.

Billy's performance can be analyzed further. From the Error Type scores we note that his difficulty includes all types of errors—Additions, Omissions, Substitutions and Word Order. Nevertheless, his greatest problem is Omissions. Of his 22 errors in Word Usage, 10 were caused by the omission of necessary words. The remaining 12 were distributed as follows: 3 Addition, 3 Substitution, 6 Word Order. When total scores are computed for Error Types we find: Additions, 3; Omissions, 11, Substitutions, 3⅔: Word Order, 6.

The remainder of the computations on page three are used in deriving the Syntax Quotient. *Number of Words* is added to *Total Omissions* to obtain the *Total Unit*. Then *Total Errors* is subtracted to obtain the *Total Correct*. The *Syntax Quotient* is found by dividing *Total Correct* by *Total Unit;* Billy's Syntax Quotient is 59.

Page *four* allows for the recording of special errors. These are useful when planning remedial education. The total findings and interpretations should be discussed under *Examiner's Comments*—discussion such as given above would appear here.

It is important that all of the scores be derived and recorded. Only when all of the data have been obtained can best interpretation be made.

ORIGINAL

CORRECTED

A boy played on his living room table.
He had a box of toys on a chair.
He had a girl doll in a chair.
He had a boy doll playing with a dog.
He had the family eating lunch at the table.
He had a mother doll pushing the baby in the buggy.

RECORD FORM
PICTURE STORY LANGUAGE TEST

NAME _Billy_   Sex _M_   Date _1964_ _5_ _10_
                                                   Year   Month   Day

Residence _2 Oak Street, Albion_   Born _1953_ _3_ _6_
                                                   Year   Month   Day

School _Brown_   Age _11_ _2_ _4_
                                                   Years   Months   Days

Parents _John and Alice_   Siblings _Brother, 13 yrs._

Occupation _Farmer_   Descent _American_

Family Physician _Dr. X_   Referred by _School_

I.Q. _112_   Grade _5_   Reading Scores _3rd grade_

SUMMARY OF SCORES

	Raw Score	Age Equivalent	Percentile	Stanine
PRODUCTIVITY Total Words	47	8	10	3
Total Sentences	6	8	27	4
Words per Sentence	7.83	8	10	2
SYNTAX QUOTIENT	59	−7	−2	1
ABSTRACT-CONCRETE	12	9	35	4

DIAGNOSTIC CLASSIFICATION: _Learning Disability-Dyslexia_

PRODUCTIVITY	Raw Score	Age Equivalent	Percentile	Stanine
TOTAL WORDS (TW)	47	8	10	3
TOTAL SENTENCES (TS)	6	8	27	4
WORDS PER SENTENCE (WPS) = $\frac{TW}{TS}$	7.83	8	10	2

ABSTRACT-CONCRETE	Level Attained	Raw Score	Age Equivalent	Percentile	Stanine
LEVEL I: MEANINGLESS-LANGUAGE		12	—7	35	4
LEVEL II: CONCRETE-DESCRIPTIVE					
LEVEL III: CONCRETE-IMAGINATIVE	✓				
LEVEL IV: ABSTRACT-DESCRIPTIVE					
LEVEL V: ABSTRACT-IMAGINATIVE					

SYNTAX SCORES

ERROR TYPE	ERROR CATEGORY			TOTALS
	WORD USAGE (WU)	WORD ENDINGS (WE)	PUNCTUATION (P)	
ADDITIONS	3			3
OMISSIONS	10	2/3	1/3	(TO) 11
SUBSTITUTIONS	3	2/3		3 2/3
WORD ORDER	6			6
TOTALS	(WU) 22	(WE) 1 1/3	(P) 1/3	(TE) 23 2/3

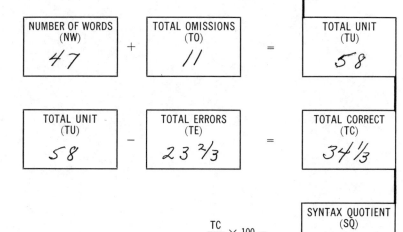

| NUMBER OF WORDS (NW) 47 | + | TOTAL OMISSIONS (TO) 11 | = | TOTAL UNIT (TU) 58 |

| TOTAL UNIT (TU) 58 | − | TOTAL ERRORS (TE) 23 2/3 | = | TOTAL CORRECT (TC) 34 1/3 |

$$\frac{TC}{TU} \times 100 =$$

SYNTAX QUOTIENT (SQ)
59

SPECIAL NOTATIONS

Meaningless Language   _____

Naming Level   _____

Lists   _____

Run-On Sentences   _____

Undue Use of Connectives   _____

Other   _____X_____ *Sentence formation and structure*

EXAMINER'S COMMENTS:

Examiner: _____*mHm*_____

Tables for Converting Raw Scores into Age Equivalents

TOTAL WORDS
Mean and Midpoint Scores by Age and Sex

Age	7	8	9	10	11	12	13	14	15	16	17
Male	22	52	83	94	106	124	143	133	123	140	158
Female	33	65	97	111	125	140	156	154	153	158	164

TOTAL SENTENCES
Mean and Midpoint Scores by Age and Sex

Age	7	8	9	10	11	12	13	14	15	16	17
Male	3.6	6.1	8.6	9.3	10.1	10.6	11.1	9.7	8.4	9.1	9.9
Female	5.0	7.7	10.5	11.0	11.5	11.5	11.5	11.2	10.9	11.2	11.5

WORDS PER SENTENCE
Mean and Midpoint Scores by Age and Sex

Age	7	8	9	10	11	12	13	14	15	16	17
Male	6.7	8.1	9.5	10.6	11.8	13.0	14.2	14.5	14.8	15.1	15.4
Female	6.3	8.1	9.9	10.5	11.2	12.5	13.8	14.6	15.4	16.1	16.8

SYNTAX
Mean and Midpoint Scores by Age and Sex

Age	7	8	9	10	11	12	13	14	15	16	17
Male	85	89	94	95	97	97	97	97	97	97	98
Female	89	92	96	97	98	98	98	98	99	99	99

ABSTRACT-CONCRETE
Mean and Midpoint Scores by Age and Sex

Age	7	8	9	10	11	12	13	14	15	16	17
Male	7	10	13	14	15	16	16	17	17	18	19
Female	8	11	14	15	16	16	17	18	19	19	18

263

Tables for Converting Raw Scores into Percentiles

TOTAL WORDS

Percentile Equivalents for Males

Percentile	Age					
	7	9	11	13	15	17
98	61	184	280	430	308	340
95	50	162	272	366	288	336
90	42	124	178	246	190	268
85	36	115	168	225	177	232
80	31	106	162	203	173	214
75	28	102	144	188	168	199
70	26	95	136	175	159	196
65	24	90	128	162	146	189
60	22	86	122	155	133	180
55	21	82	115	148	124	174
50	19	77	106	132	118	159
45	18	70	92	121	113	140
40	15	67	83	113	106	125
35	14	63	78	108	102	121
30	12	60	77	105	96	113
25	11	54	67	100	91	105
20	10	48	62	86	87	97
15	9	44	53	81	73	92
10	6	40	44	73	66	83
5	4	28	35	54	50	75
2	1	10	22	37	40	65

TOTAL WORDS

Percentile Equivalents for Females

Percentile	Age					
	7	9	11	13	15	17
98	97	286	308	354	248	348
95	84	208	276	276	228	340
90	64	174	228	264	205	304
85	49	156	204	234	192	252
80	45	143	180	216	185	215
75	41	128	172	198	179	202
70	38	120	160	192	175	196
65	36	96	146	186	172	180
60	35	84	139	168	160	170
55	34	80	129	162	152	162
50	32	76	110	149	148	158
45	30	70	100	138	144	155
40	28	68	94	126	140	144
35	27	65	88	114	137	134
30	25	62	81	100	132	130
25	24	58	78	87	126	124
20	19	54	74	80	122	116
15	14	50	69	76	118	98
10	11	44	60	66	96	84
5	4	31	48	58	80	70
2	1	29	42	42	57	56

TOTAL SENTENCES
Percentile Equivalents for Males

Percentile	Age 7	9	11	13	15	17
98	9	27	27	39	25	28
95	8	18	24	33	21	23
90	7	13	19	24	17	18
85	5	11	18	19	14	16
80	5	10	16	14	11	15
75	4	10	15	13	10	14
70	3	9	13	12	9	12
65	3	9	12	12	9	11
60	3	8	10	11	8	10
55	3	8	10	10	7	9
50	2	8	9	9	7	8
45	2	7	8	9	6	8
40	2	7	8	8	6	7
35	1	6	7	7	6	6
30	1	6	6	7	6	6
25	1	6	6	6	5	6
20	1	5	5	6	5	6
15	0	4	4	5	4	5
10	0	3	4	4	4	4
5	0	2	3	3	3	3
2	0	1	1	2	2	2

TOTAL SENTENCES
Percentile Equivalents for Females

Percentile	Age 7	9	11	13	15	17
98	11	30	34	33	28	42
95	10	20	27	24	25	40
90	9	18	25	19	16.	21
85	8	17	18	18	15	18
80	7	15	16	16	13	16
75	6	13	15	15	12	15
70	5	12	14	14	11	13
65	5	11	13	12	11	12
60	4	9	12	11	10	11
55	4	9	11	10	10	10
50	4	8	10	9	10	9
45	3	7	9	9	9	9
40	3	7	9	8	9	9
35	3	6	8	7	9	8
30	3	6	7	7	9	8
25	2	6	6	6	8	7
20	2	5	5	6	7	7
15	1	5	4	5	6	5
10	1	4	4	4	6	4
5	0	3	3	3	5	3
2	0	2	1	2	5	2

WORDS PER SENTENCE
Percentile Equivalents for Males

Percentile	Age					
	7	9	11	13	15	17
98	10.8	16.0	20.4	29.0	34.0	25.4
95	10.2	15.5	19.7	27.0	33.0	24.8
90	9.1	13.4	16.3	20.0	22.4	22.4
85	8.7	13.0	14.5	17.8	19.0	21.4
80	7.8	11.5	14.1	16.8	18.2	20.8
75	7.6	11.4	13.6	15.9	17.5	20.0
70	7.3	11.0	12.4	15.4	17.1	19.0
65	7.1	10.7	11.6	15.0	16.6	18.2
60	6.8	10.5	11.3	14.8	16.0	17.6
55	6.5	10.2	11.0	14.1	15.7	16.5
50	6.2	9.7	10.7	13.9	15.4	16.0
45	5.9	9.4	10.5	13.4	14.6	15.8
40	5.8	9.1	10.1	12.6	14.4	15.4
35	5.4	8.5	9.8	12.0	14.2	15.0
30	5.0	8.3	9.4	11.4	13.4	14.4
25	4.6	8.1	9.2	11.1	13.0	13.4
20	4.3	7.7	8.9	10.8	12.4	12.8
15	3.9	7.4	8.4	10.2	11.8	12.4
10	3.7	7.0	8.0	9.6	10.9	11.9
5	3.0	5.8	7.2	8.6	9.1	10.4
2	0.3	5.3	7.0	7.1	6.4	9.4

WORDS PER SENTENCE
Percentile Equivalents for Females

Percentile	Age					
	7	9	11	13	15	17
98	13.0	14.4	23.4	22.0	22.1	28.4
95	11.4	13.5	20.8	19.0	20.5	27.2
90	9.7	12.8	18.2	18.2	18.6	21.6
85	8.6	11.6	14.7	17.6	18.0	19.6
80	8.3	10.9	14.3	16.8	17.6	19.0
75	8.0	10.5	14.0	16.2	16.9	18.0
70	7.7	10.4	13.2	15.9	16.2	17.3
65	7.5	10.1	12.5	15.6	15.8	16.8
60	7.2	9.8	12.2	14.9	15.4	16.5
55	7.0	9.6	11.6	14.3	15.0	16.0
50	6.9	9.2	11.1	13.9	14.5	15.6
45	6.8	8.9	10.8	13.6	14.2	15.2
40	6.2	8.7	10.6	13.4	14.0	14.6
35	6.0	8.4	10.2	13.0	13.6	14.2
30	5.6	8.2	9.8	12.2	13.0	13.4
25	4.9	7.8	9.7	12.0	12.5	12.6
20	4.5	7.5	9.4	11.4	12.2	12.1
15	4.1	7.2	9.0	10.6	11.3	11.6
10	3.8	6.7	8.6	10.2	9.8	10.4
5	2.8	6.2	6.4	8.9	8.9	9.0
2	2.4	6.1	5.2	8.4	8.4	8.3

SYNTAX
Percentile Equivalents for Males

Percentile	Age					
	7	9	11	13	15	17
98	99	100	100	100	100	100
95	99	100	100	100	100	100
90	99	99	99	100	99	100
85	98	99	99	100	99	99
80	97	99	99	99	99	99
75	96	99	99	99	99	99
70	96	98	99	99	99	99
65	94	98	98	99	99	99
60	94	98	98	99	99	99
55	93	97	98	98	98	99
50	92	97	98	98	97	99
45	91	97	98	98	97	99
40	89	96	97	97	97	99
35	87	95	97	97	97	98
30	84	94	96	96	96	98
25	80	93	95	96	96	97
20	76	90	94	95	95	96
15	72	88	92	94	93	94
10	68	85	90	93	91	93
5	12	79	87	92	89	90
2	2	62	84	90	84	86

SYNTAX
Percentile Equivalents for Females

Percentile	Age					
	7	9	11	13	15	17
98	100	100	100	100	100	100
95	99	100	100	100	100	100
90	99	100	99	100	99	100
85	98	100	99	100	99	99
80	98	99	99	99	99	99
75	98	99	99	99	99	99
70	98	99	99	99	99	99
65	97	98	99	99	99	99
60	96	98	99	99	99	99
55	95	98	99	99	98	99
50	95	98	99	99	98	99
45	94	97	98	98	98	99
40	93	96	98	98	98	99
35	92	96	98	97	98	98
30	90	95	96	97	98	98
25	84	94	96	97	98	98
20	84	93	95	96	97	97
15	80	92	95	95	97	96
10	73	88	94	93	96	94
5	30	85	91	92	95	92
2	17	79	86	84	88	86

ABSTRACT-CONCRETE
Percentile Equivalents for Males

Percentile	Age					
	7	9	11	13	15	17
98	19	22	24	23	25	24
95	13	20	23	22	24	23
90	10	19	21	21	23	23
85	9	19	20	20	22	22
80	8	18	19	20	22	22
75	8	18	19	19	20	21
70	8	17	18	19	20	21
65	7	16	18	18	20	21
60	7	15	18	18	19	20
55	7	14	17	17	18	20
50	6	12	17	17	18	20
45	6	11	16	17	18	20
40	6	10	14	17	17	19
35	6	9	12	16	17	19
30	6	8	11	16	16	18
25	5	8	9	15	15	18
20	4	7	8	13	14	18
15	3	7	7	10	11	17
10	2	6	7	8	8	15
5	1	6	6	7	7	8
2	0	3	6	6	6	4

ABSTRACT-CONCRETE
Percentile Equivalents for Females

Percentile	Age					
	7	9	11	13	15	17
98	17	21	24	22	24	25
95	16	20	22	21	23	24
90	11	20	21	21	23	23
85	10	19	20	20	22	22
80	10	19	19	20	21	22
75	9	18	19	20	21	21
70	9	18	18	19	21	21
65	8	17	18	19	21	21
60	8	16	18	18	20	20
55	8	14	18	18	20	19
50	8	12	17	18	19	18
45	7	12	16	17	19	18
40	7	11	16	17	18	18
35	7	10	15	16	18	17
30	6	10	13	16	18	17
25	6	9	12	15	18	16
20	6	8	11	13	17	15
15	5	8	10	10	16	14
10	2	7	8	8	13	11
5	2	6	7	7	10	8
2	1	5	6	6	7	4

Tables for Converting Raw Scores into Stanine Ranks

TOTAL WORDS
Stanine Ranks for Males

Stanine	Age 7	9	11	13	15	17
9	55–up	172–up	276–up	366–up	280–up	336–up
8	42–54	118–171	176–275	237–365	188–279	256–335
7	29–41	104–117	150–175	195–236	170–187	204–255
6	22–28	86–103	122–149	155–194	133–169	180–203
5	15–21	67–85	84–121	113–154	106–132	125–179
4	11–14	52–66	65–83	93–112	90–105	102–124
3	8–10	41–51	45–64	75–92	67–89	84–101
2	3–7	24–40	32–44	48–74	48–66	72–83
1	0–2	0 –23	0–31	0–47	0–47	0–71

TOTAL WORDS
Stanine Ranks for Females

Stanine	Age 7	9	11	13	15	17
9	97–up	218–up	294–up	282–up	232–up	338–up
8	63–96	168–217	222–293	252–281	200–231	294–337
7	43–62	134–167	176–221	204–251	182–199	208–293
6	34–42	85–133	138–175	168–203	160–181	170–207
5	29–33	68–84	94–137	126–167	140–159	144–169
4	23–28	57–67	76–93	85–125	124–139	120–143
3	12–22	44–56	64–75	67–84	100–123	85–119
2	10–11	30–43	45–63	54–66	79–99	68–84
1	0–9	0–29	0–44	0–53	0–78	0–67

TOTAL SENTENCES
Stanine Ranks for Males

Stanine	Age 7	9	11	13	15	17
9	8–up	25–up	25–up	33–up	21–up	27–up
8	6–7	13–24	19–24	23–32	16–20	18–26
7	4–5	10–12	15–18	13–22	10–15	14–17
6	3	8–9	11–14	11–12	8–9	9–13
5	2	7	8–10	9–10	6–7	8
4	1	6	6–7	6–8	5	6–7
3	0	4–5	4–5	4–5	4	5
2	0	2–3	2–3	3	2–3	4
1	0	0–1	0–1	0–2	0–1	0–3

TOTAL SENTENCES
Stanine Ranks for Females

Stanine	7	9	11	13	15	17
9	11–up	22–up	33–up	24–up	25–up	32–up
8	9–10	18–21	23–32	18–23	16–24	21–31
7	7–8	13–17	16–22	15–17	12–15	15–20
6	5–6	9–12	12–15	11–14	10–11	12–14
5	4	8	9–11	8–10	9	9–11
4	3	6–7	6–8	6–7	8	7–8
3	1–2	4–5	4–5	4–5	6–7	5–6
2	0	3	3	3	5	3–4
1	0	0–2	0–2	0–2	0–4	0–2

WORDS PER SENTENCE
Stanine Ranks for Males

Stanine	7	9	11	13	15	17
9	10.5–up	15.7–up	19.8–up	28.8–up	33.0–up	24.8–up
8	9.0–10.4	13.3–15.6	15.9–19.7	19.2–28.7	21.6–32.9	21.9–24.7
7	7.6–8.9	11.4–13.2	13.9–15.8	16.2–19.1	17.6–21.5	20.4–21.8
6	6.8–7.5	10.4–11.3	11.3–13.8	14.5–16.1	16.0–17.5	17.6–20.3
5	5.8–6.7	9.1–10.3	10.1–11.2	12.5–14.4	14.4–15.9	15.4–17.5
4	4.5–5.7	8.0–9.0	9.2–10.0	11.0–12.4	12.7–14.3	12.2–15.3
3	3.8–4.4	7.1–7.9	8.1–9.1	9.6–10.9	11.2–12.6	12.0–12.1
2	2.3–3.7	5.6–7.0	7.1–8.0	8.4–9.5	8.4–11.1	10.4–11.9
1	0–2.2	0–5.5	0–7.0	0–8.3	0–8.3	0–10.3

WORDS PER SENTENCE
Stanine Ranks for Females

Stanine	7	9	11	13	15	17
9	12.0–up	13.6–up	21.8–up	19.3–up	21.0–up	27.0–up
8	9.5–11.9	12.8–13.5	17.0–21.7	18.0–19.2	18.2–20.9	20.0–26.9
7	8.1–9.4	10.8–12.7	14.1–16.9	16.4–17.9	17.2–18.1	18.4–19.9
6	7.2–8.0	9.8–10.7	12.1–14.0	14.8–16.3	15.4–17.1	16.6–18.3
5	6.2–7.1	8.7–9.7	10.5–12.0	13.3–14.7	14.0–15.3	14.6–16.5
4	4.7–6.1	7.7–8.6	9.6–10.4	11.9–13.2	12.4–13.9	12.4–14.5
3	3.8–4.6	6.8–7.6	8.6–9.5	10.2–11.8	10.2–12.3	10.6–12.3
2	2.5–3.7	6.2–6.7	6.4–8.5	8.8–10.1	8.8–10.1	8.8–10.5
1	0–2.4	0–6.1	0–6.3	0–8.7	0–8.7	0–8.7

SYNTAX
Stanine Ranks for Males

			Age			
Stanine	7	9	11	13	15	17
9	99–100	100	100	100	100	100
8	99	100	100	100	100	99
7	97–98	99	99	99	99	99
6	94–96	97–98	98	99	99	99
5	89–93	96	97	98	97–98	99
4	79–88	91–95	94–96	95–97	96	96–98
3	69–78	86–90	90–93	93–94	92–95	93–95
2	7–68	74–85	86–89	91–92	88–91	89–92
1	0–6	0–73	0–85	0–90	0–87	0–88

SYNTAX
Stanine Ranks for Females

			Age			
Stanine	7	9	11	13	15	17
9	99–100	100	100	100	100	100
8	99	100	100	100	100	100
7	98	99	99	99	99	99
6	96–97	98	99	99	99	99
5	93–95	97	98	99	99	99
4	87–92	94–96	96–97	97–98	98	97–98
3	76–86	89–93	95	93–96	96–97	95–96
2	16–75	84–88	91–94	91–92	95	90–94
1	0–15	0–83	0–90	0–90	0–94	0–89

ABSTRACT-CONCRETE
Stanine Ranks for Males

			Age			
Stanine	7	9	11	13	15	17
9	16–up	20–up	24–up	23–up	24–up	23–up
8	9–15	19	21–23	21–22	23	22
7	8	18	19–20	20	21–22	21
6	7	16–17	18	18–19	19–20	20
5	6	11–15	14–17	17	17–18	19
4	5	7–10	8–13	15–16	15–16	18
3	3–4	6	7	8–14	8–14	16–17
2	1–2	5	6	7	7	7–15
1	0	0–4	0–5	0–6	0–6	0–6

ABSTRACT-CONCRETE

Stanine Ranks for Females

Stanine	Age					
	7	9	11	13	15	17
9	16–up	20–up	23–up	22–up	23–up	24–up
8	10–15	19	21–22	21	23	22–23
7	9	18	19–20	20	22	21
6	8	16–17	18	18–19	21	20
5	7	11–15	16–17	17	19–20	18–19
4	6	8–10	12–15	15–16	17–18	16–17
3	5	7	8–11	8–14	14–16	11–15
2	2–4	6	6–7	7	9–13	7–10
1	0–1	0–5	0–5	0–6	0–8	0–6

Name Index

Amatruda, C., 14
Anderson, C., 69

Birch, H., 14, 69
Bloomfield, R., 100, 109, 112, 129
Boder, D., 69
Bonkowski, R., 6, 69
Boshes, B., 32
Braddock, R., 72, 78, 99, 128
Brown, R., 80

Callewaret, H., 16
Campbell, R., 19, 134
Carmichael, L., 1
Carlton, S., 69
Cassirer, E., 80
Ceram, C., 70
Chomsky, N., 78
Clodd, E., 70
Cobb, S., 14, 18
Critchley, M. 19
Curme, G., 112

Davis, E., 95, 128
Dearborn, W., 1
De Jong, R., 15
de Reuck, A., 1
Diederich, P., 69
Diringer, D., 2, 70
Doll, E., 13, 14, 134

Exner, S., 17, 19

Fernald, G., 1
Flesch, R., 134
French, J., 69
Fries, C., 76, 100, 112

Galanter, E., 9, 19
Gates, A., 1, 16, 31
Gaynor, F., 109
Gelb, I., 2, 70
Gesell, A., 13, 14, 15
Goodman, J., 69

Goldstein, K., 26, 134
Guiler, W., 69
Guilford, J., 152
Guttman, L., 150

Halverson, H., 14
Harris, T., 16
Heath, S., 15
Hebb, D., 6, 7
Heider, F., 69, 71, 76, 105, 147
Heider, G., 69, 71, 76, 105, 147
Hermelin, B., 69
Herrick, V. 16, 93
Hillocks, G., 71, 147
Hinsie, L., 19, 134
Hunt, J., 111, 128

Ilg, F., 13, 15

Jesperson, O., 112
Johnson, W., 95
Jones, H., 15

Kaplan, B., 8, 9, 10

LaBrant, L., 69
Langer, S., 2, 10
Lefford, A., 14, 69
Lenneberg, E., 8, 57
Lennon, G., 147
Lloyd-Jones, R., 72, 78, 99, 128
Lord, E., 1

McCarthy, D., 1, 75, 95, 128
Miller, G., 9, 19, 78, 129
Monroe, M., 31
Monroe, W., 1
Mowrer, O., 2, 8, 9, 10, 134
Murphy, T., 16
Myklebust, H., 3, 6, 8, 22, 25, 32, 37, 75, 78, 81, 105, 109, 117, 134, 148, 162, 163, 165

Nielsen, J., 12, 19, 20, 26, 109, 132

O'Connor, N., 1
Okada, N., 16, 93
Oléron, P., 134
Orton, S., 14, 21
Oseretsky, N., 15, 134
Osgood, C., 69, 73, 80, 133
O'Shea, M., 71, 75, 76, 78, 105, 128, 147

Pei, M., 109
Penfield, W., 5, 14
Perrin, P., 100, 103, 111, 112
Pimsleur, P., 6, 69
Pool, I., 73, 133
Pribram, K., 9, 19

Rarick, G., 16

Rioch, D., 1, 8
Roberts, L., 5, 14

Schoer, L., 72, 78, 99, 128
Smith, K., 16
Stalnaker, J., 69
Stormzand, M., 71, 75, 76, 78, 105, 128, 147
Succi, G., 69, 73, 80, 133

Tannebaum, P., 69, 73, 80, 133
Templin, M., 1, 75, 76, 95
Thompson, W., 69, 111

Weinstein, E., 1, 8
Warner, H., 8, 9, 10

Subject Index

Abstract-Concrete
  defined, 133
  See also Abstract-Concrete Scale
Abstract-Concrete Scale, 73, 133
  Conversion Tables, 263
  Illustrative Scored Stories, 233
  interpretation of scores, 162
  Levels, 135
    Abstract-Descriptive, 140
    Abstract-Imaginative, 142
    Concrete-Descriptive, 136
    Concrete-Imaginative, 138
    Meaningless Language, 133, 135
  mean age scores, 183
  norms, 80
  percentile scores, 184, 268
  Record Form, 259
  reliability, 149
    interscorer, 159
    trained and untrained examiners, 159, 160
  results
    by age and sex, 80
  scoring, 135
  Scoring Guide, 233
  stanine ranks, 186, 271
  validity, 147
Agraphia. *See* Dysgraphia.
Aphasia
  formulation, 26, 109
    Illustrative Story, 27
    word finding, 133
  motor, 5
  receptive, 27
    Illustrative Story, 28
  semantic, 109
  sensory, 5
  syntactical, 22, 109
Apraxia
  type of, 18
Ataxia
  cerebellar, 15
    case, 16
  Illustrative Stories, 17, 18
  See also Psychomotor Aspects

Auditorization
  dyslexia and, 29
  Illustrative Story, 29
  inability in, 29
Auditory processes, 23
  blending, 31
  sequentializing, 30
  spelling disorder, 31
  syllabication, 31
  See also Differential Diagnosis

Capitalization, 122
Content. *See* Abstract-Concrete Scale
Cross-cultural Studies, 65
Culturally Deprived, 64

Deaf, 57
  Illustrative Scored Stories, 225
  Illustrative Stories, 57
Differential Diagnosis, 12
  adults, 65
  agraphia, 17
  aphasia, 19
    formulation, 26, 109
    receptive, 27
  apraxia, 18
  ataxia, 15
  auditory aspects, 23
  auditorization, 25
  auditory sequentializing, 30
  cross-cultural, 65
  culturally deprived, 64
  deaf, 57
  developmental deviations, 13
  dysgraphia, 19
  dyslexia, 29
  dysnomia, 25
  inadequate teaching, 64
  mentally retarded, 47
  paralytic disorders, 15
  psychomotor aspects, 14
  reading disability, 37
  reauditorization, 28
  screening, 13
  socially-emotionally disturbed, 52

Differential Diagnosis—Continued
    speech defective, 42
    spelling disorders, 31
    visual aspects, 21
Dysgraphia, 8
    defined, 17, 19
    developmental, 21
    history of, 19
    identification, 21
    Illustrative Story, 21
    See also Apraxia, Written Language
Dyslexia, 29
    auditorization, 29
    auditory, 29
    auditory blending, 31
    Illustrative Stories, 29, 31, 32
    syllabication
Dysnomia
    defined, 25
    Illustrative Stories, 26
Dysphasia. *See* Aphasia

Echolalia, 133
Error Categories, 73
Error Types, 73, 114
Error Type Symbols, 124

Formulation Aphasia, 26, 109
    Illustrative Story, 27

Illustrative Stories of
    agraphia, 21
    aphasia, formulation, 27
            receptive, 28
    ataxia, cerebellar, 17, 18
    auditory spelling disorder, 31
    deaf, 58-63
    dysgraphia, 21
    dyslexia, 29, 31, 32
    dysnomia, 26
    mentally retarded, 48-51
    normal children, 82-91
    phonetic writing, 24
    reading disability, 38-41
    scored, 189-255
    socially-emotionally disturbed, 53-56
    speech defective, 43-46

Language
    ability, 12
    auditory, 2
    defined, 10
    development, 2
    disorders, 1, 2
    hierarchical relationships, 3
    meaningless, 109, 133
    measurement, 69
    psychoneurological aspects, 5
    read, 3, 33
    spoken, 3, 33
    systems, 3
    theoretical constructs, 1
    written, 1, 4
Language Behavior, 4
    psychological processes, 8
    psychoneurological aspects, 5
Learning, 5
    psychoneurological aspects, 5
    semi-autonomous systems, 6
    theory, 7
    transducing, 7, 18
    transmodal, 6
Learning Disabilities
    auditory processes, 30
    memory defects, 23
    neurogenic, 6
    phonetic writing, 24
    phonetizers, 23
    visual processes

Meaning, 72, 108, 133
    See also Abstract-Concrete Scale
Meaningless Language, 109, 133
Mentally Retarded, 47
    Illustrative Scored Stories, 221
    Illustrative Stories, 47
Morphology, 109, 133
    word formation and, 111

Normal Children
    Illustrative Scored Stories, 189
    Illustrative Stories, 81
    results for, 75
Norms, 75

Paralytic Disorders, 15
Phonetic Writing, 24
    Illustrative Story, 24

Picture Story Language Test, 69
  Abstract-Concrete Scale, 80, 133
  administration of, 92
  aspects of language measured, 72
  Illustrated Stories by Normal Children,
    81
  interpretation of scores, 162
  norms, 75
  Picture, 71
  Productivity Scale, 75, 95
  purpose, 71
  raw scores, conversion of, 165
  Record Form, 256
  reliability, 147
    interscorer, 151
  results, 75
  Sample, 74
  scoring, 95, 111, 135
  sex differences, 81
  standardization, 69
  Syntax Scale, 78, 108
  validity, 147

Productivity, 108
  defined, 72
  See also Productivity Scale

Productivity Scale, 75, 95
  contractions, 99
  Conversion Tables, 263
  hyphenated and compound words, 98
  Illustrative Scored Stories, 189
  lists, 96
  meaningless language, 97, 102
  names, abbreviations, initials, 98
  naming level, 98, 103
  norms, 75
  numbers, 99
  Record Form, 259
  reliability, 150
    interscorer, 152
    trained and untrained examiners, 152
  results, by age and sex, 76
  run-on sentences, 103
  Scoring Guide, 188
  scoring, principles for, 95
    divide into sentences, 101
    style, 102
  titles, 199
  Total Sentences, 99
  Total Words, 95

  validity, 147
  Words per Sentence, 105

Read Language, 2
Reading, 4

Reading disability, 39
  Illustrative Scored Stories, 212
  Illustrative Stories, 39
Reauditorization, of letters, 28
Receptive aphasia. See aphasia.

Sample, 74
Sentence, defined, 100
Socially-Emotionally Disturbed, 52
  Illustrative Scored Stories, 216
  Illustrative Stories, 52
Speech Defected,
  Illustrative Scored Stories, 208
  Illustrative Stories, 42
Spoken Language, versus written, 33
Syntax, 78
  defined, 109
  mean age scores, 179
  norms, 79
  percentiles, 180
  punctuation, 110
  results, by age and sex, 79
  stanines, 182
  word choice, 110
Syntax Quotient, 73
  formula, 131
  rationale, 128
  reliability, 155, 156, 158
Syntax Scale, 73, 108
  accuracy types, 111
  designation of errors, 124
  error type symbols, 124
  Illustrative Scored Stories, 189
  intended meaning, 113
  interpretation of scores, 162
  mean age scores, 179
  morphology, 109
  norms, 78
  percentiles, 180
  punctuation, 110, 120
  Record Form, 259
  reliability, 150
    interscorer, 153

Syntax Scale—Continued
    number sentences required, 154, 156, 158
    trained and untrained examiners, 153
Scoring, accuracy only, 113
  designation of errors
  Error types, 73, 111, 114
  Error categories, 73, 111, 114
  penalty score values, 123
  principles of, 111
  least penalty rule, 114
  special situations, 123
  stanines, 182
  Stringency Level, 112
  Syntax Quotient, 128, 131
  validity, 147
  word choice, 110
  word endings, 118, 125
Syntax Score, rationale for, 128

Theoretical constructs, 1
Total Sentences, 72, 99
  conversion tables, 263
  mean age scores, 171
  norms, 76
  percentiles, 171
  results by age and sex, 76
  scoring, 99
  stanines, 174
  See also Productivity Scale
Total Words, 72, 95
  conversion tables, 263
  mean age scores, 166
  norms, 76
  percentiles, 167
  results by age and sex, 76
  scoring, 95
  stanines, 169

See also Productivity Scale
Transducing, 7, 18
  visual to auditory, 31
Transmodal, 6

Visual Processes, 21
  letters and, 30
  monitoring, 22
  See also Auditory Processes.

Word Endings, 73, 118
Word Order, 73, 117
Word Usage, 73
Words per Sentence, 72, 105
  conversion tables, 263
  formula for, 106
  mean age scores, 175
  norms, 76
  percentiles, 176
  results by age and sex, 76
  scoring of, 105
  stanines, 178
  validity, 148
  See also Productivity Scale.
Written Language, 2
  acquisition of, 6
  aspects measured, 72
  cerebral dominance and, 5
  disorders of, 7, 12
  handicapped children and, 36
  normal children and, 75
  readiness for, 8
  spoken versus, 33
    Illustrative Stories, 34, 35, 36
  theoretical constructs, 4
  through processes and, 133
  See also Differential Diagnosis, Dysgraphia, Language